PENGUIN BOOKS

funny' *Irish Examiner*, Books of the Year

'Foster has the courage, and the historian's skill, to tackle all this stuff, make sense of it and entertain his readers too'
Economist

'A remarkably succinct analysis of change, cultural and political, delivered with characteristic elegance ...
Evening Standard

'Vivid and beautifully written' Olivia O'Leary, *Irish Times*

'Hugely enjoyable . . . Shot through with insight and convincing analysis . . .[Ireland's] present inhabitants can count themselves fortunate to have their story told in such a memorable fashion by one of their own' Brendan Smith, *Tablet*

'A fascinating trawl through a changing society . . . Rigorous and incisive' Pádraig Kenny, *Sunday Tribune Review*

'A compelling and beautifully written exploration of Ireland's late-twentieth century' Richard English, *Irish Times*, Books of the Year

'Original, engaging and brilliantly written' *Irish Examiner*

'Foster proves that being a great stylist doesn't mean there's any diminution of substance' Paul Muldoon,
The Times Literary Supplement, Books of the Year

ABOUT THE AUTHOR

R. F. Foster is Carroll Professor of Irish History at the University of Oxford and a Fellow of Hertford College, Oxford. His books include *Modern Ireland, 1600–1972*, *The Irish Story* and *W. B. Yeats: A Life*.

R. F. FOSTER

Luck and the Irish

A Brief History of Change
c. 1970–2000

PENGUIN BOOKS

PENGUIN BOOKS

Published by the Penguin Group
Penguin Books Ltd, 80 Strand, London WC2R ORL, England
Penguin Group (USA) Inc., 375 Hudson Street, New York, New York 10014, USA
Penguin Group (Canada), 90 Eglinton Avenue East, Suite 700, Toronto, Ontario, Canada M4P 2Y3
(a division of Pearson Penguin Canada Inc.)
Penguin Ireland, 25 St Stephen's Green, Dublin 2, Ireland
(a division of Penguin Books Ltd)
Penguin Group (Australia), 250 Camberwell Road, Camberwell, Victoria 3124, Australia
(a division of Pearson Australia Group Pty Ltd)
Penguin Books India Pvt Ltd, 11 Community Centre, Panchsheel Park, New Delhi – 110 017, India
Penguin Group (NZ), 67 Apollo Drive, Rosedale, North Shore 0632, New Zealand
(a division of Pearson New Zealand Ltd)
Penguin Books (South Africa) (Pty) Ltd, 24 Sturdee Avenue, Rosebank, Johannesburg 2196, South Africa

Penguin Books Ltd, Registered Offices: 80 Strand, London WC2R ORL, England

www.penguin.com

First published by Allen Lane 2007
Published in Penguin Books 2008

1

The extracts from unpublished writings by Hubert Butler on pp. 56 and 58 appear by permission of
Julia Crampton and the Estate of Hubert Butler; the extract from Brian Lynch's 'Pity for the Wicked'
on p. 115 appears by permission of the author and Duras Press; the extract from a letter by Sean
O'Faolain on p. 167 appears by permission of Julia O'Faolain; the extracts from Paul Muldoon's
'Rapparee Rap' and John Montague's 'The Siege of Mullingar' on pp. 182–3 and p. 186 appear by
permission of the authors and the Gallery Press.

Printed in Great Britain by Clays Ltd, St Ives plc

A CIP catalogue record for this book is available from the British Library

978-0-141-01765-5

For Thaddeus O'Sullivan

Contents

... 'This is not,' I say,
'The dead Ireland of my youth, but an Ireland
The poets have imagined, terrible and gay.'

– W. B. Yeats,
'The Municipal Gallery Revisited' (1937)

Prosperity has come to the land of Joyce and Yeats, creating a kind of country they could never have imagined: rich and happy. – *Newsweek*, 20 April 2001

Preface

This book has its origins in the Wiles Lectures, delivered at Queen's University Belfast in May 2004. The idea for the subject had come when I was, more or less simultaneously, asked if I would add a section to my book *Modern Ireland 1600–1972*, first published in 1988, taking the story up to the present; it did not take much thought to show me that what was needed was a new book rather than an addendum. I also found the astonishing transformation of Ireland after 1972 a subject of endless interest. However, I probably under-estimated the task. Lytton Strachey's remark that the history of the Victorian age could not be written because 'we know too much about it' might be adapted for Ireland since the 1960s. Though much of the period remains under a thirty-year rule as regards official records, there is already a huge literature of commentary, memoir, investigative records, statistical abstracts, sociological analysis and journalism, while for the early part of the period the admirable National Archives have already accumulated a treasure trove. In preparing the lectures three years ago, I scraped the surface; since then much more has come to light. The interim has also seen the publication of some first-rate general treatments of the period, in books by Terence Brown, Henry Patterson and Diarmaid Ferriter, and on television by Seán Ó Mórdha.* The treatment that follows is necessarily thematic and selective.

In putting it together I owe debts to many people. I am grateful to

---

* Terence Brown, *Ireland: A Social and Cultural History 1922–2002* (London, 2004); Henry Patterson, *Ireland since 1939: The Persistence of Conflict* (Dublin, 2006); Diarmaid Ferriter, *The Transformation of Ireland 1900–2000* (London, 2004); Seán Ó Mórdha, *Seven Ages* (RTÉ DVD, 2002).

the Wiles Trustees and the Boyd family for the invitation to deliver the lectures, and to Queen's University for providing such a stimulating, thought-provoking and comfortable environment. In particular I am grateful to Alvin Jackson and the late Peter Jupp for going to a great deal of trouble on my behalf, and to the colleagues and friends who added to the mix in Belfast: they included Paul Arthur, Toby Barnard, Paul Bew, Maurice Bric, Seán Connolly, David Fitzpatrick, Ultán Gillen, David Hayton, Matt Kelly, Ian Kershaw, Jane Leonard, Edna and Michael Longley, Fearghal McGarry, Gill McIntosh, Anthony Malcomson, Marc Mulholland, Margaret O'Callaghan, Senia Paseta, Rob Savage, Charles Townshend and Graham Walker. Marianne Elliott deserves additional thanks for beginning the train of thought by asking me to give the David Quinn Lecture at the University of Liverpool. She also, along with Tom Dunne, Richard English, Ian McBride, John-Paul McCarthy, Max McGuinness, and Cormac Ó Gráda, read drafts of this book; I owe them all thanks for providing insights and suggestions. I am also indebted to Catriona Crowe for her interest, encouragement and information. I should also like to thank Brendan Barrington, Rosheen Callendar, Eamon Delaney, Sarah Foster, Catherine Freeman, Grey Gowrie, John Horgan, Michael Kennedy, Mary Kenny, John McBratney, Tina Mahony, Daithi Ó Corráin, Rory O'Donnell, Simon Prince, Joe Spence, Colm Tóibín and Maurice Walsh for various kinds of enlightenment. My secretary Jules Iddon helped enormously in getting this into book form. My wife, Aisling, who read and advised with characteristic incisiveness, and my children, Nora and Phineas, put up with a great deal, and I appreciate them more profoundly than they know. The dedication to Thaddeus O'Sullivan celebrates both an ancient friendship and a body of work that has reflected many of the changes recorded in this book.

Once again I owe a great deal to my matchless agent Gill Coleridge; to Simon Winder, most cheering, perceptive and encouraging of publishers, who made many valuable suggestions; and to Donna Poppy, who should be the Nobel laureate of editors. This book would never have seen the light of day without them, and only I can be blamed for what is in it. When I suggested the topic to the Wiles Committee, they gently intimated that the series had not usually been given on Irish history and that I would be creating a precedent. I might have reassured them by pointing out that some might think that much of the material in this book is not, in fact, 'history' at all. I freely admit that a survey of such recent events must inevitably be interspersed with opinion, speculation and forecast. But I remain convinced that it is history none the less.

Roy Foster
Oxford, April 2007

Introduction
Culture and Anarchy in Ireland
c. 1970–2000

At the Fianna Fáil Ard-Fheis of 1998 the party leader and taoiseach of the Republic, Bertie Ahern, memorably observed, 'The cynics may be able to point to the past. But we live in the future.'[1] While this Spielbergian concept may have surprised some of his hearers, he was expressing the zeitgeist more profoundly than perhaps he knew. Even if we are in some doubt about living in the future, we know we live in 'contemporary history'. There are those who think historians should not trespass into it, and, though several have written studies of Ireland carrying the story up to 2000, it is considered a risky endeavour. But there is no 'thirty-year rule' of the mind, no self-denying ordinance that stops us from analysing things that have happened over the last genera-tion. And what will preoccupy historians in the future – where we now apparently live – is the transformation of Ireland during the closing decades of the twentieth century. It should be possible for a historian to look at the latest period in Irish history from a historical standpoint, as opposed to that of a sociologist, or an economist, or a political scientist – though the insights of all these disciplines must be employed. There are already sources available (the reports of investigative tri-bunals, Dáil debates, a plethora of statistical studies, the memoirs of the 1960s generation); and it may be enlightening to juxtapose such evidence with testimony from other, less conventional sources, as this book tries to do. But there is also a sense that we are experiencing history in fast-forward mode, as transformations accumulate in econ-omic practice, in social and religious experience, in cultural achieve-ment and in political relationships, both at home and abroad.

Those of a historical turn of mind might also be tempted to use parallels and comparisons from the further past as well as analyses of events just behind us. In a precocious essay of 1928 Isaiah Berlin argued that history

moves not in continuous straight lines, but in folds. These folds are not of equal length or substance, but if we venture to examine the points in which these folds touch one another, we will often find strong and real similarities between the points. If we attempt to look through our own age at the layers which are, as it were, in a vertical line below it, we shall see the eighteenth century, and the Roman world in the third century AD, and the Alexandrine culture in the third century BC; the comparison must not be pressed too hard, but the resemblance between these periods and ours is peculiarly profound and precise in this, that the spirit of slavery and convention lies on all.[2]

The idea that there are past periods that carry an uncanny assonance with our own sense of the present chimes strongly with the symmetries and repetitions of Irish history.[3] Reviewing Irish change over the last generation recalls the way Ireland in 1845 appeared to Thomas Davis, after bewildering alterations in the social and political position of Catholics, the interventionist policies of British Whig governments and the adjustments of the Irish economy after a long period of international war. 'The knowledge, the customs, the superstitions, the hopes of the People are entirely changing. There is neither use nor reason in lamenting what we must infallibly lose. Our course is in the open, and a great one, and will try us severely; but, be it well or ill, we cannot resemble our fathers.'[4] Another period that suggests parallels with our own recent past is the very early twentieth century in Ireland – too often seen in Joycean terms, with Dublin as the centre of paralysis in a moribund society. We might consider instead the astonishing upward curve of cultural achievement since the 1890s, the proliferation of magazines and forums for discussion, the arrival of avant-garde drama, the experiments in political cooperation, the revival of Home Rule, the interest expressed by foreign commentators in Irish conditions and Irish possibilities. This is the period to which F. S. L. Lyons attached the suggestive identification 'culture and anarchy'.[5]

In both the 1830s and the 1900s 'modernization' was in the air, coinciding with cultural experimentation and new political initiatives; so, especially in the 1900s, were aspects of what was not yet called 'globalization'. And in both eras a contemporary political critique was being mounted against the governing consensus. There are many parallels here with our own day. Both these eras also ended with unforeseen and apocalyptic events (in one case, the catastrophic Famine, in the other, the advent of world war) that brought in their wake, for Ireland, attempted revolution. This might serve as a reminder that history is not a predictive science and is at its most illuminating when written with the full consciousness of what people wrongly expected to happen. That is one insight denied to the historian of the very recent past. The post-history paradigm of Francis Fukayama, based on the idea of a benign new world order after 1989, was shown up – if such a thing needed to be done – as speciously unhistorical on 11 September 2001.

What was the expected Irish future around 1970? In 2000 the Central Statistics Office published a volume called *That Was Then, This Is Now: Change 1949–1999*, which showed – unsurprisingly – that the Ireland of 1949 might have existed on another planet when compared to the country at the turn of the millennium. But the same would be true for most European countries. For Ireland, it is the rate of change in the last thirty years of the twentieth century that is most bewildering. Partly because of the archaic nature of life in Ireland up to then, the shock of the new could only be all the more radical. Much as the sheer lack of accumulated industrial encumbrance enabled the Irish economy to leapfrog into the microelectronic age, the sudden embrace of revised moral codes allowed the new Irish laws on homosexuality to become, at a stroke, more liberal than those in Britain. Perhaps because so much of the Irish stereotype (and the tourist brand-image) conjures up an unchanging land where time stands still, the Irish faculty for changing practices or expectations with bewildering rapidity has been underestimated. Laws relating to metric measures, or European-style car registrations, or smoking in public, or the use of plastic carrier-bags, are passed with a speed and a lack of recrimination that would not be possible in the more cautious political culture of Britain (or England, at least: here, as in other areas, new-look Scotland presents some intriguing parallels to Ireland). This is in part due to the relentless centralization of Irish government; Joe Lee has astutely pointed out that this is one way in which Ireland remains wedded to a British rather than a European model.[6] But there are other suggestive questions of political culture behind this readiness to adopt change, indicated informally by a senior civil servant who advised the government on European policy-making: 'We don't have a bureaucratic system like the French or the Germans. We're just opportunistic future-grabbers.'[7]

When did the future present itself to be grabbed? Looking back, we can see that certain statistics suggest where change was likely to begin; for one thing, the 1971 census recorded the first population increase since the foundation of the state, and the demographic profile of Ireland over the next thirty years was not only to become exceptionally young but also to demonstrate a level and variety of immigration whose effects have been phenomenal. The other kind of transforming immigration would be the inflow of capital, and in analysing Irish change there is an understandable tendency to give great weight to the idea of 'Waiting for Microsoft'.[8] But offshore investment is only part of the story, and though this book begins with the economic miracle, there are other motors of change that must be measured – in the areas of religion, family patterns, sexual attitudes and politics. Accompanying this has been, as in the early twentieth century, a striking efflorescence in the creative arts. The achievements and insights of writers are themselves part of the story, and so is the marketing of the culture industry.

Nothing is irreversible (while the number of multimedia companies in Dublin quadrupled between 1997 and 2001, they subsequently went into a symmetrically steep decline).[9] Nor is it insignificant that the idioms and metaphors used by those creative writers who have used the new Ireland as their canvas often involve corruption, incest, exploitation and disorientation, while the themes of inequity, inequality of opportunity and the fracturing of social integuments are as prominent in Ireland as in any other boom economy. But the economic and psychological boundaries that defined the country have altered and expanded: Ireland has been declared by the National Competitiveness Council, at the time of writing, the most globalized country that ever yet was seen.[10] What has changed, perhaps decisively and for ever, is a question of attitude. In 2004 the *Economist* cheer-fully ranked Ireland's 'quality of life' as the best in the world, a conclusion arrived at by feeding economic statistics and family patterns into a computer along with such factors as life expectancies and divorce rates. The result was a top score of 8.33 out of 10, beating Switzerland and Norway into second and third place. Gratifyingly for many Irish people, the UK languished at twenty-ninth.[11] As this vividly illustrated, Ireland was now identified as the location of happiness – an increasingly fashionable concept for economists and sociologists. After centuries of victimhood and misfortune, by the early twenty-first century the Irish had got lucky: not only in lifestyle and earning power but in sport, music-making, international literary acclaim and even (thanks to global warming) the weather.

This book tries to chart some of these changes and their implications, without predicting how far all this apparent good fortune is likely to exist in steady state. There is also a large area where the Irish experience from 1970 was not identified with feel-good economics and sunny expectations of a liberal future opening out into pluralist new horizons: for much of the period under review, the country's image was inseparable from violence in the North. And if, for the Republic, 1972 ushered in an era of change symbolized by constitutional alterations regarding Europe and the position of the Catholic Church, as well as the impending retirements of Archbishop McQuaid and President de Valera, the year also saw Bloody Sunday in Derry and ended with bombs in Dublin and the establishment of the Special Criminal courts. This book is about the Republic of Ireland. But one central question concerns the connection between seismic change south of the border and the eventual acceptance of the necessity for change in the North, as well as the whole question of the relation between the two political entities. Paul Bew has written about the stealthy advance of 'partitionist history' – the way that historians project into the past the assumption of the border, with which we have all grown up but that formally entered Irish history only in 1920. One of the themes of this book concerns the extent to which the period sees the entrenchment of that partitionist history, and the acceptance of a partitionist attitude in 'the South'.

In the language of the sociologists and economists, Ireland has become a 'Flexible Developmental State',[12] but how far does flexibility – and development – stretch? Again, images from Irish writing come to mind, strikingly (from the poets Paul Muldoon and Nuala Ní Dhomhnaill) the traditional idea of a magic island appearing in the Atlantic, whose outline and boundaries expand or disappear in the act of observation. Surveying the fluctuating contours of contemporary Irish history, and charting the diverse energies that have driven it through a period of flux and change, recalls, again, Lyons's definition of Irish 'culture and anarchy': 'a diversity of ways of life which are deeply embedded in the past and of which the much advertised political differences are but the outward and visible sign'.[13] Conflicting cultures, in this view, were crammed together in an island too small to hold them. Written in the late 1970s, Lyons's analysis emphasized that – in the early twentieth century at least, and by implication even in the present day – the resources of the country were stretched to breaking point by the resultant tension. If regarded from the early twenty-first century, these intense conjunctions can be seen as a sign of strength, not weakness. Borders have expanded in various ways, not least by the intense interest in Ireland sustained by the Irish diaspora, projecting back images of the island to itself. This book may itself be part of that process. Certainly, one of the striking changes that it surveys is the alteration and expansion of the Irish national narrative in several ways: the perception of the North, the internationalization of the economy, the shattering of the Catholic Church's 'moral monopoly'. It is possible that the 1990s may come to be seen by future historians as the period when the resources of the country – cultural and political as well as economic – expanded in a way that made them able to accommodate what Lyons diagnosed as the anarchy threatened by competing cultures. But it is also possible that the last convulsive quarter of the twentieth century might be seen in Ireland, North and South, as not so much a Great Leap Forward as a series of interconnected crises, whose outcome must remain unknown.

I

The Miracle of Loaves and Fishes

I

In the late 1990s, Colm Tóibín has remarked, as Irish people turned away from the Church, they looked to another kind of miraculous intercession: the economy. 'The word was no longer made flesh, it was made into a set of astonishing statistics.'[1] Output in the decade from 1995 increased by 350 per cent, outpacing the per capita averages in the UK and the USA, personal disposable income doubled, exports increased fivefold, trade surpluses accumulated into billions, employment boomed, immigrants poured into the country. As the twentieth century reached its end, Ireland's transformation was an established fact. Between 1987 and 2001 the annual growth rates of Gross National Product exceeded 7 per cent and sometimes touched double figures. Change had made itself felt in many areas – religious practice, sexual mores, cultural production – that will be considered in this book. But above all, and behind everything, was the most surprising metamorphosis of all: the country had apparently become vastly rich.

Interpretations of Irish history have always faced a difficulty from the starting gate: how far back does one go to understand the past? Reviewing the astonishing changes over the last thirty years of the twentieth century does not simply concern near-contemporary events; the backwards look should ideally review events and themes since the founding of the two states in 1920–22. In terms of economic change, several competing dates may be advanced for the moment when change was set in motion: the foundation of the Industrial Development Authority of 1949, the Whitaker Report of 1958, the entry into the EEC in 1973. The approach of Tom Garvin in *Preventing the Future* is more persuasive: from the late 1950s, gathering force through the sixties, a series of initiatives was embarked upon by a new generation of politicians, unhampered by the shibboleths that had constrained the de Valera generation.[2] Nor should these predisposing factors be limited to the sphere of economic policy pure and simple (if it can ever be either of these things). Garvin's thesis stresses above all the liberalization, extension and funding of education, and it is hard to disagree.

In coming to terms with the phenomenon of Ireland's economic miracle, the historian's preoccupation intersects with those of the sociologist, the economist and even the psychologist, and they have all had their say. But, particularly for a historian, moving into this territory raises the age-old Hegelian metaphor that the owl of Minerva flies only at nightfall, or James Anthony Froude's less celebrated image of a lantern hung over the stern of a ship, illuminating the waves in its wake. Historians tend to believe that we can understand something only when it has gone. Here, there are some signs that this time has come. In 2001 Maurice O'Connell, governor of the Central Bank of Ireland, pronounced: 'The era of the Celtic Tiger is over.' Other authorities have seen that year as a watershed, and certainly there was a brief pause in the euphoria: plant closures appeared in the headlines rather than factory openings, inflation threatened, and a reckoning began.[3] The banker's caution seems excessive, but it echoed several analysts who had decided that the gravy train must surely be rolling to a halt. It is worth beginning by looking at some of the schools of interpretation of the recent Irish past.

Like protagonists in the venerable debate in British historiography about living standards in the Industrial Revolution, they can be divided into optimists and pessimists and, as with that debate, this rift coincides with a certain ideological divide too. For Irish purposes we might think of the contesting sides as 'Boosters' and 'Begrudgers'. Some of the Boosters are obvious, and come with obvious baggage: Ray MacSharry, for instance, an influential Fianna Fáil finance minister in the late 1980s, in a subsequent book on the making of the Celtic Tiger, has claimed the animal's pedigree resoundingly for his party's *in vitro* fertilization of the Irish economy in that period. Less predictably, economists such as Rory O'Donnell have produced an analysis of the process of Irish modernization that not only projects an optimistic future but links it historically back to the cultural process of self-assertion posited in Declan Kiberd's influential literary history *Inventing Ireland*.[4] Kiberd himself has made this connection with audacious directness. 'The Celtic Tiger was born', he tells us, when, in the 1990s, the ideals of the Gaelic revival of a hundred years before were rediscovered by fusing 'the sense of local pride with the idea of self-help'; he identifies the key events as the establishment in 1986 of the James Larkin Centre for the Unemployed, when 'members with specific skills' began 'setting up businesses in order to put their comrades back to work', and the setting up of the Irish-language television station TG4 in 1996.[5] What happened in the intervening three quarters of a century is skipped over, and altogether this seems a somewhat mystic interpretation. But it has been enthusiastically adopted by the Industrial Development Agency, which announced in 2005 that it intended to brand Ireland to the wider world as 'a creative economy', attributing to the Irish workforce an innate mindset reflecting literary and artistic genius. Eurocrats like the commissioner David Byrne present an equally celebratory view,[6] as one might perhaps expect, but so do some left-inclined commentators who find the originating impulse in the workings of so-called 'social partnership' structures between the representatives of labour and capital in the Republic. But, whatever their ideological orientation, the optimistic Boosters put their faith for continued prosperity in fundamental changes in the infrastructure, the accumulation of technical experience and cultural capital, and the flexibility of the new-style economy.

Against them are those whom the Boosters would categorize as Begrudgers.[7] Often coming from the left, or from the nostalgic shores of neo-nationalism, part of their argument stems from a suspicion of creeping Anglicization, and a dislike of what an earlier age would have called 'rootless cosmopolitanism' and liberalism. A more hard-headed side of this analysis revolves around the disparity between the huge profits made by Irish business in the 1990s and the state of public services, especially healthcare; and the illusory nature of these profits, channelled back to the foreign investors who set up plants in Ireland in the first place. Thus the strange conundrum, whereby Ireland has a greater Gross Domestic Product than Gross National Product – since the former statistic includes all the money made by multinationals such as Hewlett-Packard, Dell and Intel, which then is exported back to the USA, and the latter figure simply adds up what is left for the natives. As the statistics became ever more miraculous in the late 1990s, the distance between these two rising graphs widened accordingly. The difference between these two measurements, which can more or less be used interchangeably for many national economies, has long been uniquely wide in Ireland. Since 2000 it has begun to narrow – partly because the construction industry has taken over from the multinationals as the main engine of growth. But by the turn of the century just under a quarter of GDP in Ireland was accounted for by the profits of foreign-owned companies operating in the Republic.[8] The parallels with colonialism are obvious here, and it is striking how the USA plays the part, in this interpretation, that Britain did for an earlier generation of national pundits. Not all the Begrudgers may project the analysis to the point that Kieran Allen does, hoping for militant class action by workers 'to move from economic struggles to a revolutionary challenge to the system as a whole',[9] but the use of such language awakens a frisson of nostalgia. (What became of the Irish left will be addressed later in this book.)

Peadar Kirby and others prefer to target what they call 'neo-liberalism' as the malign force that has entered Ireland along with globalization and Europeanization, at uncounted human cost. This is in marked contrast to Commissioner Byrne's Pollyanna view: 'From the earliest introduction of equal pay in compliance with EU laws, which was spearheaded by Ireland's first commissioner, Dr Patrick Hillery, through to the ongoing development of various social policies to protect workers' rights, to increased workers' benefits and the introduction of the Social Charter, Ireland and the Union provide an example of how economic progress can be achieved without the necessity to curtail advances in social policy.'[10] Denis O'Hearn is one economist who sharply disagrees, arguing that the state 'abjectly failed to mobilise the fiscal resources that were created by rapid growth in order to reduce inequality and improve social welfare', instead funnelling these windfalls back through tax reductions that favoured the wealthier members of Irish society.[11] Like the late economic historian Raymond Crotty, in many ways the father of the Begrudgers, O'Hearn argues a variety of dependency theory that sets modernized Ireland adrift in the slipstream of the US boom cycle.

Certainly transnational companies generated much of Ireland's growth in the 1990s: 45 per cent of it in the first half of the decade, 85 per cent in the latter. The opening of the economy created a situation where exports grew twentyfold in the thirty years from 1970 to 2000, and imports eightfold.[12] Trade data are, however, decisively distorted by the way US multinationals use Ireland as a tax haven. One area where controversy flourishes is how far this is translated into growth in indigenous sectors of the economy. Several commentators emphasize the removal of profits from the Irish economy by multinationals repatriating their winnings; but not everyone agrees. In 1998 the Central Statistics Office estimated that while the thirty-four largest multinational companies accounted for exports worth £25 billion, they imported £16 billion. After tax their profit came to £7 billion, and their eventual contribution to the Irish GNP was about £3 billion out of a total figure of £53 billion – only 6 per cent. Thus William Keating argues that we exaggerate the extent of dependence on multinationals, and the extent of their exploitation of the Irish economy.[13] Others, such as Michael O'Sullivan, argue that, although foreign firms account for the lion's share of export figures, business research and development in Ireland, they exist against a background of very many small businesses providing business and consumer services that operate in an 'old economy' style, starkly different from the miracle-working of the multinationals.[14]

Eamon de Valera once testily contradicted a journalist who suggested that economic self-sufficiency might bring about a lower standard of living – not because this assumption was untrue, but because he disagreed with the very concept. 'You say "lower" when you ought to say a less costly standard of living. I think it quite possible that a less costly standard of living is desirable and that it would prove, in fact, to be a higher standard of living. I am not satisfied that the standard of living and the mode of living in Western Europe is a right or proper one.'[15] The Begrudging tendency would not take things so far, but another area of disagreement concerns what has happened to the social integument in Ireland over the last quarter-century. One of the most persuasive of the Begrudgers (and certainly the best writer among them), Fintan O'Toole, argues that the price of achieving prosperity has been paid by the poor, literally and figuratively: much as Kirby argues that economic 'success' (in neo-liberal terms) and social failure are linked.[16] Certainly the CIA *World Factbank 2000*, surveying inequality in ten European countries, put Ireland in the unenviable top place. The UN's *Human Development Programme Report* in 2003 concurred, and other authorities have stressed that, though absolute poverty has clearly decreased over the last thirty years in Ireland, relative poverty has increased.[17] This is less immediately obvious than the generalized sense of prosperity. By the turn of the century the Economic and Social Research Institute's analysis, and the Central Statistics Office, showed dramatic falls in absolute poverty, an increase in the values of social benefits, unemployment slashed to a quarter of its 1980s levels and an overall rise in after-tax household income.[18] This is to concentrate upon the lower- and middle-income earners. How very rich the rich have got is another and more strato-spheric affair entirely. It will be addressed, logically enough, in the chapter on Fianna Fáil politics.

It cannot be denied that the nature of Irish poverty has changed drastically over the last quarter-century, since the magazine *Magill* produced its shocking issue on Irish poverty in 1980, which estab-lished just under a million people (of a total population of 3.2 million) living below the poverty line.[19] Social inequality was the greatest in the EEC; the proportion of total income going to the poorest 30 per cent was the smallest in Europe, while the richest 30 per cent of the population received a far higher proportion of the total income than the EEC average. It was found that 800,000 people, a third of them children, lived an existence dependent on weekly social welfare or health board payments. The real revelation of this inquiry was, per-haps, the large number of wage earners who lived below poverty levels, for all the Irish Congress of Trades Unions' recurrent attempts to address the problem of low-paid workers. Simultaneously, un-employment had been rising steadily since the mid-1970s recession, and there was general agreement that the statistics underestimated the number actually unemployed. (Statistics overall were a problem; the Central Statistics Office in fact stopped compiling information on the distribution of incomes in 1969, despite the fact that the *Third Programme for Economic and Social Development* declared the need for it, and Patrick Lyons's 1972 study of the distribution of wealth declared that Ireland was unique among developed nations in having no centrally collected information about wealth distribution.) Statistics about farm incomes are also notoriously evasive, but it does seem that even in 1978, towards the end of a supposed boom period for farm income, half of farm households earned less than £2,000 p.a., and the picture of aged people existing on supplementary benefits in a depopulated and under-resourced countryside spoke vividly for itself.

II

Population matters. Jonathan Swift long ago pointed out that the wealth of a nation consisted in its people, and proceeded to argue that economic logic dictated that the impoverished and undernourished Irish should therefore turn to eating their children. Today's economists similarly see 'human capital' in terms of sustenance, supplying one of the explanations for Ireland's economic miracle. A well-educated, highly literate, English-speaking labour force was not only on the spot to work for enterprising foreign companies tempted in by tax breaks; their elder brothers and sisters, reared for emigration rather than the table, were prepared to return home and bring their skills back to the domestic marketplace. Irish education, denounced by Sean O'Faolain a half-century before as an ignorant, narrow, unrealistic parody imposed by morons on the 'hopeless putty' of Irish children,[20] had been converted into a process of enablement.

This happened as part of the generational shift that occurred in Irish politics as well as in Irish life during the 1960s. In 1965 a ground-breaking OECD-financed investigation produced a report called *Investment in Education*. This sidestepped the usual clerical guardians of received educational wisdom and revealed the brutal inadequacy of traditional Irish education as well as its inbuilt class bias and its archaic obsession with Gaelicization and religion. De Valera's all too representative minister for education, Tom Derrig, who monopolized the office up to 1948, had believed privately that 'education beyond the elementary level destroyed children's ancestral cultures'.[21] In-equalities were certainly sustained by the traditional structures of the Irish educational system. But *Investment in Education* called attention to the fact that by the early 1960s a new generation of politicians, notably minister for education Patrick Hillery and his successor Donogh O'Malley, were determined to use educational policy as a way of declaring their independence from the old Fianna Fáil dispensation. Seán Lemass had already pressed for raising the school-leaving age to fifteen in 1960; his younger colleagues pioneered the introduction of free post-primary education from the mid 1960s, followed by the upgrading of vocational schools, the introduction of community schools, regional technical colleges and, eventually, two new univer-sities. In 1968 a suggestive (and controversial) article in the Jesuit jour-nal *Studies* by the assistant secretary at the Department of Education drew attention to the quiet revolution under way. The changes in school-leaving age and the introduction of free post-primary education (and free transport) meant that the numbers enrolled in secondary edu-cation went from 96,058 to 116,859 in the decade 1958–1968.[22] Numbers of those attending university more than doubled between 1961 and 1971, and attendance at technical colleges quadrupled. Be-tween 1961 and 1991 third-level student places increased twentyfold, an expansion that took off in the 1980s and was turbocharged by the removal of university fees in the next decade.

Thus reforms in educational provision and access were well in place by the early 1980s (a gloomy point for the Irish economy), though the figures of those leaving school before the age of fifteen, in working-class areas such as Ballyfermot, argued against a total transform-ation.[23] This was to improve over the next twenty years. But how much? Looking at the results of the Celtic Tiger in 2000, the Begrudgers emphasize that one of the prime boasts of the Boosters, Ireland's superior education system, has not been able to stand the strains of modernization. There are signs that Irish education, for all the boasting of the IDA, is not keeping pace with the demands of the growing population, and government expenditure (which is very low in comparative European terms) has not combated this.[24] For years Irish educational standards have been touted as one of the reasons behind the economic miracle; but in 1995 an International Adult

Literacy test put Ireland ninth out of ten European economies, beating only Portugal, while in 1997 an OECD literacy survey administered another severe shock, showing that more than 50 per cent of those surveyed fell into the two lowest brackets.[25] Achievements in mathematics and science are also well below average. Moreover, as in Britain and the US, middle-class parents are paying more and more for fee-paying schooling (enabled in part to do so by the abolition of university fees). In education, as elsewhere, inequality of opportunity may have changed its forms but not its essence.

And the question of inequality forms the main plank of the Begrudgers' platform. Statistics apparently bear them out. Ireland currently has the highest proportion of its population living in 'relative poverty' in the EU, and one of the highest rates 'at persistent risk of poverty' (exceeded only by Greece and, again, Portugal).[26] As for the share of the national income received by the poorest 10 per cent of the population and by the richest (the so-called Robin Hood index), the Irish pattern continues to adhere much more closely to the American than to the Western European model. By 2000 the richest 1 per cent of the Irish population had seen their share of total disposable income more than double, compared to the 1970s and 1980s; the disparity between incomes in the top 20 per cent of the population and in the bottom 20 per cent was greater than anywhere else in Western Europe except (by half a per cent) Britain.[27] The Tiger does not devote much care to its more puny cubs: even some noted Boosters admit the recent decline in social services.[28] The picture here may suggest a two-tier society, of a kind recognizable to analysts of boom countries elsewhere in the world but new for Ireland.

Granted, social mobility looks striking within the Republic in 2000 compared to, say, 1973. Yet a survey of the phenomenon over this exact period shows that, though the proportion of workers in professional or managerial roles rose dramatically, the underlying structures stayed much the same. 'Almost all of this mobility is due to the changing occupational structure and the sheer number of higher class positions available, rather than being due to increasing openness in the way that higher class positions are allocated.'[29] Yet one of the traditional beliefs about Ireland is that it does not have a class system in the way that Britain does. To anyone who has actually lived in

Ireland, the notion of class is hardly alien; though its structural base may operate differently in Cork than in Cheltenham, the stratifications, codes, signals and exclusions are no less complex and rigid. What is true is that class politics, in the sense of ideological divides, are not manifested in the same way, and the unideological nature of the Irish Labour Party, and to a certain extent of the Irish trades union movement (though, unlike in Britain, it developed separately), needs to be considered in this context. For one of the alleged bases for Irish prosperity is the phenomenon of so-called 'social partnership': the recurrent initiatives of government and the unions to make agreements whereby wages, taxation and productivity are linked in a structure that ensures growth and inhibits industrial unrest and inflation.

Again, this is a development that goes back further than many Tigerish analysts recognize. The National Wage Agreements of the 1970s are often ignored, perhaps because (as the political scientist Niamh Hardiman has pointed out) both parties to the agreements often ignored them themselves (particularly private employers and the white-collar unions). The emergence of employers' organizations in the 1960s is also an important development.[30] And so is the background of epic strikes in that decade. The maintenance workers' six-week strike in 1969 seemed to herald an era of anarchic free-for-all bargaining, despite the existence of the National Industrial and Economic Council since 1963. (It would lapse in the 1970s.) Still, though the Federated Union of Employers would run into conflict with the government over issues like an Unfair Dismissals Act and the Employment Equality Act, a structured approach to the thorny issue of pay regulation was precipitated in the 1970s, when the country was faced with crisis-level unemployment and the threat of inflationary pay rises. Seven National Wage Agreements were constructed in the years 1970–78, setting norms, phases, conditions of employment and productivity targets, and attempting to prohibit above-the-norm claims. These involved, from the union side at least, some social-engineering content, but that seems to have had little enough effect. Certainly promises of welfare reform were included in the tortuous outlines of the 'National Understanding' of 1979, which was intended to be the most ambitious attempt at an integrated policy yet. But everything was conditional on pay policy, itself conditioned by the returning threat of an oil crisis and the ever present terror of inflation, the spectre that stalked the newspaper columns of the age but was so insouciantly forgotten when it seemed to have melted away in the new dawn of the 1990s.[31]

It was also in the late 1970s that ordinary taxpayers took to the streets in protest, and that the Dublin Economists' Workshop issued warning after warning of the need for drastic remedial action, faced with the huge foreign debts and precarious balance of payments incurred by Fianna Fáil governments.[32] None of this inhibited the astonishingly bullish forecasts of Martin O'Donoghue, minister for economic development in this era (and, as such, Mephistopheles to his taoiseach Jack Lynch's Faust).[33] In fact, the pressure behind a concordat with organized labour – an Irish solution for a not entirely Irish problem – was actually imposed by the guidelines for avoiding inflation laid down by the EEC since Ireland's recent entry into the European Monetary System. The 1979 'National Understanding' was not achieved easily, and when the Irish Congress of Trade Unions initially rejected it Brian Lenihan on behalf of Fianna Fáil was ready to blame 'reds' with 'alien ideologies'.[34] But much of its origins lay in 'alien' Europe, and here too was a pointer for the future. In some ways *étatisme* came easily to Ireland, a country with a tradition of governments restricting property rights, compulsorily acquiring land, monopolizing energy and transport on behalf of the state and forcing people to land at Shannon Airport at no obvious convenience to themselves. A corporatist approach to labour relations was not an illogical development and proved to be something of a life-saver.

Yet the early 1980s saw a falling growth rate, rising unemployment, polarizing farm incomes and government borrowing at 14 per cent of GNP – the unwelcome result of Fianna Fáil's pump-priming measures on the basis of increased government borrowing and their propensity – as one observer put it – to spend their way out of a boom. In June 1980 an ESRI forecast expected 20 per cent inflation and soaring unemployment; a year later, five leading Irish economists prophesied even worse figures. The balance of payments deficit was running at 13 per cent of GNP, and a budget deficit of IR£800 million was projected: the Irish pound itself had effectively devalued by 14 per cent since Ireland entered the EMS.[35] The workforce accordingly became restive. A second 'National Understanding' collapsed in 1982, and collective bargaining returned to a decentralized model for five years. Hardiman would argue that Ireland's peculiar class structure and unideological variety of labour politics made 'National Understandings' harder, not easier, to sustain. Economic policy had remained random and ad hoc; overall, the upward trend in public expenditure since the 1960s, and the failure to arrest it, 'had nothing whatsoever to do with the influence on government of imaginary Keynesian ideologues but with the infinitely more mundane pressures of realpolitik and vote-catching'.[36] It is also true that the analysis of how inflation worked from the shop-floor perspective left something to be desired; the general secretary of the ICTU later recalled that his members instructed him to 'Secure a really *big* increase this time, so big that inflation *can't* catch up.'[37]

But the wind was changing. One indication was that 1980 represented a peak of trade union membership, which thereafter declined spectacularly as a percentage of the workforce.[38] By 1987, when the next centralized agreement was negotiated, economic decline seemed to have reached a critical level. In fact, it now appears that this was when the miracle was just about to happen. Over the following sixteen years, three- or four-year pacts were consecutively arrived at, pioneering a new language that attempted to combine industrial peace, competitiveness, fairness, inclusiveness and 'promoting an entrepreneurial culture'. This was accompanied by a dramatic decline in strike activity, as well as a reversal of fortune in unemployment statistics. By this stage too the shifts in Irish industry were becoming apparent: in terms of ownership, a shift from indigenous to foreign, and in nature, from the old industries of food, footwear and clothing to the miracles of microelectronics and chemical engineering, conducted by companies that did not care for unionization. The IDA had been targeting such people since 1974; in 1980 they had just landed the Fujitsu Corporation, lured by sweeteners worth a reputed IR£20 million. By that stage 13,500 people were already employed in the microchip industry.[39] These were straws in the wind. The kind of growth rate that would radically reduce unemployment (and dilute confrontational ideology) had not been delivered by the late 1980s, but it appeared, like a miraculous beast materializing in a forest clearing, from 1990, and economists are still not entirely sure why. Nor can sociologists agree whether it has been an entirely good thing. And revisionists are beginning to wonder why the unicorn stayed hidden within the sacred grove for so long, and if its ultimate appearance was really such a miracle after all.[40]

But how modern, after all, is modernized Ireland? And how might historians approach the themes that contemporary analysts (both optimists and pessimists) agree have dictated the seismic changes in the island of Ireland? One way is to look yet again at outside influence, and to consider how much Irish transformation owes to Europe and to the USA; and to what extent the closest neighbour and ancient oppressor still plays a role in the Island of Destiny.

III

The importance of the entry into the EMS in 1979 has been instanced as one of the preconditioning factors behind attempts at 'social partnership', and the more general view does interpret the entry into 'Europe' in 1973 as a key point of transformation – sometimes to the point of ignoring underlying changes (such as the population rise and the stabilization of emigration) that were already under way. It is also worth remembering that the desire to join what was then the Common Market was distinctly articulated in several quarters from 1957, the year *before* T. K. Whitaker's legendary argument for planning and economic expansion. Ireland's first application came as early as 1961, and it was already clear that the Common Agricultural Policy held out the prospect of converting Irish cattle and sheep into so many golden geese. General de Gaulle's 'non' derailed this; by 1967 the reaction was more favourable, though Ireland's fate still seemed to be associate membership only. Finally, however, all the winning symbols came up on the European fruit machine in 1973, and a shower of money was confidently expected into the milking parlours of Ireland.

This followed the referendum of May 1972, showing 83 per cent support for joining. We hear less nowadays about the firm opposition of certain political and other interest groups, notably Sinn Féin as well as various coteries of the Labour movement. While some arguments were put forward about 'rich men's clubs' and the like, there was also a distinctly nativist reaction against dilution of Irish essences – countered by the government with the argument that attachment to the great European entity would actually extend Ireland's sovereignty rather than decrease it, especially if Irish people played a large role in the EEC's institutions. (So they did, providing commissioners who ran the gamut of substance and talent down the scale of evolution from Peter Sutherland to Pádraig Flynn.) Some leftist opposition lasted on into the later 1970s, but at voter level a certain antipathy persisted about EU membership; the first to recognize its potential, apart from farmers, seem to have been voluntary groups. Ahern's romantic belief that Ireland's relations with Europe have been from the beginning 'dynamic, yet sensitive'[41] (as in a Barbara Cartland love-story) needs some reconsideration. His forerunner Jack Lynch put it more interestingly, remarking that for Ireland to join Europe was like Robinson Crusoe finally coming off his island.[42] This is dangerously near the controversial image employed by F. S. L. Lyons to describe Ireland during the Second World War, when the outside world appeared only as the reflected images thrown up on the wall of Plato's Cave (suggesting to Lyons's critics an unacceptably Anglocentric view). But Lynch, as it turned out, would show a surprising readiness to challenge some ruling pieties, if in a characteristically low-key way.

Another taoiseach (and passionate European), Garret FitzGerald, subsequently remarked that in many Irish quarters the advantages of going into Europe were drastically underestimated in the early 1970s. FitzGerald unequivocally credits EU membership with putting the spring into the step of the Celtic Tiger.

Had it not been for the opening of the European market to Irish-made products as a result of EC membership, none of these advantages, natural or policy-created, could have produced the kind of economic growth that Ireland has experienced during most of the period since the 1960s – running well ahead of that of the rest of Europe during most of this period. It was the availability of this European market that initially created the scale of demand for labour in Ireland that eventually became such an extraordinary feature of the 1990s ... Has there been any economic downside to our membership? Whilst one can argue that the rapidity of the transformation of the Irish economy from by far the poorest in Northern Europe to one of the most prosperous in what is now the European Union has created some social stresses and strains, in purely economic terms it has been almost all sheer gain.[43]

It does seem clear that the government soon focused upon the treasure ship of the European Structural Funds designed to develop economic infrastructure, and the National Development Plan of the late 1970s was aimed at luring this galleon into an Irish harbour.[44] The European Monetary System would remove Ireland's link to an apparently plummeting sterling and support the Irish 'punt' to keep it within the allowable band of fluctuation. That malign doppelgänger, inflation, would remain attached to sterling and detach itself from the freed 'punt'.[45] (The old language of irredentist nationalism seems at this point to elide into that of new-style economics.) As more European economies became more integrated, things would get better for Ireland. In any case, both the main parties argued from the late 1970s that Ireland would need an annual subsidy of at least £600 million to facilitate this new arrangement. Eventually, by embracing the euro, Ireland would concede to Europe some powers over monetary policy and currency – which has mostly proved a good thing, in terms of government debt and budget deficits. Currency movements in the wider world have also, so far, kept interest rates low in Ireland and initially slowed inflation, though the low interest-rate regime has sustained an unhealthy bubble in house prices. If the economy overheats dangerously, the picture may look rather different. Moreover, the kind of underlying suspicion and resentment of 'Europe' shown in some leftist and Republican quarters persisted through the Tiger years, and eventually rebounded with force when the populace rejected the Nice Treaty by referendum – a severe shock to the system.[46] The way that a positive vote was subsequently engineered in late 2002 did not argue very convincingly for democratic autonomy. 'Europe' had also come to stand for other kinds of inputs into the Irish system – including in the legal sphere. Not everyone either realized or appreciated the importance of the European Court of Justice, which, while it could provide a useful stick with which to beat Britain's rule in Northern Ireland, could also threaten a certain constitutional instability in Irish law.[47]

But the perceived downsides of full EU membership were as nothing compared to the obvious advantages. Here the arguments remained firmly grounded in agrarian economics, always a special case in Ireland, and always packing a powerful political punch. In some ways the golden shower of Euromoney into the Irish countryside replicated earlier government strategies regarding the farmer backbone of the country, for whose sake the sharp wind of taxation was tempered even to the well-fleeced lamb. The *Second Programme for Economic Expansion* in 1964 initiated bonus schemes targeted at small farmers as well as direct income support. Farms under twenty-six acres were exempt from having to keep account books, let alone return taxes, though generally the bigger the farm, the more it benefited from special tax status. Rural poverty was a 'given', and the state felt the responsibility keenly. This would change dramatically when the Common Agricultural Policy enveloped rural Ireland: one commentator has described it as 'the main influence on the Irish state since the early seventies'.[48] In its origins it was, after all, a protectionist scheme to ensure good prices for farmers and reward productivity, just as de Valera would have vehemently approved. The levels to which prices were driven up were not originally anticipated when the CAP was drafted in 1962, and nor was the crisis of overproduction. But both were clearly indicated when Ireland joined ten years later. 'Intensification' and 'productivism' became keywords, and so did changes in scale. In the 1970s, 81 per cent of the funding received from Europe was directed towards agriculture, and by 1978 real farm incomes had doubled. But the way the subsidies worked reflected and reaffirmed long-standing Irish patterns of farming activity, geographical as well as economic. Price-support structures favoured large milk producers and capital-intensive activities requiring large acreages. The same pattern was evinced in structural handouts, where most of the money for farm improvement went to highly commercialized farmers in the better-off eastern half of the island. Nearly all the 'headage' subsidies, on the other hand, went to 'the western package' in a welfarist initiative that encouraged animal rearing and, eventually, overgrazing. Even in dairy production, the small producers went to the wall – as was obvious by the end of the decade.[49] Farmers with more than a hundred acres (the top 17 per cent) secured 40 per cent of all price-support funding.[50]

In a manner long familiar to Irish rural observers, the more you had, the more you got: a process that has been exacerbated with time.

This polarization, and the persistence of much real poverty among small farmers, was not obvious to Ireland's non-farming population, where a general assumption persisted that all farmers were not only gently treated by the state but were now being royally supported by Europe. This took a political form in the late 1970s. The share of national income tax paid by those conventionally taxed at source went up from 71.4 per cent to 86.5 per cent in the years 1975–8; by the last year, they were providing £1,800 million of the tax take, the self-employed £320 million and the farmers a modest £20 million. In fact, companies tax was even more disproportionately low: corporations paid only 5 per cent of the total tax take, though by some computations it should have been nearer 46 per cent.[51] (Here again was a pointer for the future.) From 1975 white-collar workers were agitating for income-tax reform at trade union conferences; by 1979 they had taken to the streets. The government's reaction was to suggest a 2 per cent levy on farm profits (a previous, unsuccessful attempt to tax farmers had been made by Richie Ryan in 1974). But the levy was abandoned in March 1979, for purely political reasons.[52] Had the farmers got away with it again?

Efforts to tax farmers had, in fact, been made before the revolutions of the 1970s. Before 1969 the approach had been decidedly notional. Farmers could opt for an impost based on one and a half to two times the rateable valuation of a farm – which in itself was based on calculating the rental value vis-à-vis agricultural prices of twenty years before then. This was recognized as spectacularly irrelevant by 1970 and recalculated, but many loopholes were left open. The idea of notional assessment based on a multiplier applied to rateable valuation persisted; the number of farmers paying tax went up from 9,200 in 1975 to 27,000 in 1979, though inequities were still glaring. Farmers claimed that basing tax on farm income ignored all sorts of hidden expenses, reinvestments, loans and so on, upon which modern farming depended; ordinary taxpayers countered that there was nothing modern about the farmers' approach to tax and their expectations of special treatment. The arguments would sputter on through the 1980s. The reason why resentment burst out in 1979 was, of course, because the effects of entry into the EEC were becoming apparent. A survey by the economist Alan Matthews at the end of 1978 had calculated that under the CAP, Irish farmers profited by about £800 million, of which half came in direct subsidy from the EEC and half through higher prices for domestic produce (in other words, from Irish consumers).[53] But it did not raise the question of uneven development, or anticipate how the effects of the CAP and then the Tiger would change the face of rural Ireland.

This had been anticipated in some other quarters. In 1965 the legendary name of the National Land League was actually revived in an association of small farmers who opposed entry into Europe; they set their faces against multinationals and 'intensifiers', in place of the landlords or graziers of the late nineteenth century. Over the next decade membership rose to 7,500, still unconvinced by EU economics. In the early EU years, while farm prices rocketed, output had lagged behind; for those without broad acres, the intervening space was too often filled by endless credit from 'the banks'. Meanwhile traditional modes of farming continued in many areas, and so did the flight from the land. In the mid 1970s, 80 per cent of Irish land still changed hands within the family, and the small proportion that came on the open market was outrageously overpriced. But a process was under way whereby farm sizes were inexorably creeping up. Nearly half of Irish farms were over fifty acres in size by 1991. Demographic shifts were coinciding with the advent of Eurofunding and agribusiness. By the end of the 1970s a survey of farmers' lifestyles could be titled 'Peasants No More'.[54] It was obvious that the CAP and the Farm Modernization Scheme had helped bring about phenomena such as a fivefold increase in milk prices, and profitable switches to dairying and sheep-rearing (the latter transformed by the opening of the French market to Ireland in 1978). But that same decade of miracles had seen the number of dairying cooperatives decline by two thirds, as big-business techniques took over. As the 1980s dawned, a perceptive observer forecast that Irish rural sociology, traditionally preoccupied with analysing the world of the small producer, should turn its attention to 'the culture of a corporate elite extending into agribusiness, industrial, commercial and political circles'.[55]

None the less, the history of Irish farming, when it comes to look at the revolutionary effect of EEC membership, will not see unalloyed advantage for everyone. The arrival of the European Monetary System in 1979 was just about to introduce a further critical effect on Irish agriculture, and 'Green Pound' devaluations were no longer there to take the brunt. For all the advent of apparent prosperity in the 1970s and the continuation of special treatment, in the 1980s Irish agriculture still looked like a peripheral region, and the Irish food-producing industries had not yet made their mark. Crucially, all the reform of the CAP from the mid 1980s moved the goal posts further. Overproduction was now critical; high consumer costs had proved to be an integral result of the policies of the past twenty years; the CAP was absorbing 70 per cent of the EU budget; the marginalization of smaller farmers as well as the environmental costs of intensification were obvious in Ireland as elsewhere. New patterns of land use and zoning were prospected in an attempt to reduce production, but so far these seem generally to have been taken up by medium-sized farms rather than acting as lifelines for the smallest. At the end of 1998 the EU was paying 40 per cent of direct aid for arable crops to just 4 per cent of farmers; 70 per cent of the direct aid budget was swallowed up by just 10 per cent of farmers.[56] At the beginning of the new century subsidy (the Single Farm Payment) would be decoupled completely from a directional policy allied to subsidizing certain activities, along with cuts in prices. Commercial farmers have continued business as usual; smaller farmers are paid by the EU and, as long tradition dictates, the Irish state, simply to survive. The Irish countryside is one area where prosperity has had a divisive effect over the last thirty years, and interacted potently with the demographic revolution that has accompanied economic transformation.

Part of that transformation has been a shift away from the emphasis on rural production that had characterized Ireland for so long. At the end of the 1990s, Irish export figures showed food products trailing a long distance behind electrical equipment and pharmaceuticals – a statistic that concealed the fact it depended increasingly upon 'miscellaneous food', which included US-owned cola concentrate products as well as new-look yoghurts and low-fat *crème fraîche* manufactured by giants like Glanbia and Kerry Foods.[57] By the turn of the century those two agribusinesses, with three smaller organizations somewhat behind, were the only food producers to make it into Ireland's thirty top companies, ranked by turnover: a list headed by builders, computer-chip manufacturers, packaging and computer software, which by then accounted for 40 per cent of all exports from Ireland. The graph of those in non-agricultural employment between 1973 (when it was 27 per cent of the population) and the end of the century, when it was heading for 40-plus, soared.[58] The Irish economic miracle has been analysed in terms of simple time-warp: this interpretation argues that it happened when the productivity of non-agricultural workers belatedly reached the levels of other industrialized countries. The same analysts add that productivity within the agricultural labour force has risen too, but this conceals a drastic reordering within the Irish countryside.[59]

In 1966, during the celebrations for the half-centenary of the Easter Rising, Charles Haughey declared, 'What finer end could there be for a boy who aspires to become a man according to Pearse's ideal than to follow the calling of the land?'[60] Like jesting Pilate, he did not stay for an answer. When the century ended 3,000 farmers a year were leaving the land. One Mayo farmer, reviewing his options, recently decided to turn his few remaining animals into a 'mobile farm', to be taken on tour around primary schools in the county, demonstrating to the children what their forefathers did for a living.[61] Others have rented out their small farms to larger operators or taken to selling sites. The face of the country has changed, first in the 1990s with subsidized afforestation and setting designated land aside; now in place of a field of beasts there are likely to be fields with brand-new houses rained down into them, often let out on short-term rents to the workforce staffing a nearby town's new software plant, or standing empty against the hope of capital accumulation or an emigrant's return. The right of local people to build houses and sell land, without benefit of sustainable planning guidelines or observing vernacular architectural style and practice, is fiercely articulated by county councillors, often to their own profit. And they know they speak on behalf of a constituency whose fields are now seen in terms of bricks and mortar rather than annual crops or fattening cattle. There has been, since 1973, the most far-reaching revolution in the Irish countryside since that created by the Land Acts between 1881 and 1909. It was the product of a conjunction between Irish traditions and European policy, but the importation of American business practices also contributed something to a development whose outcome is as yet uncertain. In this, the revolution in the land might stand as an image of the economy as a whole.

IV

It also raises the question of how far Ireland's transformation has been influenced by America rather than Europe. Approval of the idea of Europe is consistently high in Ireland, though there are indications that this approval falls along lines that are to a certain extent dictated by class as well as by political ideology.[62] At the same time, one of the chief Begrudger arguments about Ireland over the last thirty years (the exact period of EU membership) is that the country has repudiated the social-democratic European model of high taxation and liberal spending on social provision in favour of the American model now supposedly embraced by Britain too: low taxation and, in terms of the social security and healthcare safety-net, the devil take the hindmost. This means opting, in the fashionable shorthand, for Boston rather than Berlin. And this implicitly raises another popular Begrudger argument: has the historical shadow of Britain's evil empire, stunting Ireland's growth, draining her resources and imposing degraded cultural standards on a dependent population, simply been replaced by an equally enervating cloud from the West? Is the real historical phenomenon of the last generation not the Europeanization of Irish society but the Americanization of the Irish economy, and much else?

By 2001 Ireland would feature at the top of a list of countries most intensively 'globalized', and would remain there.[63] The criteria considered involve economic integration, trade statistics, foreign direct investment, capital flows, travel and tourism, international telephone traffic, internet use, cross-border financial transfers, membership of international associations and so on: but the weight falls most heavily on economic indicators. Michael O'Sullivan has argued that Ireland's experience of globalization is different from the usual cases presented for analysis, which tend to be from the Third (or, at best,

Second) World. Ireland's peculiar history as a kind of metropolitan economy, and its First World credentials since cooption into the core of the EU, have enabled the country to experience globalization in an essentially positive way – partly through pragmatism and partly through keeping state involvement at a low level.[64] Less positively inclined commentators argue that in the context of Irish cultural orientation, as well as economic activity, globalized simply means Americanized, and for some time cultural critics such as Fintan O'Toole have been asserting that modern Ireland was, in a real sense, unimaginable without the defining dimension of America.[65]

Certainly there are tempting arguments to assert this in cultural terms; anyone who reads Daniel Boorstin's prophetic study *The Image* (1962) will recognize the cult of self-presentation, the worship of celebrity, the odd derivative kitschiness that infects many areas of Irish life today and is served up every week in the pages of the *Sunday Independent*. The street names adorning a new Irish suburb, or one of those Potemkin Villages mushrooming up in the countryside, may, to the annoyance of the *Irish Times* letters page, borrow references from English history or the novels of Sir Walter Scott, but the spatial layout and eclectic architectural references rendered in perdurable PVC materials suggest a transatlantic derivation. At a more quantifiable level, 75 per cent of all Foreign Direct Investment in Ireland was American-based by the 1990s.[66] If earlier multinational companies had been lured by cheap labour, the Americans were especially seduced by tax advantages under a US–Ireland double taxation agreement, which continued to give Cathleen Ni Houlihan the edge over other foreign sirens. In turn, Irish companies began to follow American organizational patterns, and to expand.[67] The leftist critique claims that the US invasion was the result of various levels of over-absorption having been reached in the American economy, and the availability of economic breaks for fat-cat businesses, offered by collaborationist fat-cat economic advisers in Dublin. This results in enormous levels of profits repatriated back to the USA. The optimists, on the other hand, argue that not only money and jobs but also expertise and new business models are disseminated into the indigenous economy. They also argue that the mating of the Celtic Tiger with the lean, mean prairie wolf of American international capitalism was facilitated by local infrastructures and abilities. These native advantages particularly feature high educational standards, and the traditional Irish facility for verbal communication.

W. B. Yeats liked to remember Oscar Wilde announcing to him over Christmas dinner, 'we are a nation of brilliant failures, but we are the greatest talkers since the Greeks.'[68] The failure has been replaced by success, but the talk goes on. From about 1990 the traditional mantra for self-sufficiency, 'Ourselves Alone', mutated into 'Ourselves Online'. This was an astonishingly sudden leap. In 1949 there were 43,000 exchange telephone lines in Ireland; those who grew up in the subsequent era remember the single phone in the freezing hallway, the crisis aura that surrounded every trunk call. As late as 1970 Dublin house-sale advertisements could be enhanced by the alluring promise that the property actually possessed a telephone line. But the communications revolution, like so much else, really began in the 1970s. In 1978 the Posts and Telegraphs Review Group announced an ambitious programme to bring the telephone system up to European standards by 1985: subscriber lines were to be doubled, 200 new sites and 560 buildings acquired for enhanced facilities, and new automatic systems introduced. This was heavily promoted by the Industrial Development Authority; a third of the Irish industrialists interviewed by the Confederation of Irish Industries in 1975 cited telecommunications as a primary inhibitor of economic development. This was hardly surprising: there were 16 phone lines per 100 population, compared to 39 in Britain and 69 in Sweden, and a waiting list of at least 85,000 people; while, of the two exchange systems used, one went back to the end of the nineteenth century.

The microelectronic revolution was about to transform all this, but in Ireland it was aided by cutting the red-tape of civil service structures that had obstructed development in the department of Posts and Telegraphs, and by creating a new body to deal with maintenance and industrial relations difficulties. By 1997 the Irish network was handling a billion calls a year. In 1998 an Advisory Committee on Telecommunications told the minister for public enterprise:

Electronic commerce will migrate towards those countries which are to the fore in providing low cost, high quality telecommunications and Internet services, supportive legal and business regimes, and a highly entrepreneurial and technically skilled workforce. Given that neither physical size nor location primarily dictate success, Ireland can, with appropriate strategic positioning, sustain its position as Europe's premier knowledge economy.[69]

Five years later the country possessed nearly one and a half million exchange lines, and one of the highest rates of mobile phone usage in the world. As in other areas of economics, starting from a low base rate actually enabled a qualitatively enormous advance – though the privatization of Eircom left Ireland with arguably the worst broadband infrastructure in the industrialized world. Much as the lack of industrialization left the Republic with no redundant heavy-duty plant or antediluvian labour practices to impede a Great Leap Forward, the microelectronic age was embraced without impediment, and with one bound Ireland was modern. By 2006 Kerry County Council, not content with rezoning unspoilt landscapes for one-off housing, enthusiastically gave permission for the erection of a 123-metre receiving mast in front of the marvellous 'Ladies View' of Killarney, to help with mobile-telephone reception in the Black Valley.

These priorities were embraced with a conscious reference to American precedents. As in the 'knowledge economy', so elsewhere in the world of economic activity. Moreover, much that we think of as Tiger-territory stretches back further in time, and a great deal can be laid at the door of the Industrial Development Authority, set up in 1949 in order to provide research and strategic analysis for economic expansion.[70] In the late 1950s, after it was revamped and closely linked to the Central Statistics Office, it began to play a vital part in the quiet revolution that would bear fruit in the 1960s – though transformation really began in 1970 under the dynamic leadership of Michael Killeen, who played a decisive part in revolutionizing Irish industrial practices, directions and attitudes. For most of the history of the Irish independent state, protectionism had been intensely favoured and inward capital investment viewed with deep suspicion. But from early on the IDA looked to American examples, American contacts and American markets – originally symbolized by the duty-free zone instituted at Shannon Airport, the American gateway to Ireland. Marshall Aid had already started the process of exposing

Irish economic analysts to American business culture.[71] By 1970 the young hawks of the IDA were more interested in bringing the wisdom of American MBAs to bear on the Irish situation, while the organization had developed its own ethos, and a practice of targeting certain areas of industry as deserving of expansion.

Food processing was one predictable choice, spearheaded by the charismatic Tony O'Reilly; less expected, but brilliantly far-sighted, were electronics and pharmaceuticals. The IDA was impatient with the sclerotic approach of government departments, and in 1970 it became an independent organization, though with a direct link to the government, devoting its impressive intellectual horsepower to tempting foreign business investment into Ireland. Not all the inducements were well thought through, and not everyone tempted into the spider's parlour became profitably entangled in the web. But it is certainly one of the key elements in the transformation that paid such dividends twenty years later, by which time the offer of a 10 per cent corporation-tax rate interacted with the huge expansion of high-technology firms in the USA looking for expansion abroad.

By the turn of the century, according to some reckonings, 70 per cent of Irish manufactured exports were by US-owned firms.[72] However inflated by the use of Ireland as an American tax haven, the figures are arresting. But the revolution so evident in the 1990s had been coming, courtesy of the IDA, for some time. In 1978, of 200,000 industrial jobs in Ireland, 25 per cent were controlled from abroad; the IDA's four-year plan projected 65,000 new jobs, all controlled from abroad, which would have raised the proportion to 50 per cent.[73] Gerry Adams, his gaze at this point still firmly fixed on the past, liked to claim that Irish profits were being sucked away by 'England', but in fact it was America that predominated. By 1983, 17.5 per cent of the *entire* manufacturing workforce were employed by American-based firms. Ten years later it was 25 per cent.[74] These tended to be in the fields of electronics, pharmaceuticals, healthcare and software – flexible, easily shifted and with high rates of return. The Boosters, or celebrants of the Celtic Tiger, lay great emphasis on the achievement of the IDA in attracting this inward investment; the Begrudgers (including in this case the doyen of Irish economic historians, Cormac Ó Gráda) take a more jaundiced view of that emblematic association.[75]

To take one example, in 1979 the IDA tempted the American electronics company Mostek to establish a plant in Ireland, which would employ 1,100 people over three years. But this involved £42 million in grants, well over the guidelines – because they had to counter-bid against the Scottish Development Agency. Begrudgers pointed out that this would mean a cost per job of £19,500.[76] There was a tax-relief break up to 1990; and all of Mostek's major customers were outside Ireland. It was also an example of a very mobile and footloose organization that could relocate or contract almost overnight, and in the early years of attracting investment, this happened on several occasions.[77]

But the important point is that even as early as 1979 it was clear that the IDA's policy was heavily reliant on American responses, demonstrated by companies like Analog in Raheen, Burlington in Tralee, and Merck, Sharp, Dohme in Clonmel. (The last would prove highly controversial in terms of pollution, and there were contemporary allegations that Ireland's lax pollution laws were an added inducement for certain chemicals companies to relocate.[78]) Between 1960 and 1979 a quarter of all foreign factories established in Ireland were American, and American capital supplied 18 per cent of the 230,000 manufacturing jobs at the end of that period. In 1978 alone, more than half of the new jobs created by the IDA came from America. In 1980 the computer giant Wang set up at Limerick, along with Varian Associates; Ireland was now established as the primary European base for US microelectronics firms.[79] Certainly, recent years have shown that many of these jobs were singularly vulnerable to challenges from other low-cost countries, as well as shivers in the American economy. But another reason for Begrudger scepticism about the American input may be that with the newcomers came a robustly transatlantic view of labour relations, which could be non-union (like Intel's) or positively anti-union (like Ryanair's, which modelled its practices on the American firm Southwest Airlines). Nor did European legislation always sit easily with the IDA's policy of wooing transatlantic companies. In 1981, for instance, new EEC regulations meant that tax was levied on exports despite the sweetener deals on offer when companies started up. And from 2003 Ireland's extra-low corporation-tax rate was ruled illegal too, though this at least meant that new European competitors might be inhibited from stealing the Celtic Tiger's clothes. But by then Ireland's manufacturing economy had been looking westward for some time. 'While Ireland has become more integrated with the EU in macroeconomic terms,' it was judged in 2000, 'the microeconomic structure of its industrial economy has evolved more closely to resemble a region of the US.'[80]

This shift towards America was of symbolic as well as pragmatic importance. Throughout the first fifty years of independence, Ireland's exporting and importing economy had remained tilted towards Britain, and this persisted into the early years of the opened-up Irish economy of the 1960s. Between 1960 and 1970 British-owned companies represented 22 per cent of new industrial enterprises in Ireland. But by 1980 they accounted for less than 2 per cent. Significantly, the proportion of exports to Britain from Ireland halved between 1956 and 1981. True, the open economy meant that there were areas of the economy where British influence remained and grew – including the arrival in Ireland of nearly all the major British retail chains, with considerable implications also for the way people dressed and looked. But by the end of the twentieth century, when analysts began to look at where Ireland stood, they presented – in a paradigm that already sounds clichéd – the two polar alternative models as America or Europe. In fact, what had gone to shape the new-look Irish economy was a hybrid of the two; though the creation of Ireland as a classic small open economy owed much initially to the Free Trade Agreement with Britain of 1965, removing all tariffs by 1975. From 1970 too we see a new and freer use of capital, the autonomous energies of the IDA trying to sell Ireland as a destination for foreign capital investment – and the emergence of the Irish banks as central players, generating huge profits for a few people and exploiting tax loopholes. Meanwhile the Irish agricultural sector, for so long the economic as well as the cultural backbone of the country, was being altered in a way that created more losers than winners and must be counted into any consideration of the inequalities that the various booms left in their wake.

It seems clear overall that much of what has brought about economic transformation goes back to the 1970s rather than arriving suddenly in the readjustments of the late 1980s.[81] It is also obvious that the weight of influence, in terms of economic involvement and business practice, derives from Pittsburgh rather than Paris. The 1990s, after all, were the decade of declining input into the Irish economy from EU structural funds, which peaked in the late 1980s. Danaë's shower of gold was, essentially, replaced by investment from Uncle Sam. Equally striking is the extent to which some of the predisposing factors towards economic expansion have little to do with deliberate policy – the elastic labour supply, for instance, and the demographically favourable conditions that underpinned the transformation of the employment situation in the 1990s. Economic migrants to Ireland, along with asylum-seekers, constituted a rapid and obvious phenomenon. At the beginning of the 1990s annual applications for asylum were fewer than fifty, whereas by 2000 they had reached nearly 11,000. This new element in Irish life was matched by the advent of guest-workers. With the expansion of the Irish labour market a critical shortage of workers was highlighted by several surveys at the turn of the millennium. A work-permit scheme for immigrants was hastily devised, and by 2001 more than 36,000 had been issued, mostly to natives of Latvia, Lithuania, Poland, the Philippines and Romania.[82] Immigration, especially from other EU countries, was aggressively encouraged by recruitment fairs organized by the Irish government abroad. The large majority of incomers were destined for unskilled work, or the health service. They were not always appreciated for it. A xenophobic tinge entered into local politics, especially where asylum-seekers were concerned, and racist incidents mushroomed. Those cosily termed the 'New Irish' have not always received a hundred thousand welcomes. The immigration figures conceal the fact that many 'immigrants' are in fact Irish-born people returning to the country from abroad. None the less the 2006 census showed that out of the Republic's four million residents, 400,000 were born outside Ireland – about three quarters of them in the EU or the USA.[83] This was a pattern undreamt of twenty years before.

Nor was the rapid turnaround in the national fiscal picture from 1987 anticipated: economists expected a long, hard slog to rectitude. A decade earlier, of course, many of them had similarly miscalled the effect of entering the EMS (essentially a diplomatic-political decision), which was supposed to lead to an appreciation of the Irish pound against sterling. This did not happen, though decoupling was advantageous in other ways.[84] Economists, like the rest of us, do not necessarily get the future they expect. Reading, for instance, a large and apparently authoritative study of Ireland and the Single European Market written in the late 1980s, one can only note how many of its forecasts are sublimely wrong.[85] As it turned out, the Irish economy got a future that it had not expected, and may not have deserved.

But the Tiger economy was not born out of nothing, and nor were the attitudes that encouraged it. The figures for the 1990s remain more or less unassailable: a growth rate outperforming that of other EU countries; numbers at work increasing by 45 per cent between 1987 and 2001; unemployment down from 17 per cent to 4 per cent over the same period; the standard of living going from two thirds the EU average to comfortably equalling it; the highest net immigration into the EU; and so on.[86] There remain disagreements about how statistics are compiled, and the varying bases used to calculate even something as fundamental as GNP.[87] This has clear implications for the viability of forecasting. And some things do not change: the Irish inflation rate was double the Eurozone average in the year 2000, for instance (even though Irish house prices are not fully computed into the figures), competitiveness was supposedly faltering, personal debt was running at unparalleled levels, and Irish demography may yet enter another of its unpredictable lurches. History has also shown how previous periods of expansive globalization can be ended by international crisis and war. Still, the evidence of our eyes, as well as the arithmetic up to, say, 2001, shows a transformed country.

The historical perspective might be kept in focus, since it can raise knotty questions of cause and effect: Cormac Ó Gráda, for instance, has mischievously suggested that Ireland's low-tax, low public-debt economy, and indeed the development of social partnership, is the result of the Celtic Tiger rather than its cause, which turns MacSharry on his head.[88] From this angle, Ireland's belated economic success might more reasonably be seen as just that – belated. Finally, at a time when other Western European countries were experiencing de-industrialization, the Republic began to industrialize, if in a distinctively modern, or post-modern, way that turned out to suit its circumstances perfectly (the minute scale of many of the most profitable products of the new economy, for one thing, meant that Ireland was no longer disadvantaged in geographical terms when it came to transporting them). Wilde's 'nation of brilliant failures' got lucky and decided to become successful, not before time.

'Irish political economy', it has been said, 'unfortunately sometimes tends to be more political than economic.'[89] A historian might also note that many of the issues raised about Ireland since 1970 actually highlight ancient arguments, antipathies and prejudices, even if expressed in the language of supposed globalization and postmodernism. Nor, in excitedly debating proximity to Boston or Berlin, should Birmingham be forgotten: much of the sociocultural as well as the economic pattern of the new Ireland is easily assimilable to an Anglo-Saxon model, unwelcome though this sounds. From the early nineteenth century on, the position of Ireland under the Union attracted endless analysis and inspired much debate, a great deal of it hingeing upon the problem of poverty: the extent to which it was indigenous and the possibility of alleviating it by social engineering (at various levels of ruthlessness). The problem of poverty raised in turn questions of national psychology, religious influence, ethnic stereotyping and the inheritances of history. In some ways this kind of discussion would continue throughout the years of Union with Britain, and persist into the frugal era of the first half-century of independence. The Irish now find themselves addressing these issues again but from the vantage of the equally mysterious achievement of prosperity. This prosperity, which was denied the country under policies of economic autonomy, is closely connected to Ireland's unofficial membership of the global economy, and its official membership of a much larger Union than that of the United Kingdom. This basic transformation underlies, and is paralleled by, metamorphoses in spheres of national life that transcend the economic sphere, and they will form the subject of the rest of this book.

2

How the Catholics
Became Protestants

I

'Conversion' might be a metaphor for Irish experience from 1970 to 2000, if not in the strict religious sense of a mission to heretics. Those thirty years saw a transformation of cultural expectations, based not only on a new confidence in the wider world but also on the rejection of old authoritarian formations: patriarchy and the Catholic Church. These two great monoliths came under siege from feminism and secularism after 1970, and the connection and interaction between the threats form the subject of this chapter. In the widest sense the transformation of attitudes to authority, which found its way into the mainstream of politics with surprising speed, suggests a reassertion of attitudes in some areas of life in the Republic that are – with a lower-case *p* at least – protestant.

The notion of Catholicism as indivisible from Irish nationalism and even from Irish identity might be counted as one of the casualties of the last thirty years' cultural upheaval. This sails dangerously near the stormy seas where Horace Plunkett found himself when he launched his book *Ireland in the New Century* in 1904, controversially arguing that the Irish Catholic world-view and ethos retarded economic progress. But his analysis is not so far from the kind of ideas floated by Tom Inglis eighty-odd years later in *Moral Monopoly*, where he relates the forms and practices of Irish society up to the late twentieth century to the images, ideals and dictates of the Catholic Church with regard to occupational structures, the organization and differentiation of social space, even the expression of emotions.[1] Inglis also argues for a definition of 'modernization' that concentrates upon Irish life since the 1960s, rather than the more conventional view of a social and economic 'modernization' taking place from the mid nineteenth century and mediated by the Catholic Church in the post-Famine era. In this he differs from Joe Lee's influential *Ireland 1912–1985*. Inglis also argues against Lee in putting the Catholic 'habitus', rather than the Irish economy, at the basis of Irish fertility and family patterns: 'it was through a rigid adherence to Church teaching on sexual morality that Irish mothers were able to inculcate in their children the type of stem-family practices which were essential to the consolidation of farm sizes and an improvement in the standard of living.'[2]

Even more decisively, he specifically contradicts Lee's assertion that Catholicism or even religiosity had nothing to do with Ireland's laggard economic performance, which Lee puts down to laziness, inefficiency and the 'possessor' mentality (as well as the failure of Irish intellectuals to play their part in the national life). Inglis's countering argument carries an intriguing echo of Horace Plunkett:

Up to the 1960s and in many cases after then, religious belief and practice were often not rationally differentiated from economic and political activity. If it was differentiated it was quietly at the level of practice, but what was done economically and politically was within the ethos and rhetoric of the good Catholic life . . . Even if people were ambitious and successful, they had to deny continually that they had done so deliberately. The state may have decided in its economic policies to pursue unashamedly economic growth and success. But the residues of Catholic culture lingered for longer in the Irish collective consciousness, in their view and understanding of the world and of what constituted the good life and a good person.[3]

The connections between changes in the practice and status of Catholicism in Ireland and the modernization of Irish society over the last decades are still being debated. Louise Fuller's magisterial study of Irish Catholicism since 1950 establishes the stirrings of change among Catholic intellectuals grouped around the *Furrow* magazine, founded in 1950, and forcefully aired by a Jesuit in 1959: 'Too many people in Ireland today are trying to make do with a peasant religion when they are no longer peasants any more; we are a growing and developing middle-class nation, acquiring a middle-class culture, and we must have a religion to fit our needs.'[4] This, it was probably thought at the time, was all very well for Jesuits. But to understand the upheavals to come we must look back at least to the 1960s, and the advent of international radicalism and youth culture – not to mention a native television network. Pope Pius XII himself had taken a lively interest in what state television would mean for the Irish faithful: he enthusiastically anticipated a bulwark against irreligion, materialism and communism, and sent an envoy to Dublin to make the point. His hopes were raised by the fact that the new service was, to the surprise of many, firmly placed under the control of a public authority rather than a commercial company.[5] None the less, the Catholic primate Cardinal D'Alton was acutely aware of the dangers and determined to avert them. On the first night of broadcasting, 31 December 1961, he appeared before viewers, dressed in full regalia, and assured them that they had nothing to fear from the chairman of the new RTÉ Authority, Eamonn Andrews, who

made it clear that he would be a very unhappy man if he sponsored anything that would be either corrupting or might be a cause of scandal . . . I am sure that he and the director-general, Mr Roth, can be depended upon to provide programmes that will be enlightening, entertaining, reflecting high ideas, and not presenting us with the caricature of Irish life such as we have had from some of our writers in recent years.[6]

But hairline cracks would shortly appear in episcopal authority. Archbishop McQuaid of Dublin could still expect to be obeyed when he forbade the young Emmet Stagg in 1962 to take up a job in the godless Trinity College. Stagg, however, defied him; as did the young UCD academic Sister Benvenuta, OP, three years later, when McQuaid demanded to inspect her lecture notes.[7] Stagg would go on to a prominent career as a Labour politician, and 'Sister Ben' (aka Margaret Mac Curtain) would become an immensely admired public figure, both as a distinguished historian and an influential feminist. The changes in attitudes of the 1960s not only stemmed from cultural shifts abroad but also built on little-noticed elements of continuity in Irish life. Among these was a preoccupation, in some quarters at least, with the position of women in the world.

Inglis emphasizes the traditional role of Irishwomen as one of the founding building blocks in the construction of Catholicism's 'moral monopoly', and traditional conceptions of Irish society certainly could not survive the revolution in Irish women's attitudes that gathered speed in the early 1970s. But the traditional image of the Irish Catholic mother began to be eroded from the early 1960s, well before the Women's Liberation Movement, by a gathering change in Catholic devotions. In 1967 the *Irish Catholic* magazine noted that the nightly rosary was slowly being displaced by the impact of television on family life, even in the countryside. This process was hastened by Vatican II's introduction of vernacular liturgy – and the accompanying process whereby Marian devotions went into decline (including the Brown Scapular, the Miraculous Medal and Marian processions). Steep falls in the membership of the Legion of Mary and Our Lady's Sodality followed in the 1960s and 1970s.[8] Vatican II also, of course, introduced a new language where Protestantism was concerned, and even a new inflection about ecumenicism in its third session in 1964: no longer were Protestants defined as heretics and schismatics but as 'separated communities'. This was unwelcome to McQuaid, who miscalled the new spirit abroad in Rome and was left somewhat stranded at the end of his career. Elsewhere in the Irish priesthood, however, a distinct liberalization was manifested in the 1960s, and even an interest in ecumenics – a reassuringly easy option in the Republic, it might be thought, where Protestants then mustered only 3.5 per cent of the population. (Enthusiastic ecumenists must have sometimes wondered if there would even be enough Protestants to go round.) The events of the next decade make it easy to forget just how prevalent, if transient, the language of Church unity was in the early 1960s.[9] So was a completely new attitude from the Church of Ireland's hierarchy towards Rome, the Pope and their Catholic opposite numbers: attending each other's churches and initiating friendly debates about ecumenics suddenly became the norm. Garret FitzGerald has noted that from the 1960s Irish Catholic intellectuals (like himself) were more and more inclined to 'do their own theology'.[10] This did not stop Irish Catholic bishops from following a much harder line on 'mixed' marriages than in other countries of divided Christian faiths, such as Holland – as was aggressively spelt out even in the supposedly landmark ecumenical discussions at Ballymascanlon in 1973. Meanwhile, any impulses that the Protestant bishops in the North might have felt towards ecumenical initiatives were jealously monitored by their laity. To find the roots of enduring change we have to look elsewhere.

From the 1960s also, the worldwide movement querying the position of women began to make itself felt in Ireland. In 1972 the Commission on the Status of Women presented a report tackling the stereotyping of women's roles in Ireland, discrimination in employment, inequities in taxation and pension schemes, and much else.[11] It had been sitting since 1970 and was strongly influenced by the activities of Irishwomen in the International Alliance of Women's Conferences in the 1960s. But it reflected local traditions too. Recent historiography has shown the importance of long-standing traditions and structures of female authority in Irish society, even if located in highly specific and limited areas such as the convent and the Irish Countrywomen's Association.[12] The organizations that came together to form an ad hoc committee to press for women's rights in 1968 were widely representive, ranging from the Association of Business and Professional Women to the National Association of Widows.[13] Change followed fairly quickly. The year 1973 saw the Civil Service (Employment of Married Women) Act, removing the promotion and employment bar, and there was further legislation the next year – though the equal-pay issue necessitated a legal action against the government by the chair of the Women's Political Association represented, inevitably, by the barrister Mary Robinson. These advances were not before time, and attitudes remained fairly unreconstructed. In 1977 the WPA sent a questionnaire on women's issues to serving TDs; the reply of Tim O'Connor, FF, was fairly typical: 'In my own county the women are doing a great job of work in keeping their homes going and bringing up their families. This I think is just what Almighty God intended them to do.'[14] Whatever Almighty God wanted, over the next twenty years the numbers of women in work would more than double; many of these, however, were part-time jobs, and the increase rate for 1976–96 was far below that in, for instance, Scandinavia for the same period.[15]

But pressure was kept up by the Council for the Status of Women, founded in 1972 and government-funded from 1977. 'On the eve of the resurgence of the women's liberation movement in Ireland,

organised representation on women's rights was a part of institutionalized politics.'[16] But already, as with the suffrage movement a
century before, a radical wing was developing. The Irish Women's
Liberation Movement had been formed in 1970, with a more leftward
slant. As Ann Marie Hourihane has recalled, this ideology essentially
came with the territory. 'You didn't have to be a socialist to be a
member of the Irish Left; you just had to want contraception. Through
this modest commitment you'd end up knowing the entire membership
of a Maoist group called Revolutionary Struggle.'[17] Thus procreation
became politics.

II

The prospect had been looming for some time, certainly since the
crusading journalist Michael Viney aired the question of Irish people's
right to family planning in a 1966 series of articles. In February 1971
McQuaid's Lenten pastoral rose to the challenge, announcing that
'Civil divorce is evil and contraception is evil; there cannot be, on the
part of any person, a right to what is evil'; thus nobody had the right
to practise contraception, 'be he [sic] Christian, non-Christian or
atheist'. A few days later the young Trinity law lecturer Mary Robinson (the first Catholic to become a senator for the university, and legal
adviser to the Irish Women's Liberation Movement) gave notice
that she had drafted a bill to legalize contraception. Introduced on
30 March, it aimed to repeal Section 17 of the 1935 Act, along
with the Censorship of Publications legislation of 1929 and 1946,
but failed to get the requisite support of six senators. Following
McQuaid's pastoral, the IWLM picketed his house, while Mary
Robinson announced to the Christus Rex Congress in Bundoran that
the Irish Women's Liberation Movement 'constitutes the only radical
force in the stagnant pool of Irish life . . . the only untapped source of
new ideas and initiatives left in the country is its women'.[18]

A couple of weeks later this was demonstrated with élan. May
1971 saw the legendary Contraceptive Train initiative mounted by
the IWLM: women made the day-trip to Belfast, purchased a variety
of contraceptives (or pretended to) and surged through Dublin's

Connolly Station defiantly brandishing them. Though the ban on importing contraceptives was lifted three years later, a Fine Gael bill allowing limited sale was defeated when the taoiseach himself, Liam Cosgrave, with six other FG deputies, opposed it on a free vote. Direct pressure had been brought from the highest circles in Rome when the question of liberalizing legislation arose from the early 1970s. But by 1978 there were open reports of a deep split in the hierarchy, and remarkably even Fianna Fáil was not falling completely into line. Jack Lynch had already privately indicated that laws on contraceptive sales would have to be amended, and the issue removed from the Department of Justice and brought under the Department of Health – a highly symbolic decision. In 1976 the Supreme Court overruled the Censorship Board, declaring that the IFPA's book *Family Planning* (1971) should not be banned because it was neither indecent nor obscene: the first such challenge brought under this legislation in fifty years.[19]

The attitudes of male politicians to the issue remained piquant, to say the least, and it is fitting that the bill finally allowing partial access to contraception in 1979 was introduced by Charles Haughey. 'This legislation opens no floodgates ... [it] seeks to provide an Irish solution to an Irish problem. I have not regarded it as necessary that we should conform to the position obtaining in any other country.'[20] Archbishop McQuaid would have been disappointed in him. Several years before he had summoned Haughey to his palace in order to show him a copy of Edna O'Brien's scandalous novel *The Country Girls* and approvingly noted the rising politician's disgust. 'Like so many decent Catholic men with growing families,' McQuaid recorded, 'he was just beaten by the outlook and descriptions.'[21] By 1979 Haughey had acclimatized himself thoroughly to the world of Edna O'Brien (though she, like many of her crusading kind, had by then left the country). Unreconstructed feeling elsewhere was represented by the Knights of Columbanus (including the property-dealing politician Ray Burke), who marshalled an undercover opposition, and the pioneering Mrs Dunne of the 'Christmas Day Anti-Contraception Fast'.[22] But she might just as well have enjoyed her turkey. The pamphlets of Opus Dei, the anti-contraception march of Limerick Priests on the feast of the Immaculate Conception and the arguments of, for instance, Leslie Quelch, president of the League of Decency, that 'contraception indirectly promotes abortion', did not prevail. Though ridiculed by the worldly, and strongly criticized for its limitations by feminists such as Mary Robinson, the bill passed, in a welter of discussion about the Billings Method of measuring ovulation by temperature and other arcane refinements.[23] The debates make fascinating reading and provoked an epic reaction from the sardonic John Kelly (FG). 'I think it fantastic and something one would find only in a country inhabited by leprechauns whom life had spared from most of the decisions the rest of the world had to face. That a handful of ageing men could sit around here talking about moral decisions that would be right or wrong depending on whether something was right or wrong with a urine dipstick . . .'[24]

Kelly gestured towards the feminist position, but feminism was in many quarters branded as an anti-Catholic, and therefore anti-Irish, plot. 'Looking at the woman's page [of the *Irish Independent*],' wrote one incensed (female) reader in 1971, 'you would hardly suspect Ireland is a Catholic country. For months you have been brainwashing married women to have careers outside the home and pressing for a change in the laws relating to contraceptives with, once, even a suggestion that we take "a new look" at abortion. I believe it is all part of a plan to prepare the ground for "permissive" legislation, directly contrary to the teaching of the Catholic Church.'[25] It was similarly unusual for TDs to acknowledge that there was a non-Catholic dimension to Irish life as well. Oliver Flanagan declared that it was utterly immoral for the legislators to advocate *any* adults living together 'without entering into the bond of sacrament of marriage in accordance with the Catholic faith'. Only Jim White (FG) argued that the current situation was an invasion of the civil rights of non-Catholics, and, though he called on the Jewish TD Ben Briscoe for confirmation, no support was forthcoming. In these debates, which were in this respect unlike those on divorce in the 1920s, the position of non-Catholic Irish people was seen as somehow irrelevant.

Yet 'family planning', as it was delicately called, was a directly political arena: and the practice of the family planning clinics signalled a dissonance between Irish life as perceived in Kildare Street and in the world at large. The two clinics in Dublin saw 25,000 patients in 1978, the year before Haughey's bill made contraceptives partially legal, and had 50,000 on their files. This did not count casual sales of contraceptives or the estimated 70,000 people availing themselves of the seven other clinics in Ireland.[26] Indeed, considering that the clinics were sustained by voluntary payments and gave their services free to medical card holders while keeping doctors' fees very low, they must have been underpinned by very large sales of contraceptives. (They also provided sterilization services, upon which statistics are not available, and advice on vasectomies, as well as smear tests unavailable elsewhere, and psychosexual counselling.) Increasingly the vexed issue of abortion came into focus, where there was a similar dissonance between the perceived reality and actuality (an admittedly uncertain estimate of women from Ireland having abortions in Britain in the thirty years between 1967 and 1998 totalled 95,000).[27] In 1979 the 'Women's Right to Choose' campaign began, opposed in 1981 by the Pro-Life Amendment Campaign – supported initially by both Haughey and, less expectedly, FitzGerald. In 1983 a referendum on a constitutional amendment to 'defend the life of the unborn' was carried by two to one, creating Constitutional Amendment 40.3.3. This battle was christened by one commentator, not hyperbolically, 'The Second Partitioning of Ireland'.[28] The divisions laid bare were between rural and urban opinion, as well as between secular and confessional. A heated debate developed about the right to disseminate literature on the subject, or to travel abroad in order to terminate a pregnancy (rights confirmed, rather doubtfully, by a further amendment in 1992 after a traumatic and widely publicized case involving a fourteen-year-old rape victim). Meanwhile, in 1986 a referendum to allow divorce was defeated after a bitter campaign. It would not be introduced into Irish law until the narrow victory of 1995.[29]

This indicates what is evident from other quarters: that in some ways the liberalizing legislation of the 1970s was perceived as a false dawn for liberalism (or a temporary lurch into permissiveness, depending on your view). The pioneers of the Women's Liberation Movement felt that by the 1980s things had rolled back, since the heady days of the first meeting in Bewley's in 1970,[30] and subsequent explosive television appearances on *The Late Late Show* and elsewhere. Splits were developing, in time-honoured Irish fashion, but these should in many ways be interpreted as evidence of the diversity of energies released by the accelerated developments from 1970. The packed Mansion House meeting of 14 April 1971 had made six demands: equal pay, equality before the law, equal education, contraception, justice for deserted wives, unmarried mothers and widows, and one family, one home. These aims would be pursued in various ways by members of the original group, some (such as Nuala Fennell) through mainline political organizations after rancorous departures from the original movement. Others, like Monica Barnes, also entered the Dáil while continuing to campaign on women's issues and adhering to the gradualist tactics of the Women's Political Association, which by 1979 had 600 members and thirty-five branches. Americans, or those who had studied or lived in America, had taken a leading part early on. Radicalism was sustained in the Irish Women United movement, founded in 1975 and stressing socialist politics and direct action. Though it fragmented after two years, its members were influential in the subsequent Contraceptive Action Programme (CAP, appropriately enough) and the creation of Rape Crisis centres. They also took a vociferously antagonistic line towards conservative Catholic clerics.

Another continuing effect of the 1970s explosion was the established influence of feminist journalists, by far the most dominant group in the original Women's Liberation Movement. Their movement into positions of media power over the next decade would be of great importance in the battles to come over the abortion amendment and the on-off divorce campaign. Repealing the state's prohibition of divorce united a number of pressure groups, but, since it required a constitutional referendum, necessarily followed a tortuous path. The effort to achieve an all-party recommendation in 1985 stopped short of advocating straightforward repeal of the prohibition; a government effort in 1986 to push a referendum through was bitterly fought and defeated by a majority of two to one. But the campaign brought to the surface much that had lain hidden or unmentioned in Irish family life, and may have helped to keep family law reform on the agenda.[31] The fact that many avatars of Irish feminism were professional writers helped to create, as Anne Stopper has put it, 'a whole new vocabulary' to define Irishwomen's experience of discrimination.[32] The language of public debate had changed on issues previously left in the preserve of the Catholic Church as guardian of the nation's faith and morals. A prophetic instance was a lengthy discussion between Mary Robinson and Mary McAleese recorded for the avant-garde journal *Crane Bag* in 1980.[33] The brisk approach taken even by McAleese towards contraception and divorce is noteworthy, as is the secularist drift of the discussion. Had any member of the Catholic hierarchy, reading this discussion, known that these were the opinions of two future heads of state, he would not have slept easily.

It is important to clarify, once more, that the grounds for this confidence and assertiveness were laid through women's participation in professional, labour and social organizations since the 1960s and before, even if the heady days of procreation politics provided the point of departure for tackling Catholic social power head-on. 'Women's Liberation' suggested identity politics, but there were other areas in which lobbying was well established. Quite quickly women's-interest issues entered institutional politics through the well-established mechanisms of lobbying, often from a liberal–reformist rather than a radical angle. The power of Irish government ministers and their senior civil servants in policy creation, and their accessibility to pressure groups, while criticized in other contexts, can occasionally make for a swifter adoption of radical change than in other political systems.[34] And over the period under review women not only entered the workplace in large numbers (though remaining under-represented in senior positions) but arrived, belatedly and mutedly, in positions of executive political power. Nor were the portfolios assigned them purely gender-specific; stereotypes were quietly subverted below the surface. The importance of a pre-existing family connection in politics, previously almost a sine qua non, was dramatically eroded by the end of the 1990s. The proportion of women appointed by government to state boards, a key area of government patronage, had risen to one third by 1996 (though it would fall again in the following decade),[35] and state subsidies to women's organizations were now a significant part of the budget. Women were also advancing into the upper echelons of the civil service and, slowly, the judiciary.[36] By then, emblematically, there was a minister for equality and law reform (though the Department of Women's Affairs briefly established in the early 1980s had enjoyed only a short and constricted life). A concerted

campaign for equal pay begun in the 1960s progressed by fits and
starts, but united a wide range of pressure groups and was eventually
able to invoke EU law, culminating in the Anti-Discrimination (Pay)
Act of 1975; general employment equality legislation followed, mobil-
izing effective pressure from outside the political establishment.
Further moves towards statutes establishing equal rights followed
in the 1990s. All these developments were boosted by the symbolic
achievement of Mary Robinson's election as president. She had also
been prominent, during a senatorial career that began in 1969, in
pressing for changes in family law: a long campaign initiated in 1972
and spearheaded by yet another voluntary pressure group, AIM
(Action, Information, Motivation), stemming from the women's
movement. A milestone achievement in June 1981 was the abolition
of the 'Criminal Conversation' concept in law, whereby a husband
had been able to sue his wife's lover for, effectively, damages to
property.

The 1970s feminists saw the social values of Catholicism as a major
obstacle inhibiting equal opportunities for women in Ireland, however
personally devout they might be. The cover of the IWLM manifesto
in March 1971, *Chains or Change*, featured a blown-up photograph
of a pair of hands telling rosary beads – which have transmuted into
chains binding the fingers that hold them. (The editor did not broadcast the fact that the hands in the original photograph belonged to
the Pope.[37]) The question of specifically Catholic inhibitions on
women's sexual activity remained implicit, and abortion was, in the
early days, given a wide berth. The interventions and changes achieved
by feminism in politics were paralleled elsewhere in Europe during
this era – especially in Spain, where Catholic power also followed a
not dissimilar trajectory after the death of Franco.[38] But in Ireland,
perhaps more dramatically than anywhere else, the political issues of
liberalization from the 1970s to the 1990s raised the question of
religious dogma, and the period saw the effective crumbling of the
Church's decisive position. This happened with extraordinary speed.
In 1968 the encyclical 'Humanae Vitae' presented a hard line on
contraception: 'No Change!' announced a professor of moral theology
at Maynooth, with ill-concealed relief.[39] His academic colleague at
University College Cork, Revd James Good, was suspended from

priestly functions by his bishop for describing the encyclical as 'a major tragedy', but it was generally greeted with delight by the Catholic hierarchy in Ireland. In 1971, as has been seen, Archbishop McQuaid had declared that no one had the right of contraception, 'a right that can't even exist'.[40] In that same year Mary Robinson, John Horgan and Trevor West failed to mobilize enough support for their bill in the Senate, while a public-opinion poll showed a two to one majority against legalizing contraception in Ireland. However, by 1975 a similar study had shown a six to four majority in favour.[41] In 1985 and 1991 the sale restrictions under Haughey's bill were relaxed. By then Ireland was importing ten million condoms a year.

This development was accelerated by the horror of AIDS, which helped turn barrier contraception into an issue of health, and a campaign for a change in the law was spurred by the rise of an organized and articulate movement for gay rights. Irish homosexuals still lived under Victorian legislation imposing penal servitude for acts of 'indecency' between men. From 1977 the issue of homosexual law reform had been pioneered by the academic and future senator David Norris, who brought a case arguing the constitutional right of privacy as far as the Irish Supreme Court, which threw it out in 1980. But in 1988 he achieved a legendary victory in the European Court of Human Rights, in the wake of a case brought by Jeff Dudgeon from Northern Ireland (where the 1967 British reforms had not been embraced). Norris's campaign was accompanied by the simultaneous development of the Irish Gay Rights Movement, founded in 1974, and the later Gay and Lesbian Equality Network, which combated censorship as well as the illegal nature of homosexual acts. Coming out in the atmosphere of 1970s Ireland took courage, and it was rewarded by a certain advance in acceptability; previously, open homosexuality had been the strict preserve of a few celebrated figures in the world of arts and entertainment, and the denizens of a couple of dimly lit Dublin pubs. From the early 1980s a gay presence arrived in Irish public life. Marches, conferences and demonstrations accompanied the pressure for public-health awareness of the potential extent of the AIDS crisis, and an acceptance of the measures necessary to combat it. The Irish Council for Civil Liberties set up a working party on homosexual law reform in 1988, and its closely argued report advocated a simple adoption of equal rights rather than the British model. These movements would culminate in a law passed in June 1993, decriminalizing homosexuality and establishing equality with heterosexuals regarding privacy codes and the age of consent.

This was a remarkable volte-face; through the years of Norris's campaign political support from the established parties had been conspicuously lacking, apart from the usual handful of radical senators (Mary Robinson, again). The government even received advice that the AIDS crisis could be used to argue against changes in the law. But the 1990s were different. Robinson had been David Norris's legal adviser, and her presidency from 1990 targeted the gay community as part of the 'unofficial Ireland' that she wanted to incorporate. The liberalizing influence of Dick Spring in the Fianna Fáil–Labour coalition from 1992 was also decisive. But it was a Fianna Fáil minister, Máire Geoghegan-Quinn, who in introducing the 1993 bill described the previous legal situation as 'grossly and gratuitously offensive' and dismissed objections to a common age of consent as 'based on a lack of understanding of human nature'.[42] There had been, as expected, a backlash from groups such as Family Solidarity and the Knights of Columbanus. But national broadcasting had adapted speedily to public discussion of the issue (*The Late Late Show*, quick to take the pulse of the times, televised an even-handed debate in 1989). The Catholic Church kept its opposition fairly discreet. This may have been politic, given the revelations in store; but it also reflected the way that Irish opinion, particularly as represented in the press, often eschewed the prurience of tabloid witch-hunts across the Irish Sea and observed a broad-minded recognition of the boundaries of privacy.

III

Eight years after the Contraceptive Train, in September 1979, a *Late Late Show* special programme on Irish television was scheduled to deal with the issue of contraception, focusing on a bestselling book by the feminist Rosita Sweetman called *On Our Backs*. However, it was cancelled as 'inappropriate', since it would have coincided with the Pope's visit.[43] Had this been generally known, it would have given Ulster Unionist propaganda a field day. None the less, this was an aspect of procreation politics that was generally played down. The redoubtable Nell McCafferty, a Republican from Derry, was one of the very few 1970s IWLM feminists to see the campaign for contraception in the Republic as a step towards undermining Unionist arguments against a united Ireland. And when, on 27 September 1981, Garret FitzGerald as taoiseach gave a radio interview calling for a 'constitutional crusade' to make the Republic more attractive to the North, declaring that 'our laws, and our constitution, our practices, our attitudes' were all implicitly sectarian, he provoked an enormous storm as well as many pious disclaimers from Haughey.

Rather like the early days of Women's Liberation, this seemed ahead of its time. The bitter campaign over the constitutional amendment on abortion was already under way, and, though FitzGerald's position on this was ambiguous, the feelings unleashed by the issue seemed in some ways a throwback to an earlier era. The power of the Church in politics had certainly retreated since the early 1960s, when even progressive young bloods like Haughey had to defer to McQuaid on issues such as education. (Haughey characteristically tried to curry favour by sending cases of fine claret to the Bishop's Palace at Drumcondra but received the forbidding reply that the archbishop drank wine only when abroad.[44]) The power of Catholic opposition to the introduction of divorce was still formidable, and that too would represent a defeat for the liberal–secular ethos in 1986. FitzGerald had been warned, by no less a person than Pope Paul VI, nearly ten years before, in March 1977. 'In his remarks to me in French,' FitzGerald recalled,

the pope's uncompromising theme was that Ireland was a Catholic country – perhaps the only one left – and that it should stay that way. Laws should not be changed in a way that would make our state less Catholic. When at the end of his brief address I started to say that an appallingly tragic situation existed in Northern Ireland to which we in our state were trying to respond in a Christian way, he immediately intervened to the effect that he knew how tragic the situation was there – but that this could not be a reason to change any of the laws that kept the Republic a Catholic state.[45]

Italy had decriminalized contraception in 1968, France in 1974, and Spain would follow suit in 1978; the Vatican was clearly staking its faith on Ireland. Later the papal nuncio of the time would unguardedly tell a journalist of his constant efforts behind the scenes to combat FitzGerald's efforts to change Catholic social law in the Republic in the 1980s – presumably by giving instructions to bishops. As early as 1971 Cardinal Conway lodged complaints to senior diplomats about the threat presented by FitzGerald's 'liberalism'.[46] But consciousness was changing, and FitzGerald should be given credit for his part in changing it – and for the connection he unfailingly made: that a liberalization of social law in the Republic was a necessary part of a realistic accommodation with Northern Ireland. Along the way, he was making his own accommodations – as he engagingly tells us. For his own part, he has recorded, the weakness of the argument in 'Humanae Vitae' simply persuaded him that his long-standing antipathy to artificial contraception had all along been not moral but aesthetic.[47]

The future was with him, and the process of liberalizing law would eventually be accelerated by the decline of Catholic Church power in the 1990s. Plummeting vocations (first evident among nuns) and the exposure of a series of scandals had many bizarre knock-on effects, among them the development of a variety of soft-centred Celtic spirituality, marketed as self-help. More unexpectedly, a liberal form of Protestantism in the Republic achieved respectability, and even fashionability. Constitutional crusading was facilitated by the arrival of women in national politics – in their own right, rather than by the traditional route of widows' inheritance, though there remained a strange discrepancy between their visibility in front-rank roles and their under-representation in the Dáil at large. (Even by 2000, when women served as president and tánaiste, held five ministerial posts and led two parties, they still accounted for only 12 per cent of Dáil seats.[48]) The Council for the Status of Women remained in existence and was influential behind the scenes. The creation of new ministries, such as that for 'Women's Affairs and Family Law Reform' by the coalition government in November 1982, kept issues such as reproductive rights and divorce at the front of the agenda.

There was, of course, a reaction. The 1980s also saw the arrival of pressure groups trying to defend or retain Catholic social law. The Society for the Protection of the Unborn Child arrived in Ireland, from the USA via Britain, in 1980. As has been seen, the Pro-Life Amendment Campaign, founded in April 1981, was soon opposed by the Anti-Amendment Campaign, and it split political parties. The voting patterns in the successful 1983 referendum supposedly to protect the life of the unborn showed a decisive difference between Dublin and rural Ireland, reflecting a dissonance in Church influence as well as other factors. All this was also true for the next divisive issue, the divorce referendum in 1986: a 63 per cent turnout, and a two thirds victory for those who opposed introducing the possibility. Here, there seems to have been a large majority of women voting against it, in one of the last successful demonstrations of Church influence brought to bear on its traditional bulwark of support. There are many examples of extraordinarily crude manipulations by clergy at local and national levels, but such incidents were reported in several sections of the national press with a significant sense of outrage.[49] There was also an important contribution from a liberal Catholic lobby, led by the head of information at RTÉ, Louis McRedmond, who wrote a series of articles in the *Irish Times* advancing examples of permitted interpretations of state divorce, arguing in terms of religious liberty. These were the kind of arguments that would win the battle a decade later. But by then the authority of the Catholic Church had received a series of blows from another quarter.

Even before the upheavals of the 1990s, decisive change threatened several areas of Irish life traditionally colonized by the Church, such as welfare and medical care. And changes were also coming in the traditionally electric subject of education. As early as 1968 the Jesuit journal *Studies* defied McQuaid's attempt to suppress Seán O'Connor's article questioning the traditional relationship between Church and state in Irish education.[50] In 1973 the influential editor of the *Education Times* John Horgan, who was also a senator with a record of embracing liberal issues, drew attention to the gathering pressure for codifying educational practice, and the changes that the development of comprehensive and community schools implied for religious management.[51] In 1975 one of the radical Irish Women's Union demands against patriarchy was for 'state funded, secular, co-educational schools', with community control. This was a gauntlet flung down in front of 120 years of religious-dominated education. In fact, 'community schools' were already developing, especially in new urban locations and under-resourced rural areas. Though clerical opinion saw them as a Trojan Horse intended to kill off denominational education, they did involve religious management – opposed by Irish radicals but probably a necessary sine qua non to get parents voting with their feet. And, as Seán O'Connor had daringly forecast in 1968, the future role of the clergy would be 'as partners, not always as masters'. A further impetus towards change might be located in Vatican II's new emphasis on the centrality of parents' roles in school systems, supported formally by the Irish hierarchy in 1969. Pandora's Box sprang open. From 1975 new-style boards of management appeared in most national schools, spreading lay influence further into the school system. A group of Catholic parents scented danger, publishing a pamphlet attacking 'progressiveness', 'state control' and interdenominational education: it was called *Have the Snakes Come Back?* (The traditional Protestant argument that St Patrick might be seen as one of the founders of Irish Anglicanism clearly got short shrift here.) Equally worried, the Catholic Church authorities realized that the next step might be a reptilian slither towards multidenominational schools.

The path forward was shown by the Dalkey School Project in the early 1970s, which produced just such a structure; interestingly, it was eventually supported by the then taoiseach Jack Lynch, against the wishes of the Department of Education and probably the minister. (Within the department, opposition was couched in the terms that if one integrated primary school was established with official sanction, 'everybody would want one' – clearly an undesirable outcome.) Lynch in a speech at Tralee in 1974 apparently endorsed integrated education, and was rewarded by a blow from Cardinal Conway's crozier. It did not stop him repeating his endorsement of integrated education, North and South, a year later.[52] Dalkey became the first multidenominational national school to be recognized by the state since 1922, and about twenty have subsequently followed. In 1985 a National Parents' Council was established, and won consultative and negotiating rights with the Department of Education and Science. In the 1990s the question of decentralization of educational control became a live issue; new-style educational boards were floated, against the vigorous opposition of the Church. The Episcopal Commission on Education attacked this as building 'the bricks of a secularist agenda and ... an attempt by the state to push the church out of education'.[53] By the same token, the Employment Equality Bill drafted in 1996, enlarging the entire area under monitoring for discrimination, ran into trouble because it 'redefined the scope for religious control in schools, hospitals and other institutions where church authorities acted as employers'.[54] None the less, equal representation for owners, parents, teachers and community representatives was subsequently agreed and built into the Education Act of 1998.

This was supported by the Conference of Religious in Ireland (CORI), whose line on lay participation in school management (and everything else) was discernibly more liberal than many bishops. Regarding secondary education a perceptive, if brutally realistic, analysis had earlier been advanced by the Education Commission of the Major Religious Superiors (CORI's predecessor), which, in its 1973 report 'The Future of Religious in Education', prophesied with impressive accuracy the implications of the decline in vocations for Church–state relations in education.[55] The report suggested that these ominous statistics, together with the rise of community schools, enforced a policy of retrenchment. Religious orders should retreat, effectively, to running a smaller number of schools simply providing education for the upper echelons of Irish society, funded by 'hard bargaining' with the Department of Education. This suggestion caused havoc when the report was leaked to the *Education Times* by an enterprising civil servant.[56] Teaching orders such as the Christian Brothers remained antagonistic to the idea of community schools, but they were endorsed openly by civil servants and covertly by Fianna Fáil politicians, who knew from their local *cumainn* that the voters were in favour. Other parties were even less trustworthy from the Church's point of view; Cardinal Conway's worries about Fitz-Gerald's dangerous 'liberalism' were initially aroused by his views on education.

Undeniably, the last thirty years have seen the decline of the religious control of education and the rising popularity of the secular and multidenominational approach practised by what might be called the ex-Protestant schools in the Republic. This has kept pace with developments in ecumenical initiatives and, through the 1990s especially, a change in religious language. At President Douglas Hyde's funeral in 1949 (as at Yeats's reinterment the year before), Catholic government ministers dared not enter a Protestant church in order to pray for the soul of a national hero. This edict was lifted by the hierarchy in 1966, but a firm line was still imposed against taking the sacraments in a Protestant church. However, in 1997 the Catholic president Mary McAleese received communion in Dublin's Protestant cathedral. Catholic bishops complained, and Archbishop Connell referred to it as a 'sham', but they were swiftly seen to be isolated by public opinion. It was clear that most Catholics supported the gesture and rejected the reactionaries.[57]

'The President's Communion' has a nicely medieval ring to it, like 'The King's Two Bodies', but it was more than a storm in a communion cup. The moment was all the more symbolic as it came from President McAleese rather than from her less openly devout predecessor. Even before this, the sociologist John Fulton, examining the debates over multidenominational and integrated education, discerned the emergence in Ireland of what he called 'a form of pro-religious anti-clericalism' among the Catholic community, especially in its urban and middle-class sectors.[58] By the end of the 1980s he saw this as forming an oppositional tendency to the long-established sense of separateness among Irish Catholics, traditionally based on the belief that they possessed a more authentic ethno-religious identity than the 'less Irish' Protestants. Protestantism has become more 'Irish' now, converging with the new-look liberal Catholicism of the Irish middle classes. The latter looks more and more like Irish Protestantism without the name. What else, after all, is 'pro-religious anti-clericalism'? In 1970, at the start of this book's period, Hubert Butler had written to a friend: 'I am beginning to believe that we are more likely to see what used to be considered the Protestant virtues in the growing number of liberal Catholics than among our own people.'[59] He may have underrated his tribe. But, thirty years on, it sometimes seems that the relation of the once defunct Anglican Church of Ireland to the tottering structure of Catholicism resembles Hobbes's description of the early papacy: the reincarnated ghost of its predecessor and adversary, 'sitting crowned upon the grave'.

Others, such as the historically minded sociologist Tom Inglis, have similarly hinted that there is a point at which *à la carte* Catholicism becomes a kind of Protestantism:

Irish Catholics are not only becoming more Protestant – that is, devising their own spiritual and moral path to salvation – they are also becoming more secular. The decline of the influence of the institutional Church in the religious field has been matched by a decline in its influence in other social fields, particularly in politics, education, health, social welfare and the media. In terms of individual behaviour, being religious or acquiring religious capital is no longer necessary to the acquisition of other forms of capital. Irish Catholics can attain status, honour and respect, and they can attain political, economic and social power, without having to have Catholic religious capital or to have their forms of capital symbolically legitimised by the Church.[60]

Certainly the figures for decline in religious practice bear him out. From a high point of 1975, statistics of Mass attendance and religious vocations slid downwards, slowly at first but snowballing from the late 1980s. As late as 1990 it could be claimed that 85 per cent of the Irish adult population attended church once weekly (though this has been queried); but by 1997 even the most optimistic survey showed this had fallen to 65 per cent, and far lower than that among the urban young.[61] Between 1970 and 1995 the total number of religious in Ireland decreased by over a third. Even this statistic disguises a far more spectacular falling off when age structures are taken into consideration, as well the rocketing rate of departures from the religious life. (Vocations declined by nearly 100 per cent in the thirty years from 1966 to 1996.) The numbers of diocesan clergy held up rather better than those in religious orders, until about 1990; then these too plummeted (a 63 per cent decline by 1998). Again, one must look at the number of ordinations to see the real revolution: 412 in 1965; 259 in 1970; 150 in 1980; 129 in 1990; 44 in 1998. In that last year deaths and departures from the religious life outnumbered ordinations by five to one.[62] The following year there was only one priest ordained in Dublin diocese, and his career choice was seen as so unusual that the *Sunday Times* gave it an entire page.[63]

This is the kind of pattern of decline (along with the selling off and closing down of buildings previously dedicated to religious uses) that the Protestant Church of Ireland had been familiar with for many decades. But strangely, during this critical period, the Church of Ireland in the Republic seemed to find a new voice. In some ways it was belatedly fulfilling the hopes cherished by some of its intellectuals in the barren post-war years. 'Belief that is dead', Hubert Butler wrote in an unpublished fragment from these years, 'should like the phoenix consign itself to the flames, having laid the egg from which a radiant and glowing new phoenix will be hatched . . . The poor old phoenix [the Church of Ireland], moulting and blind and bedraggled, gazes mesmerized into the fire, but unable to summon up the courage to take the last leap. Yet I think it still has the power to lay a very fine egg.'[64] He was slowly vindicated, in some quarters at least, as the issues of procreation politics flared into life during the 1970s and 1980s. While some of the Church of Ireland's members (especially in Donegal) supported the anti-abortion amendment in 1983, Dean Victor Griffin of St Patrick's Cathedral vehemently campaigned against it, declaring that 'Ireland had to choose between republicanism and confessionalism.'[65] Several of his predecessors would have blanched at the word 'republicanism', but Griffin's endorsement of it was of a piece with his high-profile and unapologetic career. He represented a Church of Ireland that had long gone beyond the timorousness and detached stance recalled in so many memoirs of the 1950s and before.

Though Griffin's proactive stance had been foreshadowed by laymen like Hubert Butler and W. B. Stanford in that era (and more cautiously by clerics such as Archbishops McAdoo and Simms), Griffin was the first public representative of new-look Protestantism in the Republic. By the end of his ministry Protestantism was almost fashionable again; it was certainly distinctively Irish. And the Church of Ireland within the Republic, though formally an all-Ireland institution, had developed distinctly different attitudes from those to be found in some of its representatives in Northern Ireland. Edna Longley once remarked that 'the Northern Catholic Church, still locked into a nineteenth-century relationship with nationalism, is also pursuing its own interests, in that Northern Catholics can be kept thirty years less liberal than their Southern counterparts.'[66] It is not often enough noted that the same gap has opened in the Protestant Church of Ireland, north and south of the border.[67] The escalating Orange demonstrations at Drumcree in the 1990s, centred on the parish church there, were greeted with condemnation by both clerics and members of the Church of Ireland in the Republic. This reflects the very different political stances of the Church in both jurisdictions, not to mention the virtual disappearance of Orangeism in the twenty-six counties by the mid twentieth century. The attitudes, language and concerns of Archbishop Eames in Armagh have been, over the last twenty years, in marked contrast to those of Archbishop Empey in Dublin: moderate Unionism compared to moderate nationalism, in the words of one observer.[68] Bishop Empey had served in the Irish Army, spoken out on current issues (including political corruption) and taken a markedly liberal and ecumenical line in Church matters, enabling him to politely face down an insulting and offhand dismissal by his Catholic opposite number for his supposed lack of intellectual qualities. A turning point came with the refusal of Archbishop Eames to sever the Church's ties with the Orange Order, as declared in the Armagh Synod of 1996, where he effectively endorsed the connection between the institution and the Church. He was decisively contradicted by Empey in Dublin, when he condemned 'parades of an offensively triumphalist nature'. According to the Church of Ireland Gazette, 'The southern community feels itself to be moving with new confidence, well integrated into a rapidly developing society; it wonders why the Northern Church has been unable to divest itself of what looks like uncomfortable and anachronistic sectarian baggage.'[69]

Subsequent mayhem at Drumcree snapped whatever tightrope Dr Eames was trying to balance upon, and the attitudes of the Church of Ireland south of the border chime more and more closely with those of the liberal Catholic middle class. Yet more closely, perhaps, they comfortably reflect what the Labour politician Ruairi Quinn got into trouble for describing in 1996 as 'post-Catholic, pluralist Ireland'.[70] A Church never noted for its fashionability is now adopted by the style icons of alternative Ireland: the singer Gavin Friday, asked in 2003 to list the greatest influences on his artistic development, put as third on the list 'Protestants', and the importance of Protestant evangelical culture for his fellow musicians U2 is a matter of record.[71] Protestantism within the Republic has also received a numerical boost from certain sectors of recent immigration. Garret FitzGerald, sharp for his purposes, has pointed out that 'one of the most remarkable, although in general unremarked, features of the Irish state has been the disappearance of Protestant Unionism from most of the Republic.' 'What now differentiates Protestants politically from Catholics', he has added, 'is only the fact that they do not share the Anglophobia that is still to be found in some sections of the Catholic population.'[72]

The integration of Protestants into the life of the Republic has been much eased by the questioning of those thorny issues of Catholic social law from about 1970, largely provoked by the women's movement. A cynic might add that this integration is also eased by the major role that the community played for much of the last century in business and commercial life; by some computations, their influence actually increased disproportionately between 1926 and 1991.[73] It has also been helped by the apparent softening of the Catholic line towards ecumenicism since Vatican II, though that is a story of fits and starts. The pioneering work done by, for instance, the Jesuit Michael Hurley towards the historical and contemporary understanding of Irish Protestantism did not endear him to all his colleagues. Hurley envisaged the Irish School of Ecumenics in 1960, but it took ten years to establish; over thirty years it has done much within the academic ambit to project an ecumenical dimension into Irish life. While it does involve itself in wider community issues, its influence is primarily academic and its tendency historical as much as theological. But this has its own importance. Hubert Butler might be instanced yet again. In his very last piece of published writing, in 1990, he turned to the question of ecumenicism and remarked: 'what is likely to unite us is not the spectacle of a pope embracing a patriarch or a heretical archbishop or the return of St Andrew's skull to Petras or some holy keepsake from Byzantium to Rome. We have to venture out from the well-kept museum of symbols on to the junk-heap of cast-off clothes, broken crockery and maggoty corpses which is history.'[74]

The relative fortunes of Irish Catholicism and Protestantism were set on a new course well before the convulsive scandals that dominated the Irish media of the 1990s. Ostensibly, these came at a time when the

Catholic Church seemed to have withstood several of the challenges mounted against it from the 1970s. In 1979 came the Pope's visit, when 2.7 million Irish people turned out to see him (1.2 million alone on one day in the Phoenix Park). Foreign journalists noted his appeal against violence in his Drogheda speech (Lord Mountbatten had been killed a month before), but it is likely that several members of the hierarchy set more store by his injunctions at Limerick, where he denounced birth control and divorce, and pleaded with Irishwomen to stay in their places at home, bringing up families. The abortion amendment campaign shortly followed, with its apparent victory for Catholic values; an Irish sociologist of religion sadly delineated what he saw as the monolithic, absolutist, intolerant and conformist world-view of Irish Catholicism, along with sexual obsessiveness and prudery.[75] The victory over divorce three years later seemed to embed them still further. These were the very attitudes that could not survive the revelations of families fathered by leading Catholic churchmen, and the patterns of sexual abuse on a vast scale, ignored or covered up by the hierarchy. The novelist John Banville, asked in 2000 to nominate an iconic national figure for a re-erected Nelson's Pillar in the heart of Dublin, sardonically opted for Bishop Eamonn Casey: 'He caused the whole collapse.'[76]

But it was not a matter of a mighty edifice suddenly assailed by forces from the unknown. The barbarian hordes had actually been sapping the foundations for some time. The revelations about the secret families of Bishop Casey (1992) and Father Michael Cleary (1994–5), the infinitely more horrific exposures of the rapes of children perpetrated by Seán Fortune (1999) and Brendan Smyth (1994), and the continuing catalogue of assaults on boys by priests in positions of authority were publicized by developments in media coverage. The change in the tone of commentary considered acceptable had been developing since the 1970s. In Casey's and Cleary's cases, it was a particularly piquant irony that each man owed his fame to use of the media, much encouraged by some elements in their Church (though Cleary's particular brand of populist intolerance infuriated more thoughtful and less high-profile clerics). Programmes such as Mary Raftery's *States of Fear* on RTÉ (1999) revealed the extent of inactivity and cover-ups over abuse scandals in Catholic institutions. From about 1993 an avalanche of cases against priests for sexual abuse of children (mostly boys) had been accumulating and seemed to bear out the most fevered Protestant fantasies about the effects of celibacy.[77] The Church's moral authority was further destroyed by the hierarchy's apparent inability to apologize for its inaction in practically every case. Traumatic publications such as the Ferns Report conveyed not only appalling records of sexual exploitation by clerics but a near-criminal inability among their superiors to handle the social responsibilities they had inherited with their position. But the proliferation of articles and reports highlighting sexual abuse by clerics that appeared from the mid 1990s, and the interrogations to which senior clerics were subjected by RTÉ, would have been unthinkable twenty or even ten years before and signalled the end of a culture of deference. The television set had become the confessional box.

Not everyone took this on board. It is striking (indeed semi-miraculous) that in a book by the editor of *Irish Theological Quarterly*, published in 2003 and called *The End of Irish Catholicism?*, there is much about the dangers of the liberal agenda and nothing about disgraced bishops.[78] But the upheavals since the early 1990s, and the pervasive significance of the Robinson presidency since 1990, created a different atmosphere when divorce returned to the political arena in 1995. In the run-up to the referendum, episcopal interventions were far more muted than a decade before, and their tone was far less apocalyptic: the threats of hellfire were abandoned in favour of lessons drawn from sociology. Even the Archbishop of Cashel contented himself with warning a congregation at Holy Cross Abbey that divorced people smoked and drank more than married couples and were more liable to be involved in car accidents.[79] Taoiseach Ahern, himself a separated husband living with another partner, pronounced: 'It's a matter that an awful lot of people want or maybe an awful lot of people don't want and the people will decide ultimately.'[80] The people did decide, and thus divorce came at last to Ireland, while the media continued to print exposure stories about religious communities. A world of exploitation and abuse was revealed through scholarly research, harrowing memoirs and television interviews. The tragic images of children starved and abused in industrial schools and unmarried mothers slaving in convent laundries inevitably overshadowed the many achievements of the Church in social welfare, and the kindness and dedication of many of its personnel. Those images of religious authority abused came to stand as the picture of an Ireland before the women's movement, before the Celtic Tiger, before prosperity, before everything that the last thirty years had brought. It seemed like another country in a dark age.

IV

Much of the 1990s were, in fact, to be spent coming to terms with cultural memory. Recalling the heady days of the 1970s thirty-five years later, a founder of the Irish Women's Liberation Movement said, 'We separated church and state . . . we set the seeds that destroyed the authority of the Catholic Church, though mind you, they mostly destroyed themselves with their sexual scandals.'[81] It is hard not to agree that the challenge to patriarchy mounted by the women's movement from 1970, and in some ways climaxing in President Robinson's election in 1990, helped set the terms that enforced a revolution in the traditional Catholic Church's place in Irish life. The election of Mary Robinson, given her record as women's-rights advocate, provided an enduring symbol of this. It should be remembered that her election was probably swung by the exposure of a Fianna Fáil scandal and the subsequent lies that wrecked her opponent's campaign. But it was also given a boost by a counter-productive sneer from a particularly unreconstructed member of Fianna Fáil, to the effect that she neglected her duties as wife and mother, which caused outrage across the political spectrum. Much of Robinson's support mobilized women's votes, sometimes from unlikely quarters: there are many stories of women members of the opposing parties who canvassed for their own candidate but, when the day came, voted for Robinson. And one of her great attractions for the electorate at all levels was her refusal to bow to the usual pieties. Asked to define her religion, President Robinson remarked that she was 'not a non-practising Catholic': a new note for an Irish head of state indeed.[82]

What place is left for a non-traditional Catholic Church is another question; but part of that place is being occupied by the Protestant

Church of Ireland in the Republic. Matters in the North are, of course, different; the border has driven a deep wedge even within institutions (like the Churches) that nominally transcend it. Though movements for dialogue and ecumenicism have opened up, the languages differ, North and South. Ecumenical or mutual-understanding movements have been afoot in the North since the Troubles began, and one should note such initiatives as the Joint Group on Social Questions (founded in 1969) and the Working Party on Violence in Ireland (appointed in 1973, and led by Cahal Daly and Eric Gallagher, which reported in 1976).[83] The first inter-Church meeting at Ballymascanlon on 26 September 1973 is taken generally as some sort of landmark, though theological questions apparently presented the gathered churchmen with fewer problems than did the issue of community relations. The fortunes of ecumenicism in Northern Ireland have not altogether flourished through the 1980s and 1990s.[84] But what have the alterations in the positions of both Churches in the South meant for national identity in the Republic?

There may be a case for saying that the decline of old-style Catholicism necessarily means the decline of old-style Republican nationalism. Certainly there has been a rewriting of the language of national identity, and the parameters within which it was inscribed, or imposed, by the state have either expanded or broken down. From the sixties, one authority has claimed,

the profusion of new identities that emerged marked a vital change in identification processes. National identity lost its power to dominate other social, cultural and political identities and hence also lost the power to determine society according to a single controllable model. Where previously national identity had a transcending power, now it increasingly occupied one position in a competitive space in which other forms of identity intruded with increasing power and persistence.[85]

If this is true in Ireland, it has much to do with the decline of Catholic authority. But it does not necessarily mean that traditional nationalism has evaporated alongside it – even if it has changed its language.

None the less, these shifts have been influential in the way that Northern Ireland has been viewed from the South (the subject of a later chapter in this book). Again, much of this goes back to the early

1970s – and to the language pioneered by Jack Lynch, no less than the abrasive writings of Conor Cruise O'Brien. The recognition that Northern Unionism had a voice worth listening to has come slowly, but it is one of the striking reversals of approach over the last thirty years, and many of those who advanced it are the same people who have figured in the revolutions dealt with above, such as Mary Robinson and Victor Griffin. The Anglo-Irish Agreement of 1985 suggested a change in approach to the nation-state, and the recommendations of the Opsahl Commission a few years later advanced other forms of intellectual reconfiguration. Eric Gallagher, a moving force in inter-church negotiations, unequivocally challenged both Catholic and Protestant Churches in the North to re-examine their respective forms of absolutism and develop areas of mutual recognition. What effect, or importance, this will have 'on the ground' is uncertain; and a benign, liberal, varieties-of-Irishness agenda is contemptuously rejected by many elements that hold decisive power at the beginning of the twenty-first century. If one theme in the history of the last thirty years has been an increasing desire among Irish intellectuals to get away from the old binaries, Catholic/Nationalist, Unionist/Protestant, it must also be realized that since 1998 the idea of political progress has been attached to a weighted political system in Northern Ireland that takes a binary division as axiomatic, has in some ways redefined sectarianism into community politics and that looks like eliminating middle-ground parties from the arena altogether.[86]

The process also relies on a change in language and approach that has brought Sinn Féin into an arm of Her Majesty's Government and seen Unionist rhetoric alter beyond recognition. Such shifts have surely been facilitated by the transformations in the Republic, and by the breakdown of some of the most traditionalist paradigms that defined national identity since the foundation of the state: that calcified congruence of Irishness, Catholicism and Republicanism. This came about, since 1970, through revolutions in the religious control of education, in the expectations of women and in the structures of family life. Between the mid sixties and the end of the twentieth century the proportion of births outside marriage rose from 1.5 per cent to 33 per cent in Ireland. Since 1980 the proportion of women married by the age of twenty-five fell from 60 per cent to 12 per cent, while the age of women giving birth for the first time has also soared. Most strikingly of all, in 2002 one sixth of Irish couples with one child under five were unmarried. By the mid 1990s Ireland shared with France the lowest marriage rate in Europe.[87]

Some at least of these statistics reflect the effect of immigration and social dislocation, as well as a change in Irish attitudes towards women and their appropriate expectations: but the latter is undoubtedly a major factor. So is the rise of prosperity, the decline of Catholicism and the redefinition of non-Catholicism. The links between these developments are not always clear but political and economic transformation has undeniably helped to create the change in religious outlook. (The Inglehart thesis, which posits a close link between economic scarcity and insecurity, and a search for spiritual abundance and certainty, might be instanced here.[88]) Traditional Protestant attitudes to Catholics as brainwashed pawns of a totalitarian religious system could not survive the spectacular demonstration of individual conscience and judgement by Irish reformers of one kind or another since the 1960s. The end of monopoly Catholicism has seen the rise of a number of competing groups, some of whose legitimacy is still weak. But it is not too much to say that by the turn of the twenty-first century the authority of the Catholic Church in Irish civil society had been comprehensively destroyed. 'It was as though everything the Catholic establishment stood for had turned out to be wrong, and everything it had opposed turned out to be right.'[89] Ironically, this reflection, which is strongly tinged with regret, comes from a perceptive study of Catholic decline by a founder member of the Irish Women's Liberation Movement. The revolutions that began with the fabled 1960s started more than they knew. And, if one looks at the Republic of Ireland over the last thirty years in religious terms, it is hard not to think of that standard exam question for students of Irish history: 'Why did the Reformation not succeed in Ireland?' And answer: 'It did, but it took four hundred and fifty years.'

3

'The Party Fight and Funeral': Fianna Fáil and Irish Politics in the Late Twentieth Century

I

William Carleton, idiosyncratic but essential chronicler of nineteenth-century Irish life, provides a description in *Traits and Stories of the Irish Peasantry* of 'The Party Fight and Funeral', stressing the intimate connection between these two national rituals. His subsequent reflections upon the propensity towards hatred in Irish life and the power of party feeling strike a chord, and his talents could have done justice to the last thirty years of the twentieth century – an era dominated by Charles James Haughey, who himself seems to have stepped from the pages of a nineteenth-century novel. Haughey also changed, almost overnight, the ethos of Fianna Fáil ('Soldiers of Destiny'), the creation of Eamon de Valera in 1926. In its post-Civil War origins a 'slightly constitutional' alliance, it became the natural party of government, claiming to represent the country at large rather than sectional interests. This shifted dramatically with Haughey's leadership in 1979. At the very end of the century, in December 1999, came the funeral in his native Cork of Jack Lynch, former taoiseach of Ireland (and champion hurler). Against all precedent, the current Fianna Fáil leader and taoiseach, Bertie Ahern, was not asked to give the eulogy. That honour went instead to Des O'Malley, seen by many as an apostate who had left the party and founded the Progressive Democrats after challenging the leadership of Haughey, Lynch's successor and Ahern's mentor. Behind this funeral there lay a party fight in a very real sense, and a vital chapter in recent Irish political history.

While the party fights within Fianna Fáil since the departure of Seán Lemass in 1966 had focused on personal rivalries and hatreds, they also revolved around three enduring themes from past history: politics, nationalism and land. The way these continue to intertwine gives some pause for thought, especially in the era of the hegemony of Fianna Fáil and the recent revelations by which that party in its post-de Valera persona will be judged. The party may have become increasingly 'constitutional' in the years when it monopolized power, but descriptions of the Fianna Fáil ethos tend to rely upon some qualifying adverbs. 'We were', Charles Haughey remarked in one of his less guarded reminiscences, 'fairly sincere people.'[1]

Fianna Fáil's impressive record of hegemonizing Irish political power long rested upon what it conceived of as special and direct links to the Irish political psyche. One connection is mediated through its 'Republican' ethos, as the party of irredentist nationalism: its origins lay in opposition to the Treaty of 1921. Another claim, proudly advertised, was a traditional link to the ethos of rural Ireland, which enabled it to boast an impressively vertical profile of class support, from poor to rich. And, like all Irish political parties, it used history for its purposes. It was in fact a Progressive Democrat, not a Fianna Fáil minister, who most barefacedly invoked a link back to the Land War of the 1880s, when arguing against the introduction of planning restrictions, but he spoke on behalf of a Fianna Fáil-led government. In August 2003 Tom Parlon called up the shades of Charles Stewart Parnell and Michael Davitt, who, he said, 'gave their lifetimes' to the creation of a nation of property-owning farmers – an achievement he proceeded to use as a rationale for allowing land developers to run riot unimpeded by legislation. This subject was about to be addressed by an all-party committee – in the face of mounting scandals revealed by the tribunals then investigating political corruption. Parlon magnificently ignored not only Davitt's lifelong crusade for land nationalization but also the fact that Parnell and Davitt used state intervention *against* the contemporary rights of landlords. But it is a piquant illustration of how potent a part the issue of land can still play in Irish politics.

The politics of land were, in the late nineteenth century, intimately connected with the politics of patriotism. In the era of Haughey, an interest in land took over from a commitment to nationalism. The history of Fianna Fáil's manoeuvres around the Rock of the Republic, in the form of the question of partition, will be dealt with in the next chapter. But there is necessarily an overlap. The eruption of violence in Northern Ireland (of the kind that had been so vividly depicted by Carleton) ushered in a period of convulsion in Irish politics whose implications are still being assessed. Justin O'Brien and others (notably Vincent Browne in a series of ground-breaking *Magill* articles during 1980) have done much to relate the IRA split that produced the Provisional IRA to that other power struggle going on south of the border, down Merrion way: the battles within Fianna Fáil. Taoiseach Jack Lynch was presented with a powerful cabal within his party, led by Neil Blaney, Kevin Boland and Charles Haughey, supported unsteadily by Micheál Ó Moráin. The resentment went back to the circumstances of Lynch's succession to the legendary Seán Lemass in 1966. Lynch was not, contrary to his later mystique, a reluctant aspirant to the crown.[2] There were several rivals, the most prominent of which were Blaney, Boland and Haughey. Haughey had been a reforming minister for justice in the early 1960s and subsequently an imaginative minister for finance, much appreciated for his largesse to old-age pensioners and artists. Later he would prove less tractable to the attentions of journalists, but in his early, more unbuttoned days he was good copy. To catch a vote, the playwright Hugh Leonard wrote, he would unhesitatingly 'roller-skate backwards into a nunnery, naked from the waist down, singing "Kevin Barry" in Swahili'.[3]

Unlike Blaney and Boland, who came from established Fianna Fáil dynasties, Haughey was a self-made man. He was already known for a febrile temperament, suavity alternating with aggressive crudeness, and for his ostentatious pleasure in the good things of life. With his boon companions Donogh O'Malley and Brian Lenihan he represented in the 1960s a different ethos to the old revolutionary generation, who looked at him with deep suspicion – in spite of his apparent adoption into the Camorra through marriage to Lemass's daughter Maureen. Lemass himself apparently shared their suspicions. But one thing his son-in-law had in common with him was a belief that the business of modern Ireland should be business, and that all possible effort should be put into economic development. Haughey, however, saw other possibilities in the commercial world too. He was much involved in the 'Taca' organization: a circle of rich businessmen prepared to put money into the party through American-style funding events in public and large donations in private. They also expected to be rewarded.[4] Haughey's appointment as finance minister, essentially his reward for withdrawing his own leadership bid to succeed Lemass, made him a key figure in this alliance, which held a message for the future. And, as his colleague Kevin Boland bemusedly noted at his first Taca dinner organized by Haughey, 'the extraordinary thing about my table was that everybody at it was in some way or other connected with the construction industry.' As one such contributor would later say, 'Fianna Fáil was good for builders and builders were good for Fianna Fáil and there was nothing wrong with that.'[5]

The contempt felt by Haughey, Blaney and others for their leader Lynch, whom they saw as an amiable stopgap, took an ideological tinge too. All had Northern links, and all were prepared to attack this quintessential Corkman for unsoundness on the national question. What happened as the Northern crisis developed was that the old uncertainty within the party about where it really stood on Republicanism came uneasily into focus. The conspiracy theory that dissident Fianna Fáil politicians financed the foundation of the Provisional IRA because they were alarmed by the left-wing trend of the Official IRA is unproven. In fact, the money produced in late 1969 went to both wings of the movement. Moreover, for Haughey at least, the Northern issue presented itself primarily as a valuable strategy for destabilizing his leader.[6] But the arms-gatherers within Lynch's party did believe that their leader was too soft on the issue of partition. The astonishing series of behind-the-scenes skulduggeries that climaxed in the Arms Trials of 1970 predict, in some ways, the later scandal-racked era of Haughey's own ascendancy, when he was beset by events that he described as 'Grotesque, Unbelievable, Bizarre and Unprecedented', allowing his arch-enemy Conor Cruise O'Brien to coin the acronym 'GUBU'. By then Haughey, clinging to his Napoleonic pretensions and presiding over an increasingly rackety government, had infused Fianna Fáil with his own inimitable ethos.

But his eventual achievement of high office looked most unlikely after his fall from grace following the Arms Trial of 1970. Haughey and Blaney, sacked by Lynch, were arrested and charged with attempts to import arms illegally into the state. The charges against Blaney were dismissed at an early stage, but Haughey stood trial with three others and was acquitted in October 1970; contradictions in evidence suggested that there had been more covert government acquiescence than appeared in court. Haughey's extraordinary career was far from over, but the stage was set. Behind the events surrounding his struggle towards power and his eventual exposure there lies a larger issue, and a different power struggle, concerning the very nature of nationalism in modern Ireland. To read the language of Blaney's attacks on his leader, or the romantic rodomontade about the dead generations from Kevin Boland (another minister who resigned in sympathy), or most of all the innocent Fianna Boy Scout Captain James Kelly, fall-guy for the politicians, is to hear the last strains of Fenian rhetoric in mainstream politics. And this presaged, as will be seen, a change in the *raison d'être* of Fianna Fáil, pioneered by Jack Lynch. Haughey achieved power only because he eventually accepted this, while continuing his obeisances to older household gods. His successor, Bertie Ahern, who performed a similar step dance, has gone on record more than once as saying that he does not like revisionists. No wonder, then, that when choosing the speaker for Lynch's funeral oration in 1999, Ahern was passed over in favour of Des O'Malley. For Jack Lynch was, in some ways, the father of modern Irish political revisionism.

II

Lynch had come into politics with less rhetorical baggage than many Fianna Fáil aspirants. This meant, in Irish terms, that he was held to be 'not interested in politics', which indicates what 'politics' is taken to represent in the culture of the party fight and the funeral. Patrick Hillery, another slightly atypical Fianna Fáil member, would later recall of Lynch and himself that though they 'didn't know anything about politics', they were the cabinet members who seemed most interested in 'policy'.[7] This division of 'politics' from 'policy' deserves some analysis. Lynch was insecurely in control of a party in which atavistic feelings ran very deep. His speech in August 1969, declaring that the Irish government could not 'stand by' and see the North dissolve into anarchy, seems to have been railroaded through by nationalists in the party, and certainly did not express his own preferences. But it was probably the least he could say at the time.[8] And his subsequent addresses of July and October 1970, effectively repudiating irredentist nationalism and suggesting a bipartisan approach with Britain for an internal Northern Ireland solution, unsaid his August 1969 speech as much as he possibly could. What followed was the attempt to expel from the centre of power an irredentist Republican tendency represented by Haughey, Blaney and Boland. Though the moment when the Republic might have intervened in the North had passed, against some contemporary expectations, the 1970 Arms Trial cleared up nothing, and showed no one in a particularly creditable light.

The period starting in or around 1972, besides seeing the Republic entering the EEC, the ending of the reigns of de Valera and McQuaid, the North in chaos, Stormont suspended and rethinking on both sides of the border, was also characterized by a sense of post-stress trauma in nationalist politics. Lynch was manipulating a particularly divided and difficult party, facing into an era of political uncertainty north and south. Though the cabal of his enemies had been sidelined, they had not been expelled, and the unresolved nature of the charges brought against them enabled Haughey, at least, to rebuild his position from the ground up, using local caucuses, calling in old political debts and, as time would show, contracting new financial ones. He was rich enough to hire his own PR machine. His eventual return to the upper echelons of the party was bitterly contested by Frank Aiken, Erskine Childers and others of the old de Valera guard. Aiken, for one, was prepared to split the party and begged Lynch not to ratify Haughey's nomination in the 1973 election. Lynch was not prepared to go so far. And Fianna Fáil was about to have, after sixteen years in power, a chance of regrouping in opposition. The election of 1973 saw it very narrowly defeated by a coalition of Fine Gael and Labour under Cosgrave and Corish, which held power for four years.

This is generally seen as a new start, and it felt, at the time, rather like the New Labour advent of 1997 in Britain. The faces were new, the language was different, there even seemed to be some intellectuals in places of power; Garret FitzGerald was foreign minister at just the time that the job acquired a new meaning, with Ireland's access to Europower. But the oil crisis and 20 per cent inflation put paid to many of the brave new hopes. FitzGerald's time would come again, and in many ways he would carry forward a legacy from Lynch rather than Cosgrave. For the interim, the Soldiers of Destiny resembled more closely one of their other chosen designations, the Legion of the Rearguard. In opposition Haughey strengthened his position to the point where Lynch readmitted him to the front bench in 1975. His old enemy Childers, who had become president, had suddenly died the year before, but Childers's widow took the opportunity to sever connections with the party, declaring that her late husband 'is now close to God and will be able to ask His intercession that his much loved country will never again be governed by these people'.[9] God did not oblige. In the election of 1977 Fianna Fáil shouldered its way in front once more and reclaimed its position as the natural party of government. However, when Lynch returned to power, with a majority so large that it troubled the canny Corkman, it was at the expense of a number of hostages to fortune. The economic outlook was stormy; even Ken Whitaker, a close Lynch supporter, felt that the party leader was going awry on this issue.[10] Martin O'Donoghue, minister for economic planning and development, promised an 'everlasting boom' in December 1977, guaranteeing full employment by 1983, while admitting inflation might reach 7 per cent.[11] In fact, it went to 10 per cent rapidly, and climbed. There were profligate promises to be honoured: abolishing domestic rates, motor taxation and the like. And there was the restoration of Haughey to cabinet rank, as minister for health and social welfare.

This seemed an astonishing risk, but worse was to come. When Lynch retired early in 1979 the crown passed not to his designated successor, George Colley, but to the once disgraced and repudiated Haughey. It should not have come as a complete surprise. He had devoted himself, during the wilderness years, to nurturing local party bosses in far-flung parts of Ireland. This had been reflected in support from many of the 1977 intake of TDs, including hungry figures from the west like Pádraig Flynn and Seán Doherty, who would later be rewarded well beyond their capacities. For months *Magill* had been consistently tipping Haughey to beat Colley, and in some ways

Lynch's isolation from certain areas of the party had continued. Haughey had poured money into his campaign, employing his own press officer and trying to buy in writing talent from the young guns on *Magill* and *Hot Press* such as Colm Tóibín and Gene Kerrigan. Colley had twenty of the twenty-five ministers behind him, but Haughey had the back benches – and, more surprisingly, the support of some senatorial figures of unimpeachable probity, like Michael Yeats. Haughey benefited from a groundswell of opposition to Lynch from figures who were not necessarily Republican fellow travellers. As it gathered momentum, Síle de Valera and other opportunists came on board, attacking their leader for making security arrangements with the British government. Colley was unprepared for this heave, but Haughey capitalized upon it. He celebrated the moment of victory with the thumping lie that he had promises of unreserved support from his most prominent opponents.[12] The Fianna Fáil family, traumatically sundered behind the scenes, was hard put to present a united front to the outside world; Garret FitzGerald's celebrated attack on its new leader's 'flawed pedigree' struck a raw nerve. Lynch, who lived on for twenty years, was removed from the public photo calls and conveyed his own feelings by studiously avoiding all public party occasions, even the annual Ard-Fheiseanna. These turned into party rallies, American-style, orchestrated by Haughey's legendary press officer P. J. Mara, whose partly parodic evocations of his leader ('*Uno* Duce! *Una* voce!') provided rich pickings for satirists. From the early days of his boss's rehabilitation, Mara had laid down the ground rules for interviews: 'none of that old arms trial shite'.[13] As power was assumed by a figure variously compared by his opponents to Salazar, Nixon and Dracula, the shape of a new kind of New Ireland came into view.

By the early 1970s Haughey had apparently become astoundingly rich. From a modest suburban background, his degrees in commerce and law had initially enabled him to found a swiftly expanding accountancy practice with Kevin Boland's brother, specializing in tax-avoidance advice to the wealthy; but his way of life soon outpaced even that of the richest of his clients. Advised by his property-developer friend Matt Gallagher, in 1969 he bought Grangemore, a Georgian house on twenty-five acres in North Dublin. The land was rezoned with planning permission while its owner was minister for finance and sold back to Matt Gallagher in 1969 at a profit of about £90,000 – just a year after Haughey had himself brought in a new provision of the Finance Act that protected such profits from windfall tax. He then bought a far grander house, Abbeville at Kinsealy. Again it was a Georgian mansion adjacent to spreading suburban sprawl, but this time came with 250 acres and had been designed by Gandon, the great architect of the Dublin's neoclassical Custom House and Four Courts, for an eighteenth-century Ascendancy grandee. The stables at Abbeville were soon occupied by suitable inmates. A 127-acre stud farm in Meath was added to the portfolio, a large yacht and, most ostentatiously of all, Inishvickillane, an entire island off the Kerry coast, for £100,000. Here Haughey would build a lavish house costing £38,000 in 1977–8, at a time when his personal debt to Allied Irish Banks totalled £580,000. It would be nearly double that by the end of the decade.

Haughey's overdraft was already running at £244,000 by 1971. The construction of trusts that 'owned' his various properties did not provide protection, and the bank became increasingly desperate. From time to time it would try to call in his cheque books, but weakly accepted its client's assurances about meaningless repayment arrangements – inevitably based on projected land deals – and claims that he would be helped by rich property-developer friends. When he became a minister again in 1977, he simply stopped turning up for scheduled meetings at the bank. Michael Phelan, the manager, would call rather pathetically at the Department for Social Welfare and leave with nothing more than some doleful notes of what had transpired. ('[Mr Haughey] waffled a bit about a recent sale of a field across the road from Abbeville at a very high price ... Apart altogether from any monies from the sale of lands he told me that from a development in Baldoyle, which was now coming to fruition, there would be a sum of £2,000 coming to him ... All in all, it is my considered opinion that this client does not believe the bank will force a confrontation with him, because of his position.'[14]) By the beginning of 1979 the overdraft was touching £900,000; it topped a million in December. And at that very point the contest for the Fianna Fáil leadership opened. The directors of Allied Irish Banks knew their controversial client owed a million pounds and had proposed clearing it with the help of major businessmen like Matt Gallagher, but they sportingly kept this information to themselves. The unfortunate bank manager who had pursued him to his ministry and come away empty-handed knew he had to admit defeat. The next letter from the bank was one of congratulation. 'To say the task you have taken on is daunting is an understatement,' wrote Phelan, 'but I have every faith in your ability to succeed in restoring confidence in this great little nation.'[15]

Phelan knew more than most about the private state of the new taoiseach's finances, but his expenditure was there for all to see. Dublin watched and marvelled; the few journalists who consistently and pertinently asked how all this was managed on a politician's salary of £7,000 p.a. were seen as spoilsports. (Haughey had retired from active involvement in Haughey Boland back in 1960.) It was during his wilderness years from 1970 to 1977 that the debts had spiralled; a clear pattern throughout his career was the way money came rolling in when he possessed political power and dried up when he did not. It was widely believed that while minister for health he was a silent partner in the property-development business of John Byrne; certainly his colleague George Colley believed it, and therefore refused to allow government offices to lease space in Byrne's eyesore office blocks.[16] From Haughey's own point of view, he seems to have felt that not only did he deserve the lifestyle of the rich and famous but that it was in the national interest for him to live it to the hilt. An important part of the smokescreen relied upon the covert approval of the electorate; he was spending like a prince for the good of the country's image. Years later, when the Moriarty Tribunal inquired as to why the millionaire Dermot Desmond should have picked up the large bill for refurbishing the *Celtic Mist*, Haughey replied that he supposed Mr Desmond felt that the taoiseach's yacht 'should reflect the country in a good light'.[17] Such a thought would not have occurred to his rival FitzGerald, piloting a battered Saab to Senate meetings at the National University from his Rathmines house, cluttered with books and academic articles in progress. It was also in marked contrast to Lynch's uxorious life in a small Victorian villa (also in Rathmines), not to mention the markedly gloomy and austere style of de Valera's domestic existence. The grandeur of Abbeville's interior decoration, all Aubusson-style carpets, gilt chairs, flashy gifts from foreign potentates and portraits of its owner, was held to be essential for entertaining heads of state. By the time he became taoiseach in 1979, and throughout the rollercoaster ride of the following twelve years, Haughey never lost his sense of entitlement. In some ways he kept it to the end of his life.

III

His model of grandeur was an odd combination of Napoleonic enigma, Ascendancy hauteur, Gaelic chieftain and Tammany boss. Like his rival FitzGerald, Haughey had a certain cult of France; but, while FitzGerald's tastes had been formed by youthful holidays with French families and a keen appetite for philosophical discussions with Catholic intellectuals, Haughey's Francophilia involved lavish visits to Paris, hand-stitched shirts from the legendary Charvet *atelier*, a cellar of chateau-bottled claret and a running bill at Dublin's plutocratic French restaurant Le Coq Hardi. He also determined that the government headquarters in Merrion Street should be restored and developed as grandly as any French public building. The 'Ascendancy' component of Haughey's personal myth was more easily lampooned. A love of horses and an addiction to breeding them is a congenitally Irish characteristic and not (as in England) generally defined by class; but Haughey took it to the Ascendancy limit, even commissioning a series of portraits of himself on horseback in full hunting fig by the gifted painter Edward McGuire. McGuire, radical in his politics and subversive by nature, produced such obvious parodies that Haughey, incensed, wanted them destroyed.[18] A more unstinting admiration was lavished on him in his North Dublin political fief, which he nursed with the clientelism and occasional brutality of an American ward boss. In his Gaelic chieftain mode, installed on his western island, he held forth to his family and friends about the ancient world of gods and chieftains; this persona is preserved in a hagiographical film scripted by Anthony Cronin, one of the talented and creative spirits whom Haughey liked to include in his circle. If FitzGerald relished a seminar, Haughey wanted a court.

In all these poses, in the frantic accumulation of wealth and equally frantic disposal of it, in the unashamed demands for handouts from Ireland's growing plutocracy, in the endless commissioning of busts, portraits, memorials, in the flashes of crudeness and malevolence, even in the refusal to be photographed with colleagues taller than himself, Haughey could appear a cliché: and he was duly mocked, most spectacularly by Dermot Morgan and Gerry Stembridge in the legendary satirical radio programme *Scrap Saturday*. Irish audiences were gratified by parodies of the gravel-voiced 'Boss', intoning the descent of his clan from Arab princes, Gaelic kings and Merovingian dynasties, before breaking off to bark '*Mara!*' and order the roughing up or elimination of a luckless colleague. Some of the authorities in RTÉ were less amused, especially as they had to deal with complaints from the taoiseach's office. Charles Townshend has wittily referred to Ireland after 1948 as 'The Second Republic', but the peculiar aura surrounding Ireland's Man of Destiny from 1979 suggests, as so much of this era does, the France of the Third Republic – with a would-be-Napoleonic figure turning out to be General Boulanger instead. Already, at the beginning of the period, the elements of that 'flawed pedigree' were in place.

When FitzGerald mounted this unprecedented and ruthless attack on the new taoiseach, he concentrated upon Haughey's refusal to condemn the IRA and his close links in 1969–70 to his co-defendant the Belfast Provisional John Kelly. But, as will be charted in the next chapter, by 1979 Haughey's Republicanism had become as shadowy as much else about him. Though his family had been closely involved in IRA activity in the 1920s, and his brother Jock could have brought him the kind of embarrassment provided by the siblings of John Major and Jimmy Carter, Haughey himself seemed more interested in politics as a route to money. When he became taoiseach his financial go-between Des Traynor, a tax-avoidance expert from the family accountancy firm, transferred his bank overdraft by collecting 'loans' from businessmen like Matt Gallagher and moving the balance to the heavily shielded offshore accounts that Traynor had set up for general tax-avoidance purposes in the Cayman Islands, under the name of Ansbacher. Rumours persisted of land deals from the 1960s, and some shadowy areas marked Haughey's stint as minister for finance in 1966. Later, his supposed breakthrough in Anglo-Irish relations over the North misfired badly; he seemed ready to play the Republican card for defensive or Anglophobic purposes only (as when he attempted ineptly to smear Garret FitzGerald for lunching with 'a trained British spy' in the person of the duke of Norfolk). Once in power he was oddly indecisive and passive on key issues. Effort went instead into his PR machine, striking attitudes of Gaullist grandeur and unveiling plaques to himself in places like Castlebar. The new taoiseach also devoted a good deal of energy to getting control of party funds, with the result that donations to Fianna Fáil ended up more and more regularly in the leader's pocket – a process facilitated by the trusting party secretary, Bertie Ahern, who provided him with blank signed cheques. But in cabinet, faced with revolt from O'Malley and antagonism from Colley, he was oddly ineffectual. There was also a wall of antagonism from the Department of Foreign Affairs.

In any case, the days of secure and unaided Fianna Fáil majorities seemed to be over. Those party strategists who had tried to persuade the Irish people to give up proportional representation in 1968 must have been gnashing their teeth. Haughey lost power to a Fine Gael coalition government in 1981–2, and the election of February 1982 denied him an overall majority. He also had to head off a leadership challenge from Des O'Malley before arranging skin-of-the-teeth support from the radical (and Republican) independent Tony Gregory as well as from the Workers' Party – ironically, the slightly constitutional descendants of the Official IRA, whose cause Haughey had done so much to stymie in his gun-running days. As it was, he governed only till November 1982, which saw the third general election in eighteen months. At this stage Haughey had to give way to reality and accept a new direction for national economic strategy. But by then too policy was in danger of being overshadowed by a mounting background of scandalous events.

He was already surrounded by an entourage that included some notable grotesques and stage turns. In his first administration Lynch supporters were unceremoniously dumped, though Colley temporarily remained. The more talented and substantial figures who came to the front included Ray MacSharry, Albert Reynolds, Máire Geoghegan-Quinn, Michael O'Kennedy and Brian Lenihan. The range, size and powers of the taoiseach's department were spectacularly increased, with divisions to handle economic and social policy, cultural and legal affairs, and foreign relations (Haughey's relations with Iveagh House, which he described as a centre of 'sophistry, ambivalence and self-deception', continued to resemble Hitler's with the diplomats at the Wilhelmstrasse).[19] The wider circle included his election agent, known as 'Pat O'Connor-Pat O'Connor' (on account of a misunderstanding about duplicated voting), the clownish Pádraig Flynn and the distinctly unlegalistic minister for 'justice', Seán Doherty, who used his powers to fly very short distances in helicopters, move uncooperative Gardaí to new postings and bug the phones of supposedly 'anti-national' journalists. Telephones mattered; there was also a scandal about the taoiseach ordering override facilities for internal telephones in Government Buildings, allowing him to listen in, Nixon-like. And it would be the records of telephone conversations that destroyed his reputation in the end. Then there was Haughey's financial fixer Des Traynor, an ostensibly respectable businessman on the boards of several leading Irish companies. Future tribunals would demonstrate how this financial Leporello to Haughey's swaggering Don Giovanni conjured money in and out of Ansbacher. According to later evidence, Traynor's role in Haughey's life meant that the taoiseach did not even have to have a personal bank account. Everything was managed for him, like royalty.[20]

Haughey's manipulation of power in the late 1970s and early 1980s gave no indication that the economic crisis apparently crippling Ireland would be tackled. Unemployment had been the ghost at the Fianna Fáil feast from 1977, along with a declining GDP. By 1980 the out-of-work figure was back at 100,000 (the level inherited by Lynch), and it would double over the next three years. The borrowing requirement and national debt also soared after 1977. Nor was Fianna Fáil able to utilize its legendary vertical class profile in order to moderate union wage demands, though it tried. There was also an ominous wave of public protest about taxation, from sectors of the population unable to avail themselves of Des Traynor's advice. Not that the patrons of Ansbacher accounts were seen as the culprits. The tax burden weighed more and more heavily on urban, industrial and white-collar workers, while farmers – already, as we have seen, feeling the benefits of the EEC's Common Agricultural Policy – were further favoured by the agricultural ministers' traditional reluctance to see them pay any income tax at all. The end of Lynch's regime had been rocked by angry public demonstrations on behalf of hard-pressed PAYE workers, objecting to the government's abandonment of an attempt to levy some tax on farming profits.[21] In terms of financial policies, Haughey had no choice but to preach hairshirt measures as soon as he took over. On 9 January 1980 he made a special broadcast to the nation, announcing portentously that 'as a community we have been living beyond our means.' How the directors of Allied Irish Banks felt as they listened to this has not been recorded.

Even more piquant, in retrospect, is the continued level of public protest at taxation levels that, due to inflation, continued to bite very heavily on salaried workers. Had those calling for a national strike for tax reform known about the network of offshore trusts on the Cayman Islands whereby Fianna Fáil's Golden Circle avoided paying any tax at all on tens of millions, or about the taoiseach's failure to declare the many 'gifts' that flowed his way from Irish millionaires, their action might have taken a more direct form. And, in any case, political pressures and the vulnerable state of several sectors of Irish industry meant that the government had to soft-pedal on deflationary measures. Over 1980–81 the Exchequer borrowing requirement, targeted for reduction by IR£23 million, rose by IR£208 million instead. Government spending followed suit. Taxation rose heavily for ordinary people, but Haughey's government continued to avoid cuts. Deficits and borrowing requirements continued to soar, and there was little sign of improvement by May 1981, when Fianna Fáil lost out to a Labour–Fine Gael coalition government, committed (despite its leftist slant) to radical deflation. In opposition Haughey continued to show little sign of economic realism, provoking open disagreement with colleagues such as Charlie McCreevy. In any case, tension within the coalition helped bring about its defeat in early 1982. This precipitated a behind-the-scenes political crisis when Haughey and his supporters pressed President Hillery to instruct them to form a government rather than granting a dissolution. Hillery refused to sacrifice constitutional propriety in favour of his ex-colleagues, and the election was again a hair-trigger affair, leaving Haughey reliant on the support of left-wing independents, which tied him to public-spending promises at odds with his previous pronouncements; he had in any case sought political capital when out of office by accusing FitzGerald's government of 'Thatcherism'. As with the North, political pressures would always distract his attention away from consistent policy on the economy.

This weather-vane approach to the economic crisis was one reason for the convulsive situation within the party, where challengers constantly plotted in the wings. Matters were exacerbated by the series of scandals swirling around the ludicrous Doherty, culminating in the arrest of a psychotic multiple murderer who had been staying as a guest in the attorney general's flat in the summer of 1982. This crisis had at least three noteworthy results. It inspired John Banville's extraordinary novel *The Book of Evidence*. It called forth one of Conor Cruise O'Brien's most effective onslaughts on the Haughey ethos, when he seized upon the taoiseach's lame attempt to distance himself from the recent events to coin the acronym 'GUBU'. And finally, under mounting pressure, the Fianna Fáil government embraced a consistent policy of austerity to reduce budget deficits, accompanied by a strategy of attracting inward investment by seductive tax breaks. This was outlined in *The Way Forward* (October 1982). The government fell from power the next month, but a new course was set. It also, in a manner characteristic of Irish politics at times of crisis, turned into a bipartisan approach. It was a Fine Gael government that in 1983 began imposing deflationary policies, cutting spending and increasing taxes. A prominent Cassandra, the brilliant maverick economist Raymond Crotty continued to preach doom; his *Ireland in Crisis* (1986) prophesied 'utter economic, political and social collapse' for the Republic by the end of the decade. He did not live, alas, to see just how wrong he could be.

IV

Fine Gael and Labour were in power from late 1982 till March 1987, and, with FitzGerald as taoiseach and Labour's new hope, Dick Spring, as tánaiste, there was once more an air of a brave new world. There was also an instant spate of revelations about the late Haughey government, but the Man of Destiny retained power over the Soldiers. The last days of his 1982 government had been darkened by an attempted putsch led by McCreevy and Des O'Malley; Haughey's victory over the rebels had been accompanied by alarming scenes of physical violence by his followers. A more serious challenge was mounted a few months later; describing his enemies as 'the media, alien influences, political opponents and most of all business interests pursuing their own ends', Haughey survived this too.[22] He used his opposition days to purge his opponents within the party, a process that produced, *inter alia*, the new grouping of the Progressive Democrats under O'Malley and Mary Harney. The FitzGerald era saw the New Ireland Forum and the 1985 Anglo-Irish Agreement signed at Hillsborough – both initiatives in the spirit of Lynch's earlier statements of intent. Haughey's attempt to denounce the 1985 Agreement as unconstitutional utterly misfired when Garret FitzGerald pointed out that the clause requiring majority agreement within Northern Ireland was taken verbatim from Haughey's 1980 communiqué after his meeting with Thatcher. But another Fianna Fáil legacy remained more ominous: this period, as we have seen, was also marked by the continuation of economic insecurity and ballooning deficit figures.

Fianna Fáil returned to power on a knife-edge majority in 1987 in a rather bedraggled condition. The departure of the Progressive Democrats had set in stone the traumatic rifts in the party after Lynch's departure, and the change in the nature of its leadership. To many people the future looked gloomy but not to Haughey. Just after the 1987 election, the editor of the *Irish Times*, Conor Brady, was driven out for an audience with the incoming taoiseach at Kinsealy by his colleague John Healy – whose immensely influential political journalism had consistently supported the controversial Squire of Abbeville, while stigmatizing his opponents as 'Honest Jack Lynch' and 'Garret the Good'. Despite a quarter-million unemployed, double-digit interest figures, factory closures and a continuing stasis in the North, Haughey prophesied to the newspapermen a glowing future, forecasting a growing economy and investment of state resources in key areas. Dublin was to follow London's example by situating an international finance centre in the increasingly redundant docklands (the brainchild of his millionaire friend Dermot Desmond), and rejuvenating the run-down Temple Bar area *à la* Covent Garden. The beef-processing industry was to be launched aggressively into export markets, with the aid of another Haughey intimate, Larry Goodman. Brady remained sceptical – as he did when, some weeks later, influential figures at the Industrial Development Authority told him that a dramatic upturn in inward investment was on the way, powered by the American microchip industry.[23]

Garret FitzGerald had already floated the idea of an all-party economic forum to arrive at a consensus policy. This was not going to happen without strict fiscal economies. Fianna Fáil adhered to the austere strategy pioneered by its predecessors, helped by a new element of political will, as well as by support from across the house. In fact, the next two years saw an unprecedented degree of cooperation over economic policy from the opposition, now led by Alan Dukes: an admirable response for which today's prosperous Republic should thank him, but that earned him no political advantage at all and in fact probably cooked his goose (that distinction between 'politics' and 'policy' comes to mind once more). The new regime continued to be accompanied by particularly sanctimonious lectures from Haughey himself on the immorality of living beyond one's means.[24] How this sounded to the unpaid suppliers of hand-sewn shirts and vintage wines, or the employees of his racing stables, is again a matter for the Balzac of this era, when he or she sits down to write its Human Comedy. Moreover, the rhetoric of public probity was oddly blended with another French tradition, the exhortation given by Guizot to the subjects of Louis-Philippe: '*Enrichissez-vous!*'

On the national front, if we are to believe the MacSharry version, the genius of Fianna Fáil was simultaneously to liberalize the economy, restructure the tax system in favour of corporate profit and inward investment, and carry through the IDA plan of creating jobs and wealth by becoming the favoured destination of multinationals in search of a home. How temporary that home might be was not mentioned. Nor does this version of things feature the inflow of EU structural funds that was by now well on stream. Garret FitzGerald, in so many ways Gladstone to Haughey's Disraeli, liked to stress that *this* was the basis of the economic miracle; but here, as in other ways, Haughey looked to Boston rather than to Berlin – and even to London, as with the Financial Services Centre. (Lobbying for the contract to develop the 27-acre site between Amiens Street and the Liffey took the form of a feeding frenzy from ambitious consortia in late 1987; the winners, Custom House Docks Development Company Ltd, would later be shaken down by Haughey for a £100,000 Fianna Fáil contribution, diverted without the donor's knowledge, as so much else, via Des Traynor and Guinness Mahon to the taoiseach's personal expenses.[25] Land and its potential remained, as ever, at the centre of the party's vision. Fianna Fáil also liked to link the economic turn-around of the 1990s to the party's good relationship with labour, and its pioneering of social partnership. This was the rhetorical replace-ment of the old de Valera mantra that Fianna Fáil was a 'national movement', not a party. It might have been buffeted by traumatic splits and scandals, changed its homespun image for suits from Louis Copeland and come to be identified with millionaire builders rather than twenty-acre farmers. But it now claimed to be the party of wealth creation for all, and this was its title deed to remaining the natural party of government. However, Fianna Fáil tended to ignore one implication of the 'attracting-jobs-and-wealth' mantra: how much of the wealth actually attached itself to the people who did the jobs?

Who was actually making money in the Haughey era? There were some native millionaires like the Dunne family, of supermarket fame, who might, once again, have stepped straight from Balzac: the eccen-tric, cheese-paring patriarch Ben Dunne, riddled with envy of the Cork merchant princes whom he had supplanted, the scapegrace namesake son, the steel-willed daughter Margaret. Their lives would intersect strangely with Squire Haughey's and the link would destroy him in the end. At another social level, family businesses established in the heroin-trading flats of Weaver Court, Dolphin's Barn, rather than in the mansions of Killiney and Ballsbridge, cemented their money and power in these years: the black economy of bundles of cash trans-ported in sports holdalls operated all across the social spectrum. But the most gilded life was led by the financial entrepreneurs who were most closely involved in the Golden Circle of Fianna Fáil supporters. It was almost as if political connections helped the rich to qualify for the indulgence of the Revenue Appeals Commissioners, a body that looked with exceptional kindness upon the Dunne family trust, among other cases. Access to policy-making circles smoothly became an expected business perquisite. Similar allegations were made during the course of later legal inquiries about the exercise of political influence to lubricate possible obstructions in the way of gigantic takeover deals.[26] This coincided with the rise of big business within Ireland to a financial level hitherto undreamt of, and the dramatic expansion of the Irish Stock Exchange. But as the 1980s dawned, it was clear that one sector of the Irish economy was making money above all, hand over fist: property developers. That ancient Irish connection between land, politics and power was being exploited in a new and murky way.

Though the housing market had stagnated in the early 1970s, it began to inflate before other sectors of the economy did, from about 1976. This was linked to the working-through of the population increase that had started in the previous decade, and the pronounced demographic shift from country to town, as the number of agrarian jobs plummeted and the ancient structures of Irish family farming, sustained through the decades with so many inducements, tax breaks and varieties of income support, began to change into something more like agribusiness. Traditional patterns in land transactions persisted up to the mid 1970s, as did small-farming patterns, but these too would change. By the end of the 1980s nearly half of the farms in the Republic were fifty acres or more. The rise in farm incomes, and the structure of CAP payments, favoured large farmers above all. Farmers, under Fianna Fáil, had continued to profit from an almost unbelievably indulgent tax regime. (The threats posed by GATT and Maastricht were still in the future.) So did the kind of agribusiness represented by Larry Goodman's beef export company, early on earmarked for favourable treatment and boosted by vast sums of money paid in phoney export credits. And so did others; crucially, property developers.

Tax breaks were offered to builders of multistorey car parks, or city hotels, or seaside apartment blocks. And there was money to be made in rezoning agricultural land that lay in the path of urban development, as Dublin spread north and west. 'Greenfield sites' were, strangely, targeted for so-called 'urban renewal'. From 1981 investigative journalists were pointing out the disproportionate number of Fianna Fáil TDs who had interests in property development, or who were actually auctioneers themselves.[27] Those involved in county council politics rapidly realized how their influence could be exploited, and on this fertile ground countless corrupt relationships began to flourish. Several members of Haughey's rogues' gallery were involved, such as the TD for Dublin West, Liam Lawlor (who had helped Haughey return from the wilderness in the 1970s but later supported O'Malley's challenge against him). There was also an unlikely rising star from the wheeler-dealer world of North Dublin estate agents, Ray Burke. An insatiable recipient of sweetener payments in office, he was also prepared, as minister for communications, to ignore all normal constitutional procedures when granting a new licence to Century Radio – in return for what the Flood Tribunal would name as 'corrupt payments'.

The rumours started early on; he was targeted by *Magill* magazine in September 1979 for arranging suspect planning permissions.[28] When Haughey's government fell in late 1982, Burke as minister for the environment had swiftly packed An Bord Pleanála, the planning authority, with five apparently unqualified nominees. The subsequent coalition government's attempt to limit ministerial powers in relation to the Bord provoked Haughey's most impassioned response: he described the idea of depoliticizing the planning process as 'spiteful, dirty, mean and debasing', words that might be better applied to his and Burke's manipulation of patronage and planning. (Negotiating with the independent radical TD Tony Gregory to stay in power earlier that year, Haughey's sticking point had been a refusal to agree to an investigation into development and planning issues.) Under the aegis of such people, Dublin County Council in the 1980s itself became effectively an estate agency handling planning permissions for the highest bidder. And it is striking how national politicians liked to hang on to their local power bases, by continued association with local politics. Over 60 per cent of those returned to the Dáil in 1977 were sitting councillors, and people like Liam Lawlor moved heaven and earth to retain council seats even while active as high-profile TDs. The links of builders to politicians have become clearer and clearer in retrospect. The late Patrick Gallagher, son of Haughey's early bankroller Matt Gallagher, described it as a kind of social project, self-justifyingly manipulating an image from a now-bygone history.

'Haughey was financed', he later said, 'in order to create the environment which the Anglo-Irish enjoyed and that we as a people could never aspire to. Everything was planned.'[29]

The sanctimonious self-delusion of this trumps even Tom Parlon's claim that the Land League's aim was to ensure unrestricted profiteering by property developers. The 'Anglo-Irish' were merely a historical figment by 1974, when Patrick Gallagher inherited his father's vast building and property empire, and proceeded to spend heavily on racehorses, cars and multiple residences – to such an extent that the business was bankrupt in seven years and he was sentenced to a jail term for financial malpractice. He may have thought that spectacular improvidence was an 'Anglo-Irish' precedent too, but what he had been prevented from 'aspiring to' remains obscure. In any case, the payments to politicians created a culture of kickbacks, special access to contracts and massive tax evasion that would enable Patrick Gallagher and others to live in a style of conspicuous consumption, often at the expense of the public purse, that few of their countrymen could hope for.

It is now clear from the evidence extracted by the several government tribunals established to investigate corruption that the organization of development zoning was managed by politicians, local and national, sweetened by enormous cash bribes. The Irish political world began to feature a figure up to this time more familiar in American politics: the lobbyist. One prominent exemplar, Frank Dunlop, had come to this new profession after working as press secretary for Fianna Fáil in the early years of Haughey's ascendancy, from 1977 to 1982. This Hogarthian progress led inexorably to a career in public relations; and from 1986 he principally represented land developers. Dunlop's autobiography is brilliantly entertaining about his years as press secretary, and informative about the operations and etiquette of the Haughey court circle, but it ends before his subsequent career, which can be traced through the tribunal hearings investigating land deals and political influence.[30] Through his lobbying, figures from the building trade like Tom Gilmartin enjoyed surprising access to the centre of political power; while from their side, politicians of ministerial rank apparently became used to demanding and receiving large cash sums allegedly destined for 'party funds'. Gilmartin's dealings with the Soldiers of Destiny in Leinster House, according to one witness, 'made the Mafia look like monks'.[31] And it would be Dunlop's revelations, like those of the embittered James Gogarty, that would finally open the way to the investigations that preoccupied the Irish political world from the late 1990s. Frank Dunlop's admission on 19 April 2000 before the Flood Tribunal of huge payments to councillors began the avalanche that would carry away Liam Lawlor and others with him. It is also clear, from the evidence of the tribunals, that cabinet-rank Fianna Fáil politicians were accepting enormous bribes from those involved in the land-development world. And some of the largest bribes, literally totalling millions, were tendered to the taoiseach himself: the Moriarty Tribunal would eventually conclude in 2006 that he took payments of €11.56 million between 1979 and 1996 (equivalent to €45 million in contemporary values), and 'granted favours in return'.[32]

The connections between planning permissions, land development and political influence can be more directly and crudely drawn. When we look at the physical evidence of the boom building years, it is clear that the kind of housing produced, not to mention developments such as the Liffey Valley shopping centre, bore little or no relation to the needs of the area or its populace, in terms of social amenity, transport links or architectural vision. Dublin house prices quadrupled during the 1970s. By the nineties building firms' profitability was soaring. Sisk's increased its profits sixfold between 1994 and 97, while Cramptons' trebled in 1997 alone. Housing prices had taken off into the stratosphere, following the ancient nineteenth-century pattern whereby Irish people were prepared to pay a price for land that far outreached its intrinsic value – or, often, their ability to finance it. And in Dublin, at least, new patterns of owner-occupancy were in the making. Behind these sociological shifts lay a world that recalls R. H. Tawney's description of business and politics in Jacobean England: 'that seductive border region where politics grease the wheels of business and polite society smiles hopefully on both'.[33] The interlocking of politics and high finance began to come into focus in the 1990s, though it was still a world where members of the Appeals Committee of the Inland Revenue were nominated – very carefully – by politicians. There were Prevention of Corruption Acts in existence, such as the 1995 Ethics in Public Office Act, intended to make politicians declare gifts, but it was very loosely drawn.[34] From 1974 to 2000 only one case was considered under this legislation, and that was in order to extradite someone to face charges in the UK.

Meanwhile, Ray Burke was accumulating a series of cabinet posts under Haughey and (as the Flood Tribunal would spectacularly reveal) pocketing large donations, supposedly intended for party funds, from the builders Joe Brennan and Tom McGowan.[35] His taoiseach continued to spend money like a billionaire, on houses, his island, his yacht, his racehorses and his son's helicopter company. But by the late 1980s his own debts were causing widespread anxiety. When they were transferred from AIB to Guinness Mahon – of which Des Traynor was a director – there was some respite. But when Guinness Mahon was bought out by a Japanese firm, reality began to bite. That was the point when Traynor began, in 1987, to look for a new patron for his spendthrift chief. He found the supermarket heir Ben Dunne.

What Ben Dunne expected in return for his money is not yet established. One claim is that he provided it out of simple gratitude. The troubled supermarket heir had been kidnapped by a fringe IRA group some years before, and a ransom of £1,500,000 was apparently paid, contrary to the instructions of the Gardaí and Special Branch (who had immobilized the money in the Dunne family accounts). Later, it was claimed that the taoiseach, astonishingly, ignored this agreed policy and instructed Patrick Gallagher to provide the money for Dunne's release.[36] If this was the case, Ben Dunne may have felt cause to be grateful. But he already had a habit of paying politicians with large sums concealed from the tax authorities, as was revealed by the story of his relationship with the Fine Gael deputy Michael Lowry, exposed by the McCracken Tribunal. In 1987, when Fianna Fáil returned to power, the Dunne family trust was fighting a £30 million tax bill raised by the Revenue on the break-up of the trust, due since 1985; it was dismissed by the Appeals Commissioners in 1988. The previous year Dunne had paid Haughey more than £200,000, the first of several such *douceurs*. More would follow, just before the 1989 election (a useful time for rationalizing large inflows of money from private donors).[37] The McCracken Tribunal failed to find any hard evidence of favours directed towards Dunne in return. During the family row that erupted over the revelations of his payments to Haughey, unsubstantiated allegations flew back and forth about the reasons for Ben Dunne's generosity to the taoiseach; the issue became tangled up with the siblings' disagreement about the nature and function of the family trust. The more sensational implications were retracted under close questioning at the McCracken Tribunal, when Ben Dunne clearly testified that he had been 'under ferocious pressure to try and get what I felt was mine and I made some very, very stupid allegations'. Full clarification is unlikely to emerge.[38]

Tax threats notwithstanding, there was a lot of money to spare; the Dunne stores by the 1990s sold 48 per cent of the food consumed in Ireland, their turnover was about £900 million, and the family finances were sorted into a trust worth £600 million. But the heir lived a high-pressure life, and on the morning of 19 February 1992, at the Grand Cypress Hotel in Orlando, Florida, he cracked. After an incident involving a bag of cocaine, call girls and a violent psychotic episode on a seventeenth-floor balcony, he was carried from the hotel hog-tied to a pole. (This is the point where the story of modern Ireland demands its Zola rather than its Balzac.) Though his solicitor did his best to have charges quashed on technicalities, the Irish newspapers had a field day. Three of Dunne's siblings had had enough, and the family entered into acrimonious litigation over the vast family trust. One of the main issues regarded Ben Dunne's spending patterns. The trail led back to Abbeville, the Georgian mansion inhabited by Charles James Haughey: Dunne's sister, Margaret Heffernan, made an unwelcome call there in August 1993 and found out that her brother had handed over, for Haughey's personal use, sums totalling £1.3 million. The house of cards surrounding Haughey and other 'top people', involving a web of tax evasion, offshore accounts and lies, began its long cascade. In February 1997 the McCracken Tribunal was set up to examine payments to Oireachteas members and would eventually reveal that Des Traynor steered £38 million of undeclared money belonging to a small number of Irish people into the offshore accounts at Ansbacher Cayman. Traynor, to the relief of many, died in 1994, and his British partner, John Furze, burnt his files, to greater relief still. But after months of stonewalling, ignoring seventy letters from the tribunal and lying to his own lawyers, Haughey found his world laid bare. The revelations spread further, and quickly touched upon the whole murky area of development, planning and kickback payments involving Lawlor, Burke and many others. Tom Parlon's belief that Parnell and Davitt had devoted their lives to ensuring the unfettered ability of Irish people to exploit land development for private profit had apparently been taken by his Fianna Fáil colleagues to a very abstruse level indeed.

V

Haughey had retired from office on 7 February 1992 (a week before Ben Dunne flew to Florida). Relations within the party had been soured over his decision to hang on to power by allying with the apostate Progressive Democrats in 1989, following a disastrously miscalled election. The débâcle of the presidential contest in 1990 delivered a further blow. The Fianna Fáil candidate, Brian Lenihan, had let slip in an interview with a doctoral student that Haughey and his associates had indeed brought unconstitutional pressure to bear on President Hillery in trying to prevent a Dáil dissolution eight years before ('Charlie was gung-ho'). After unsuccessful pressure on Lenihan to resign, Haughey had fired his old friend and supporter, but this neither redeemed his own reputation nor kept Mary Robinson from the presidency. Dick Spring's subsequent Dáil speech made Fitz-Gerald's intervention of 1979 look mild. Haughey's 'greed for office, disregard for truth, contempt for political standards and grasping acquisitiveness . . . [created] a cancer eating away at our body politic'.[39] From that point the finance minister, Albert Reynolds, was positioning himself for a challenge, and within the ranks many other supporters began to shift their allegiance.

Perhaps because of this, a series of scandals linking big business to corrupt political influence began to seep into public view. A judicial inquiry had begun into the beef credits paid to Goodman a year before. The profiteering of the managing director and secretary of Greencore, the newly privatized Irish Sugar Company, also raised eyebrows. Suddenly questions were being asked about privatizations and the vast rake-offs for handling them, which accrued to the lucky and well-connected. There was also the revival of scandals from 1982 – particularly those involving the phone-tapping of journalists considered to be 'anti-national'. Here the publication of Garret Fitz-Gerald's surprisingly outspoken 1991 autobiography, *All in a Life*, should not be ignored. FitzGerald's book pulled no punches about Haughey's career and the scandals that beset it; he also demonstrated the continuity of policy on Northern Ireland from Lynch to himself, culminating in the Anglo-Irish Agreement of 1985, and showed in some detail the inept and counter-productive nature of his rival's contributions in this arena. Haughey survived the first of Reynolds's challenges, but when the embittered Seán Doherty deliberately revealed that Haughey himself had authorized the tapping of journalists' telephones in 1982, he directly gave his ex-Boss the lie. The Progressive Democrats could no longer respectably countenance coalition, and the level of opposition within Fianna Fáil had at last achieved critical proportions. Cruise O'Brien once remarked that even if Haughey were buried at a crossroads with a stake through his heart, his opponents would be wise to go on wearing garlic. Politically speaking, the point had finally been reached when garlic could be abandoned.

Despite these circumstances the passing of 'The Boss' occasioned some maudlin pieces by journalists who should have known better. Haughey himself chose to invoke *Othello*, declaring he had done the state some service, and that was enough. But it is worth considering what kind of service his squalid career had done for the image and reality of Fianna Fáil. What would the revelations mean in political terms? The membership of the party began dropping in the early 1990s, by which time the party finances were also in a bad way; but Haughey's eventual successor Bertie Ahern brought in some large donations, particularly from businessmen whose firms benefited from Fianna Fáil policies. None the less, it is certain that hardly any of the huge payments made by moguls and land developers to party politicians over the previous twenty years found their way to Fianna Fáil's coffers. Especially bitter for some of the old-style party faithful was the fact that coalition with the PDs meant it could no longer rely on its once famous vertical class profile, and its commitment to the plain people of Ireland.

A few years later this would be rivetingly demonstrated in the legal tribunals set up in the 1990s uncovering Fianna Fáil politicians' networks of kickback payments, offshore accounts and tax-haven companies with names like 'Caviar Limited'.[40] As public entertainment, these far outdid the high-minded 'Forum' of the previous era. The high point was the merciless cross-examination of Haughey at the McCracken Tribunal. Evidence furnished by Ben Dunne in March 1997 required the ex-taoiseach's attendance, but he determined to stonewall, initially refusing cooperation and determined to deny that any payments at all had been made. But the tribunal proved a tougher nut than Allied Irish Banks twenty years before. Des Traynor was now dead, but the carefully layered arrangements for concealing Haughey's gratuities through Ansbacher accounts was revealed. By late June the best he could do was admit that vast payments had been made on his behalf but claim that he had no knowledge of them: all had been handled by Des Traynor 'to ensure that I would be free to devote my time and ability to public life and that I would not be distracted from my political work by financial concerns'. Unwisely, he decided to brazen out the claims by Dunne's solicitor, Noel Smyth, that he had accepted bank drafts straight from Dunne's hand. As in the Arms Trial twenty-seven years before, he relied upon a straight disputation of the case made against him, leaving it to the tribunal to decide who was telling the truth.

But Smyth had logged and recorded a series of meetings and phone calls with Haughey from three years back, detailing the ex-taoiseach's worries that matters might become public and establishing beyond doubt that he was lying to the tribunal and to his own legal representatives. A brief statement read by his counsel destroyed his reputation for good. 'I now accept that I received £1.3 million from Mr Ben Dunne and that I became aware that he was the donor to the late Mr Traynor in 1993 and furthermore I now accept Mr Dunne's evidence that he handed me £210,000 in Abbeville in November 1991. In making this statement I wish to make clear that until yesterday I had mistakenly instructed my legal team.' His public appearance on 15 July began evasively, with the reiteration that he had not known where his money was coming from; but he did not survive a forensic cross-examination. The interrogator was the senior counsel Denis

McCullough. One of his grandfathers was that Denis McCullough who had revived Fenianism in the North in the early 1900s, fought in 1916 and was briefly TD for Donegal. Another ancestor was Seán T. O'Kelly, from that same generation of austere Republican founding fathers. It is hard not to think that McCullough's surgical demolition of Haughey was carried out in the names of those dead generations. But the party that Haughey led was irredeemably a very different entity from theirs. The party fight within Fianna Fáil, which convulsed the Lynch era from the mid 1960s, led to the funeral of establishment Republicanism in politics south of the border.

What would take its place? If we look once again for a historical parallel to the welter of scandals besetting the late Third Republic in France, it seemed likely then that the socialist challenge under Jean Jaurès and others would displace the party of personal enrichment – and so it might have, had it not been for the First World War. But no such challenge appeared in 1990s Ireland. The left had gone missing. Much had changed since 1970, when Captain James Kelly, Haughey's associate and armourer-by-appointment to the newly fledged Provos, had seen the Irish left as such a challenge to Republican probity,[41] when Cuba had seemed a reasonable model to many young Irish intellectuals, and when the Front Square of Trinity College Dublin had been occupied by the Maoist Internationalists setting out their stall. The Irish Labour Party had, by and large, remained uninfected by ideology; meriting, perhaps, Lemass's brutal description of it in 1966 as 'a nice respectable docile harmless body of men'. It had seemed to present a viable political challenge under the impressive figure of Dick Spring, but that had faded, and its detachment from the trade union movement had marginalized it from the social-partnership negotiations of the 1980s. One of the less noticed developments of the Haughey era was the manner in which the eclipse of the left worked to Fianna Fáil's advantage, and indeed ensured its survival. Haughey had skilfully cultivated trade union leaders, particularly in his 1987 *Programme for National Recovery*, and in fact they had nowhere else to go. In the 1970s, bizarrely, an estimated 80 per cent of Irish Transport and General Workers' Union members were Fianna Fáil voters.[42] This foretold the future.

The dynamic and modern-minded Spring, leader of Labour from

1982, temporarily brought the party into the limelight, but he too, after a slightly bruising experience of Fine Gael coalition, accepted the inevitability of realpolitik. With Haughey's successor Albert Reynolds he produced the *Programme for a Partnership Government 1993–1997*, which represented a public reaction to the GUBU culture, and a response to the revelations of the tribunals. It stressed the accountability of those in high office, as well as the necessity for detailed registration of politicians' financial interests, and included a range of progressive initiatives. Labour certainly needed a quid pro quo to live down its unexpected coalition with Fianna Fáil – especially since Spring had recently announced that such a step was unthinkable unless the Soldiers of Destiny, who had shown themselves 'blind to standards', 'underwent the most radical transformation'.[43] When Labour did the unthinkable, the reaction among the left-leaning *Irish Times* intelligentsia was as if a daughter to whom they had given every advantage had 'married the boy from the wrong side of town when there were some nice polite boys from good schools to choose from'.[44] Spring and company stuck with the rough boys, on and off, but finally separated company over Reynolds's insistence on fixing a controversial appointment to the presidency of the High Court. Fianna Fáil had always taken a brutally realistic line about looking after its friends, whatever the public disapprobation.

John Bruton's Fine Gael replaced it, in coalition with Labour, but Fianna Fáil would return to power in 1997 (an election that flattened Labour's rising graph) without recourse to its left-wing allies. And when Reynolds's brief hour was over, its leader would be Bertie Ahern, known for his ability to fix deals with union leaders and perfectly able to combine with the new generation of Progressive Democrats. Though initially anointed by Haughey, he would cultivate a personal style that was the very opposite of Napoleonic. Meanwhile the Workers' Party was no more. It retained some of the leftist ideology of its parents in 1960s Sinn Féin, but not enough to make it uncomfortable company in the Dáil, and had passed, by means of changing its name yet again to 'Democratic Left', into eventual alliance with Labour. On the wilder shores of radicalism, the Communist Party was still being run in the 1980s by Mick O'Riordan, an antique Stalinist who steered his sect through many changes of name while parroting the Soviet line on everything, and wisely never revealing to journalists the number of members in his party.[45] By the end of the century any leftist grouping in Irish parliamentary politics had to call itself social-democratic at most. The old radicals were by then in the position of the Tories as described by Horace Walpole in the later eighteenth century: 'In truth, all the sensible men I ever knew became Whigs. Those that remained Tories remained fools.'

Where Irish radicalism went is still up for speculation. Wealth had been created to such a dizzying degree in the 1990s that the politics of the left found little room for purchase. Green issues took up some of the slack, and by the turn of the twenty-first century the influx of immigrants from less privileged parts of the world were creating a new underclass – but not one that was yet making any indentation upon established political party lines. The strikingly youthful age profile of the electorate also argued against a high level of political activism. Labour never succeeded in wooing a popular vote away from the Soldiers of Destiny. The pursuit of power through edgy coalitions was yet another of Haughey's bequests, as was the creation of the Progressive Democrats, who were formed in reaction to his ascendancy. The departure of the PDs had seemed good riddance to the old-style Fianna Fáil element who treasured the idea of a 'national movement' denying the barriers of class and economic difference, and stretching down to the bedrock of the rural proleteriat. But these traditionalists had received a rude shock when the PDs were deemed viable coalition partners in July 1989. Viable coalition partners they remained, if also representing some of the grit in the Fianna Fáil oyster and providing free-market arguments for the policies of successive Ahern governments. Some of the party's traditional support may end up with newly domesticated Sinn Féin. The point is, however, that the Soldiers of Destiny remained in power, scandals notwithstanding, through the 1990s and beyond. They also continued to take credit for the boom – even as the tide of revelations from the tribunals lapped around their shiny shoes.

In this morality tale, which may not have travelled as far from William Carleton as may be thought, Charles Haughey is the key figure. As minister for justice back in the early 1960s, speaking in the Dáil on a bill dealing with judges' salaries, he had remarked, 'Do we not all know that a man's work or value is judged by what he earns? It is a human and natural thing and it is something which is very common here – to look down on a man who does not earn as much as you do.'[46] This tells us much about the man, but perhaps it also tells us something about Ireland. It was also remarked upon by an acclaimed novelist, who had grown up there, left and returned.

Dublin has picked the simplest rule – and made it absolute. You can be anything you like within her Four Hundred – but you must be a successful person. That is all. Successful in the plainest and commonest sense – that you make, and spend, a very great deal of hard cash in pursuit of whatever you do, and that your name is very often in the papers. That is the simple regulation which keeps the ruling class down to a very manageable, neat proportion in Dublin; it might also seem to threaten that class with monotony, but in practice this is not so – since where every kind of creature is eligible, from duke to jockey, variety and comedy are non-stop, and easily observed from the side-lines in any decently expensive public place.

This seems a recognizable portrait of the world Haughey made. In fact it is a reflection from Kate O'Brien's book *My Ireland*,[47] published in 1962, the same year as the future taoiseach's reflections upon money and respect. It brings home the point, perhaps, that what we see in contemporary Ireland has its roots further back in Irish history than we may think. But the extraordinary period that began in the late 1960s, and that witnessed unprecedented developments in culture, economics, demography and religion as well as in politics, was also indelibly marked by the interaction between those old party animosities (Carleton again) and the advent of a new kind of politics. There has been a price paid, in terms of disillusionment as well as in losses to the taxpayer. But equally significant may be the fact that those years of enrichment, GUBU and all the rest saw a progressive distancing by the Irish political establishment from the issue of irredentist nationalism north of the border, which had played such a part in the first act of Haughey's drama. In the North, the party fight would reach, by the end of the century, a stand-off between the extremes – while the funerals came, for the moment, to a halt. How this happened is the subject of the next chapter.

4

'Big, Mad Children':
The South and the North

I

Another funeral. At the obsequies for Charles James Haughey on 16 June 2006, his brother the Revd Eoghan Haughey declared that 'the problem of the North' was close to the late ex-taoiseach's heart and high on his political agenda, ever since he 'helped ignite the peace process quietly and patriotically'.[1] The minds of some mourners (including that of Gerry Adams, MP) must have gone back to that attempted ignition strategy of 1969 when Haughey, aided by another of his brothers and a ramshackle crew of fixers, appropriated £100,000 of government money destined to 'aid' the beleaguered Catholics of the North and diverted it to the venerable Republican tradition of purchasing arms in Germany for the wing of the IRA emerging as 'Provisional'. The subsequent Arms Trial featured in the last chapter.[2] Thirty-six years later, at the time of the disgraced politician's death, what seemed much clearer was how quickly he had distanced himself from the 'problem of the North'. This strategy had enabled him to return to the forefront of politics by 1979 – and, once in power, his Northern policies diverged more and more from traditional pieties. Haughey's own story reflected events and movements in the nation at large.

A dominant theme of Irish history in the last thirty years of the twentieth century has been the cementing of partitionism and the institutionalizing of twenty-six-county nationalism. Official acceptance of the border with Northern Ireland was forbidden by the 1937 constitution, so it could not be put in those terms; indeed, it often required an accompanying rhetoric claiming that the opposite tendency was in process. From 1970 Britain accepted that the Republic had a rightful role to play in the affairs of the North: privately acknowledged by London as early as 1971, publicly recognized in the Sunningdale communiqué of 1973, and set in stone by the Anglo-Irish Agreement of 1985, the Downing Street Declaration of 1993 and finally the Good Friday Agreement of 1998. But, while this was a diplomatic fact, political opinion and government practice in the Republic favoured a delicate but largely consistent strategy of detachment. What the South inherited, as the new century dawned, was a kind of watching brief on Northern affairs, with any notion of unification relegated to the realm of a very distant aspiration indeed.

This was far from the official rhetoric prevalent when the period opened, but matters were very different then. The North was heading into the maelstrom, while the Republic was just beginning to modernize its attitudes towards history and morality as well as liberal economics. The very period that would see the transforming outcomes of these processes would also see the north-east of the island convulsed by paramilitary violence and sectarian murder sprees, leading to 3,000 deaths. It would also see the destruction of the twentieth-century version of 'Protestant Ascendancy', to be succeeded by a series of failed devolutionary initiatives. By the first years of the twenty-first century the reborn IRA was receding again, as it had done in the late 1920s, to become a ghost at the feast. What had not emerged was anything like a reunited Ireland. Nor is it easy to argue that Northern Ireland had become a more harmonious place. Half a century before, the brilliant Kilkenny essayist Hubert Butler (who described himself as a Protestant Republican) had forecast that, with the mollifying of extreme attitudes on both sides, the border might 'become meaningless and drop off painlessly like a strip of plaster from a wound that had healed, or else survive in some modified form as a definition which distinguishes but does not divide'.[3] But the opposite had happened. What had peeled away were Articles 2 and 3 of de Valera's constitution, laying claim to the six north-eastern counties as part of his platonic Republic. And when they were voted away by a 96 per cent plebiscitary majority in 1998, and formally dropped by the government at the end of 1999, they left hardly a mark behind them.

One question that suggests itself is: what, if any, is the connection between the economic and social transformation of the South, and the parade of horrors in the North? And what bearing does this have upon the growth of partitionism in the Republic? Another more subtle development requires attention: the connection between Southern partitionism, Northern political events and the development of fashionable neo-nationalism in some sections of Irish opinion during the 1990s.

This requires a return to the mid 1960s, before the Northern balloon went up. The year 1965 saw another kind of craft launched: Seán Lemass's attempt to normalize relations with Northern Ireland by meeting its premier, Terence O'Neill, to discuss (at very most) some forms of cross-border cooperation on bread-and-butter issues. The significance of their agenda in 1965 was inflated by objections such as those raised by Ian Paisley, widely perceived in the South as a hilarious survival from another age. In fact, he turned out to presage the Northern future. What would prove out of step was O'Neill's clipped, pragmatic, patrician tone, which owed far more to the style of metropolitan Conservative Party cabals than to the sclerotic huddles of Ulster village politics. While he sometimes betrayed the automatic prejudices of his class and his caste, his nods towards an Orange constituency were undertaken as a necessary but distasteful insurance policy. Lemass's gritty realism, on the other hand, was in tune with the current mood of the South. The old 1916 revolutionary had arrived at a position where he was ostentatiously impatient with the knee-jerk shibboleths of his party regarding not only partition but economic self-sufficiency, frugal book-balancing and the sacred First National Language. Modernizer was apparently calling to modernizer across the petrified forest of cross-border politics.

To younger and more radical souls, the pace of this process and the limitations of their self-imposed agenda seemed pathetically inadequate; forty bloodstained years on, it all looks rather different, as some of the now middle-aged Young Turks have ruefully admitted.[4] And though it now seems as if Lemass's enterprise succeeded while O'Neill's foundered, the potency of Irish politics old-style was demonstrated the very next year. During the half-century commemorations of the 1916 Rising, the construction of an impressively coherent and democratic twenty-six-county state was celebrated with parades, addresses and intensive use of the new national television network. No one spoilt the party by pointing out that the 1916 Rising had effectively made partition inevitable (and that it was copper-fastened by the Treaty of 1921). Instead President de Valera, in his speech at the General Post Office on Easter Monday, declared that the divided island remained the great unfinished business of the state and called for the restitution of the province of the great Gaelic clans (as he conceived it). This comprehensively retreated from his statement of forty-five years earlier, when he had sensibly remarked that forcing Ulster into an Irish republic was unviable, and counties should be allowed an opt-out clause. But the rhetoric had calcified.[5] The triumphalism of 1966 helped mask the halting steps towards realism taken a year before.

That year also saw some other ominous signs – notable among them the Malvern Arms murder of the young Catholic barman Peter Ward, later claimed by Provisional IRA leader Seán Mac Stíofáin as the start of the Troubles. The riots following nationalist attempts to display the tricolour in 1964 have been instanced by other commentators as evidence of subterranean lava flows just awaiting an eruption.[6] But it is equally justifiable to look at the range of potential initiatives available in the mid 1960s that apparently indicated a more optimistic and productive shift of tectonic plates. There was a new-look Labour administration in power in London, with a premier who presented himself as the apostle of reassuring modernization, and who apparently believed that tackling minority grievances in Northern Ireland was part of his party's brief.[7] Harold Wilson also liked to stress the large number of Irish voters in his Huyton constituency, much as his successor James Callaghan enjoyed holidaying in West Cork and telling the Irish ambassador Donal O'Sullivan over off-the-record lunches that his heart was with Irish unity. But, like British politicians before and after them, the new Labour leaders found themselves pitchforked into a situation that required both a historical briefing impossible to acquire overnight and a sense of on-the-ground realpolitik not vouchsafed to visitors. And it was on their watch that the British media first called attention to Protestant ascendancy, political stagnation and discriminatory practices in Northern Ireland – with a pioneering series by Cal McCrystal in the *Sunday Times* on 'John Bull's Political Slum'.[8]

Discrimination in housing allocation may not have prevailed all over the province, but its episodically glaring inequalities could be highlighted easily enough; as could the gerrymandered electoral boundaries and inequitable voting procedures that produced baroquely unrepresentative local government bodies. If radical investigative journalists in London began the process of denunciation, politicians in Dublin were ready to join in – though it might be thought piquant that the most ostentatious condemnations came from a Fianna Fáil party trying to entrench itself in permanent power by doing away with proportional representation in the Republic. But this fitted with the comfortable doublethink that prevailed wherever the North was concerned – a sort of partition of the mind.

Official rhetoric might call for restitution of the sundered fourth province, but anti-partitionism was muted. From 1956 to 1960 there had been no visits from Department of Foreign Affairs personnel to Northern Ireland.[9] Within that department, which housed an impatient intellectual elite honed by Gonzaga, Clongowes and the Literary and Historical Debating Society at UCD, a feeling had grown that the Northern nationalist minority should adopt a more realistic and participatory approach to the statelet in which they lived. There was little comprehension in Iveagh House when Kevin Agnew, one of the more myopic 'leaders' of the Northern nationalist community, declared at a convention to choose an abstentionist candidate for Stormont that he would prefer to see local children naked and starving under the tricolour than prosperous under the Union Jack.[10] From the northern side of the border, in the mental world of Kevin Agnew, things looked different. The South was viewed with an odd compound of resentment, yearning and a sense of abandonment. But this co-existed with a more critical feeling that the Republic was in some ways archaic, backward and uncomfortable, if also diverting to visit and good for drinking. It was not only Unionists who saw it as Mexico to Northern Ireland's USA. This was a form of condescension that would not survive the 1990s, but it was very evident thirty years before. Archaism also persisted in the attitude of the British governing classes, but their nostalgic possessiveness about Northern Ireland as a surviving corner of the empire where matters were conducted old-style, and there was still honey for tea, was evolving fast. (Margaret

Thatcher, tutored by the eccentric reactionary Enoch Powell, would try briefly to rediscover this line in the 1980s, but she retreated fast in the face of the province's unbridled enthusiasm for handouts of public money. 'You mean, like Scotland?' 'Yes, Prime Minister.'[11]) By the mid sixties, as the poet John Montague has put it, old moulds were being broken all round.

II

Into this world came Seán Lemass, unmuzzled after a long and confining apprenticeship. He listened to advisers like the Northern-born T. K. Whitaker, the most brilliant and influential civil servant of his generation (and a friend of James Malley, Terence O'Neill's private secretary). Lemass also respected the opinions of Donal Barrington, a long-time advocate of recognizing Northern realities (though a defender of Articles 2 and 3). In 1963 Lemass had impatiently told his colleagues that Northern Ireland was an actual entity, existing 'with the support of the majority, artificial though that area is'.[12] In this he was echoing the opinion of intelligent diplomats like Con Cremin, who had suggested the previous year that it was time to start dealing with Northern Ireland as it was, instead of being frightened of accusations that this implied a recognition of partition.[13] 'We are today more prepared than we were, perhaps, some years ago to accept Partition for as long as it will last, as a necessary evil, and to try to improve relations between the two parts of the country on that basis.' Dublin had noted answering signs of realism among the nationalist community in the North; Eddie McAteer even declared in 1964 that the Nationalist Party was 'now anxious to step into the twentieth century', which, if still remarkably cautious, was welcome.[14] Purist abstentionism towards Stormont was no longer the full extent of strategy. Thoughtful young Catholic activists like the Derry teacher John Hume and the Queen's University history student Austin Currie were framing agendas that stressed change within the system rather than reunification, though these priorities would shift with the bewildering polarizations of future years, especially for Hume.[15] When Lemass strode into Stormont in his gangster-like wide-stripe suit and trench coat he struck the young civil servant Ken Bloomfield as a fascinating exotic, carrying the whiff of the Republic's cordite-scented past.[16] But at this remove we can discern in 1965 the promise of one of those alternative futures that hover seductively at so many junctures in Ireland's history.

The stir of events in the mid sixties was further agitated by the Northern Irish Labour Party and the Irish Congress of Trades Unions, which publicized the discriminatory practices of Unionist rule to the new Labour government. This development was precipitated by small liberal and radical organizations pushing for change in Northern Ireland since the early sixties; all these trends coalesced in the Northern Ireland Civil Rights Association, founded in February 1967. But their several agendas stipulated a 'UK rights' programme, not a charter for reunification. The language of the student radicals who were beginning to emerge at Queen's in the same years looked to more exotic inspirations (Fidel Castro, Daniel Cohn-Bendit, the SDS in America). If they now seem like the rolling pebbles that inevitably start an avalanche, the mountain did not move because oppression had become unbearable. Unrest was the result of a slightly liberalized regime, and the working-through of the 1944 Education Act. The de Tocqueville thesis of revolution happening at the point of improvement, rather than of immiseration, is distinctly applicable to Northern Ireland in the 1960s.

The avalanche came none the less. The major contribution of the student radicals, via their heady if incoherent People's Democracy organization, was that quintessential act of 1960s agitprop street theatre: the march. Their chosen exemplars may have been the SDS, but in Ireland far older traditions were invoked – of territory invaded and privileges asserted or threatened. The marches in Derry (October 1968) and from Belfast (January 1969) used the international language of civil rights, but already the campaign begun by Austin Currie's occupation of unfairly assigned housing at Caledon had raised the threat of Catholic activists arrayed against the power of the Protestant state – and seen it reproduced on the television screens of the Western world. Police connivance in attacks on marchers at Burntollet was equally widely broadcast. With these events, O'Neill's cautious initiatives in franchise reform and housing allocation came under unbearable strain, and his electoral position was irretrievably weakened after the elections of February 1969. Meanwhile Wilson's government havered as pusillanimously as Asquith's had in 1912–14. The ensuing spiral of violence and atavism on both sides has been rehearsed many times. Less often considered is its effect on the politics of 'the South'.

Here too the ritual dance of the established political parties was disrupted by new elements taking unprecedented steps. In the Republic, as in Northern Ireland, the 1960s zeitgeist was affected by imbibing avant-garde ideas aired by student radicals, who had often acquired them on the mandatory summer-job circuit of the USA. Some of these influences mutated through the Republican Clubs of Trinity and the National University of Ireland, which attempted yet again the fusion of socialism and nationalism floated unsuccessfully in the 1930s. The utopianism of the 1960s fused with historical time-travelling fantasies. The briefly radicalized Irish Labour Party, which suddenly acquired a smattering of left-wing university dons like David Thornley and Conor Cruise O'Brien, discussed whether Ireland could become a European Cuba. Cathal Goulding, the socialist chief of staff of the IRA in the Republic, was not a student, but he was similarly affected by the intoxication of the times, declaring that a radicalized Protestant working class in the North would be the Trojan Horse whereby the 1919 Dáil's democratic programme might be revived.[17] This suggested another replay of a different historical fantasy: the delusion of Patrick Pearse in 1912, when he welcomed the sight of 'arms in the hands of Irishmen' as an inevitable step towards independence, even though those arms were in the hands of the Ulster Volunteer Force.

Most of these hopes would prove as ill founded as Pearse's. But for the moment, to be youngish and left-wing, while a revolution apparently broke out north of the border, was very heaven. The euphoria passed with unnerving speed. The battle of Burntollet Bridge on 4 January 1969, between police and Orangemen on one side, and Civil Rights marchers on the other, inaugurated the end of the left–internationalist 'civil rights' phase of the Troubles, and the shift to ancient antagonism over national and religious identities.[18] From that point can be dated other reassessments – most famously that of Conor Cruise O'Brien, who was impelled to begin a ruthless interrogation of

Irish nationalism as understood by his own generation, particularly in relation to the North. He was often accused of being too clever for his own good: he was certainly too clever for the good of his less brilliant and more acquiescent political colleagues.

Other left-wing intellectuals in the South continued on a different tack, notably David Thornley. His destination would eventually be on platforms alongside the Provisional IRA, whose formal existence began in December 1969, nearly a year after Burntollet. The far left, who had helped begin much of the reassessment, wandered through the political wilderness in various directions. For a brief moment Marxism seemed as if it might let Republican intellectuals off the sterile hook of irredentism regarding the North. The British and Irish Communist Organization first evolved a 'Two Nations' theory, based on uneven economic developments in the North and South, which set it firmly against the atavistic nationalism preached by the Provos – though one or two of its most eccentric spirits would later stagger back to it with all the zeal of the returned prodigal. A more or less day-to-day account of the disorientation of the left-wing Republican Clubs has been published by the Marxist republican Roy Johnston, influential progenitor of the Wolfe Tone Society and much of the leftist rethink of Republicanism in the South during that fleeting moment. It makes for intermittently hilarious but essentially gloomy reading, recording the mounting incomprehension of the idealistic labour-history guru Desmond Greaves and his acoloytes, as they shuttle from Belfast to Dublin in 1969–71: anticipating the impending 'crisis of capital', opposing entry to the EEC and preaching a campaign against ground rents and fishing rights in order to unite the working classes of both religions against 'the real enemy' – landlordism.[19] Meanwhile the Catholic and Protestant working classes of the North unco-operatively remained as clear as ever where *their* real enemy lay. However, Johnston made a pilgrimage to Belfast as late as the 12th of July 1969 and reassuringly found 'no sense of impending pogrom' among Belfast loyalists. 'I enquired about the personalities depicted on the [Orange Order's] banners, and no-one knew who they were. I enquired "Why Finaghy", hoping to get some sense of history, but was told "Because the Orange Order owns the field." I got talking with some who had walked, and they enthused about having gone to Dublin for the Horse Show, and met with Brendan Behan.'[20] A month later the ghettoes exploded into violence with the 'Battle of the Bogside' in Derry and the invasion of Catholic areas in Belfast by B-Specials.

Johnston, Goulding and their comrades showed more prescience in their suspicion of the growing influence within the IRA of the militarist Seán Mac Stíofáin, English by origin, who, behind such smoke-screens as an insistence on conducting all discussions in Irish, was 'actively building the Northern Command structure outside of the political process'.[21] This meant killing people rather than raising their consciousness. Johnston also noted the ominously atavistic elements in Donegal controlled by the political machine of the local Dáil deputy Neil Blaney, and the determination of Blaney's Fianna Fáil colleague Charles James Haughey to support the nationalist minority in the North with arms. Blaney had taken it upon himself to declare in a speech at Letterkenny that forcible intervention from the South was 'not ruled out'. An *Evening Standard* journalist visiting Dublin that autumn of 1969 was disconcerted to find the 'most rational and least bloodthirsty' Irishman he met to be the Marxist Johnston, whereas 'a charming member of the Irish Cabinet remarked over coffee in a luxurious restaurant that he had been in favour of ordering the Army to march into Ulster'.[22]

III

This charmer was inevitably Charles Haughey. Though he had grown up in the North Dublin suburb of Donnycarney, and 'luxurious restaurants' were now his natural habitat, his roots were in Swatragh, County Derry. While the family had supported the Treaty, Haughey's youthful views were generally supposed to be Republican – in the sense that the green wing of Fianna Fáil understood the term, accommodating a comfortable sense of doublethink. Certainly by 1970 he was describing himself to British journalists as 'a Northern fenian'.[23] Despite marrying Lemass's daughter, he showed little of his father-in-law's impatience with venerable but unrealistic nationalist national blueprints. The inheritor of this approach was Lemass's successor Jack Lynch, and this may be one reason why the outgoing taoiseach shed few tears when his son-in-law did not inherit the purple. In the Republic's general election of June 1969, the North hardly figured. But from August of that year there was nothing else to think about, as violence exploded in the Northern cities and the South's traditional rhetoric was put to the test. Pressed by Blaney and Kevin Boland to send troops north, Lynch could rely on a horrified negative from the army command and from most of his cabinet colleagues. He also benefited from a well-established tradition of argument and advice from senior civil servants and diplomats, especially Eamonn Gallagher, who presented a realistic assessment of what an attempt at enforced reunification would bring. In early 1970 the army chief of staff discussed with ministers the contingency of sending troops over the border in the event of 'a complete breakdown of law in Northern Ireland'. It was clear to most politicians that even in such a case, the resources of the Irish Army were manifestly inadequate to cope with what they would find there, and that the consequences of any incursion on the basis of their current strength would be 'disastrous'.[24] Lynch's celebrated address on Irish television, following the threat of Armageddon in Derry, was drafted in this sense, and much influenced by Gallagher and Whitaker. Haughey, Blaney and Boland objected to its restrained tone, and as delivered the speech declared that the Irish government 'can no longer stand by'. What he offered by way of intervention was medical depots set up on the border, a request for a UN peacekeeping force (clearly a paper tiger) and negotiations on the constitutional position, pending an 'eventual' restoration of unity.

Behind the scenes, the Committee for the Relief of Distress in Northern Ireland was set up, funded by £100,000. As minister for finance, Haughey was its most prominent member. He rapidly commandeered it, sharing control with Neil Blaney. Not for the last time, his manipulation of public funds would lead to disaster. Money was passed through the Red Cross into Blaney's control and used to set up a vituperatively anti-partitionist newspaper, *The Voice of the North*. This was the mouthpiece not only of the Blaney wing within Fianna Fáil but of those IRA elements preparing a wholesale shift towards the 'armed struggle' and away from the socialist alternative offered by Cathal Goulding. The reports of the gung-ho liaison officer from the Irish Army, Captain James Kelly, have been much quoted. 'It would seem to be now necessary to harness all opinion in the state in a concerted drive towards achieving reunification. Unfortunately, this would mean accepting the possibility of armed action of some sort as the ultimate solution.' Kelly was 'so forthcoming in advocating the use of arms that doubts were entertained by his listeners [in the IRA] that he was, in fact, an intelligence officer'.[25] The literal-minded captain and Charles Haughey's IRA-supporting brother 'Jock', aided by Albert Luykx, a shadowy Belgian resident in Ireland, set to buying arms on the Continent, destined for the North.[26] By then their activities were being monitored by the increasingly uneasy security forces of the Republic. The result, as has been seen, would eventually be the firing from Lynch's cabinet of Haughey, Blaney and their catspaw the alcoholic minister for justice Micheál Ó Moráin, followed by the scandalous Arms Trial of 1970. Haughey and Blaney had lied to Lynch about their involvement from the start, and Haughey would lie his way through the legal proceedings as well. (He had already privately asked if the civil servant Peter Berry could be 'induced . . . directed . . . or intimidated' into not giving evidence.[27]) It was part of a successful strategy to remain in politics whatever the cost.

The Arms Trial and the political emotions that it focused have been the subject of penetrating exegesis by Justin O'Brien, Stephen Collins, Bruce Arnold and Vincent Browne. The episode takes its place in a sequence of events by which traditional Southern views about 'the North' were tested and found wanting. Initially, the government's automatic reaction to the Northern crisis had been to flood Irish embassies abroad with twenty-year-old anti-partitionist literature, duly distributed to 'the waste-paper baskets of the world's press and foreign ministries'; there was also a contingency plan to send in forces to protect the Northern minority if law and order broke down completely (the 'Doomsday' scenario), but this remained sketchy.[28]

In any case a more realistic reaction soon asserted itself. Many in government circles found Captain Kelly's posturing culpably naive, Blaney's gangsterism repellent and Haughey's opportunism contemptible. A national poll found that 82 per cent of the Irish public supported Lynch's moves against the Haughey–Blaney–Boland cabal in 1970.[29] The taoiseach's caution was not always to his advantage, and he could have moved earlier against his colleagues; he was probably inhibited by his position within Fianna Fáil, which was that of the compromise candidate who had succeeded the charismatic Lemass. But his sane and careful response to the Northern crisis has been spectacularly vindicated with time, and takes its place in a tradition begun by Lemass and continued by Garret FitzGerald – whom Lynch had anticipated in 1970 by declaring a wish to make the Republic 'a more plural society' as a step to reassuring Northern Unionists. Lynch's actions at that time were also warmly supported from across the floor by independent spirits like Noel Browne and Owen Sheehy-Skeffington.[30] Moreover, the report of the Cameron Commission in 1969 set out markers for internal reform in Northern Ireland, strengthened by the Hunt Report on policing, which led to the abolition of the B-Specials. The fact that official opinion in British government circles was relaxing about the North in 1970 may seem in line with the historical myopia and political wishful thinking reliably displayed by Downing Street and Whitehall since the crisis began. Had it been generally known that in February 1969 a British cabinet report outlining various possibilities had stated unequivocally 'in the longer term the most desirable solution from the British point of view might be a union of Northern and Southern Ireland', the reaction in the North may be imagined.[31] More surprising still is the optimism evinced in official reports from Dublin about increasing stability in the North following internal reforms from 1970.

But from this very point the Provisional IRA was growing, fuelled not only by the right-wing IRA fundamentalism represented by the born-again Englishman Seán Mac Stíofáin, in his Aran sweater and quiff, but by the ethnic antagonisms of the North's divided society. A new generation of activists would fuse the two, and for top-dressing steal some of the international–socialist posture of the increasingly marginalized Official IRA. This was not a comfortable combination for most people in 'the South'. In early 1970 Lynch had told a deputation of aggrieved Northern nationalists, 'If we were given a gift of Northern Ireland tomorrow we could not accept it'; they left convinced of his determination to keep the Republic uninvolved (at least in the traditional sense that they understood 'involvement').[32] When the Arms Trial finally came to court in late 1970, the revelations sounded a knell for comfortable Republican fellow travelling in Southern politics. While much of the material offered in the courts was contradictory – so much so that the verdicts had to acquit the defendants because of insufficient evidence – the implications were clear, underlined by further suggestions of lies and peculation during sessions of the Public Accounts Committee. As Conor Cruise O'Brien pointed out, Northern nationalists found it all embarrassing (the arms that did get through had been stored *in a monastery*, for one thing).[33] For their part, Northern Unionists had several prejudices about the South confirmed; the Republic now looked not so much like Mexico as Colombia.

The embarrassment in the South was of a different order. Some of the revelations were funny but savagely so; and the questions left open were awkward as well as confusing. Captain James Kelly was evidently telling the truth, if only because he was too simple-minded (or 'emotional', in the words of his superiors) to see how problematic it was. He seemed dumbfounded when James Gibbons, minister for defence, appeared incapable of remembering whether he knew anything about the arrangements regarding arms supplies, or whether he had informed the taoiseach. Gibbons's confusion was counterpointed by Haughey's crisp denials, and the contradictions between their evidence did not stop there. Yet both men voted confidence in Lynch's leadership shortly afterwards, one presumably from loyalty, the other certainly for survival. The doubletalk of Fianna Fáil politicians was revealed. Equally exposed was the self-proclaimed integrity of the real Soldiers of Destiny, Captain Kelly from the South and the Provisional IRA link-man John Kelly from the North, who did his best to bring the house down in a fully fledged speech from the dock, invoking 'the graves of dead generations'. 'We asked for guns and no-one from Taoiseach Lynch down refused that request or told us this was contrary to Government policy.'

It was now clear that 'government policy' under Lynch was taking a very contrary direction indeed. After the crisis of 1969–70 he regained control of the party, and the direction towards realism indicated by Whitaker and others was resumed. In his speech at the Ard-Fheis on 17 February 1970 Lynch had asked those advocating speedy reunification what they would do with a million Unionists: 'would we compel them to flee the country altogether, or else to live under our own domination in constant opposition?'[34] (The *Irish Press* a few months later actually did float the idea of 'repatriating' Northern Unionists, hopefully instancing Algeria, but few others went the distance of this kind of Republican logic.[35]) Pressing home the point, Lynch's speech on RTÉ on 11 July 1970, the eve of annual Orange parades in the North, is a landmark document of Irish history. Beginning with the poet John Montague's line that 'Old moulds are broken in the North', he stressed that the problems of that province could be solved only by the two communities abjuring violence and understanding each other.

There is no real invader here. We are all Irish in our different kinds of ways. We must not now or ever in the future show anything to each other except tolerance, forbearance – and neighbourly love.

I speak now to the Irish people, north and south, Protestant, Presbyterian, Catholic – and simply Irish. The whole unhappy situation is an Irish quarrel. I admit that others come into it, either because they misunderstand it or because they misuse it – but they are not an essential part of it. We must settle this quarrel among us.

While this was an unequivocal message both to time-warped Irish-Americans and to those who believed that British occupation was the full extent of the problem, Lynch had a particular message for 'Irish people of the majority tradition': 'Let us not appeal to past gods as if past generations had said the last word about Ireland. We have our opportunity to say for our generation what is in our hearts and minds.' This provocatively used some of Patrick Pearse's rhetoric in the Proclamation of the Republic, and turned it on its head. His appeal to Northern Unionists was also carefully crafted. They were, historically, one of many migrations into Ireland who had become 'part of our soil'; they should realize this, and note that political leaders in the South had been saying for fifty years that they 'had no wish to confront you or destroy you'. 'Do not be persuaded to sully your own great tradition. All Irish traditions are intertwined; let us cherish them all.' The appeal directed at Britain equally stressed that there was nothing to fight about, and no victories to be claimed, but a problem to be settled by peaceful means between civilized peoples. While reaffirming his own wish for ultimate unity, he balanced this with his commitment to Anglo-Irish friendship. Our two governments have surmounted many difficulties to establish a unique relationship. Our peoples know and like each other . . . This is not a job for soldiers. And let me say on this that I much regret the injuries suffered by British soldiers during the course of the duties imposed on them in the North of Ireland; these young British boys find themselves in a position which must to them seem inexplicable.

Both governments, he added, would guarantee rights and justice for the Northern minority; therefore it was not in their interests to interfere with the Orange parades. T. K. Whitaker, who had drafted an important speech of Lynch's emphasizing the consent principle the previous September, was probably closely involved. An early draft ended even more emphatically: 'Let the Orangemen parade if they must. Do not interfere with them. Old moulds are broken. The future is for all of us.'[36]

As it stood, it was a remarkable intervention, widely recognized as a call for dialogue within the North rather than as the imposition of easy 'solutions' from outside. There was an uncharacteristically warm private letter of support from the Conservative prime minister Edward Heath, which the Department of Foreign Affairs rapidly decided to use as an opening for talks with London.[37] By September 1970 Lynch had privately become convinced that for an approach to the Northern problem to succeed, it must involve internal reform and a reconciliation of the two traditions. 'He also', as an internal memo put it, 'believed that Britain no longer has an interest in maintaining the division of Ireland.'[38]

By the end of 1970 Dublin officials held out hopes that Chichester-Clark's Stormont government might inaugurate a reforming era. Reports from Eamonn Gallagher to the taoiseach's office were cautiously hopeful: 'it is now accepted openly by the British that Dublin have a legitimate interest in the situation in the North and specifically in the progress of the movement for reform in the North'.[39] But, as the Provisional campaign gained in power, violence and ruthlessness, and the loyalist response fractured into killer gangs, these beliefs held little purchase. Nor was this the only advice being directed at Downing Street, especially from the army. The disastrous policy of swooping into Catholic areas and summarily arresting and interning supposedly 'known Republicans' on the basis of out-of-date or hearsay evidence, ineptly embraced during August 1971, delivered a recruitment boost that the Provisionals could only have dreamt of. Time and again, Republican activists reflecting later on the feelings that mobilized them in the early 1970s mention 'anger . . . real rage' at the invasion of their homes.[40] And the First Paratroop Regiment compounded this by their massacre of fourteen demonstrating civilians in Derry during a march on 30 January 1972. An angry Dublin crowd, choreographed by local Republicans, attacked the British Embassy in Merrion Square and burnt it out. Within a month the Official IRA had detonated a bomb at Aldershot Barracks in England, killing six cleaning staff and a Catholic chaplain. The poet Brian Lynch, a journalist on the rabidly nationalistic *Irish Press* edited by Tim Pat Coogan, would later remember his colleagues' reaction with a shudder:

> The newsroom rang with howls of joy.
> They'd murdered us. We'd murdered them.
> And I joined in, a roaring boy
> Who cheered the butchers' requiem.[41]

Internment and Bloody Sunday did for the IRA and Sinn Féin what the post-1916 executions and conscription had done for their ancestors. At last – in the view of the 1960s radicals, still on the scene though now wearing shorter hair and IRA arm bands – the North had come South, and the moment of crisis had arrived.

IV

Of course, it had not. The year 1972 began with Bloody Sunday and the burning of the embassy, followed by Aldershot and more mayhem, but it was also at this time that Heath prorogued Stormont. Three years too late it may have been (though opinion in the Department of Foreign Affairs had been rather chary of the idea, perhaps because the Provisionals proclaimed it as a victory, clarifying Britain's 'alien claim to Ireland'[42]); but it helped to set in motion the discussions on a new political framework involving the Republic, which would climax with the Sunningdale conference of 1973. History also shifted a gear in the South during 1972–3, with the removal of the special constitutional position accorded to the Catholic Church, and the vote to enter the EEC. Behind the scenes another change of considerable symbolic importance was being canvassed: the Irish government was advised to abandon the aggressively irredentist designation 'the Six Counties' and consistently use the term 'Northern Ireland'.[43] From May 1970 there was also a newly created Interdepartmental Unit on the North, which represented the departments of the taoiseach, external affairs and finance; the last component could be guaranteed to highlight the unacceptable costs of reunification, and duly did. In the wider world, a series of articles in the *Irish Times* in the summer of 1970, opposing unification from a Southern viewpoint and calling Articles 2 and 3 'a national menace', roused strangely few objections (though this may simply reflect the kind of people who read the *Irish Times* in those days).[44]

The year 1972 also saw Conor Cruise O'Brien publish his classic examination of contemporary Irish nationalism, *States of Ireland*. O'Brien in his youth served as an Irish diplomat sent to preach anti-partitionism to the infidel, and in his middle age emerged as one of the few Irish intellectuals to embrace Labour politics and an international viewpoint. The coruscating testament that he now produced was part autobiography, part political analysis, part prophecy. Written in his uniquely mordant and mocking style, it became a national bestseller. This by no means indicated that what he had to say was universally welcome. But his icy dissection of sloppy thinking and hypocrisy, his demonstration of official insincerity towards Northern Ireland, his first-hand knowledge of Northern politics (like Garret FitzGerald, he had Protestant relatives in the North), his determination to present the view of Northern Unionists, and his delineation of 'malign' and 'benign' scenarios for the future, said much of the previously unsayable. Finally, he concluded, 'I believe that at this moment none of the main sections of the population of Ireland actually wants unity.'[45]

O'Brien finished writing in June. A month later William Whitelaw, the heavyweight secretary of state for Northern Ireland, secretly summoned several leading Provisional IRA members to London for private talks. They included Seán Mac Stíofáin and the youthful

Gerry Adams, then an inmate of Long Kesh prison camp but already a key figure in the Ballymurphy Brigade of the Provisional IRA.[46] Whitelaw's initiative had predictably little effect on IRA policy, except to confirm its belief in its own natural leadership of platonically pure Irish nationalism. Some of the issues raised at the meeting (political status for prisoners, release of detainees) would have a long and troublesome future. But the IRA's annoyance at Whitelaw's rejection of their portentous demands for British withdrawal was vented on the people of Belfast when the city centre was ravaged by twenty-six bombs on 21 July. Whitelaw's naive intervention infuriated the Irish government, just as Harold Wilson's secret meetings with IRA leaders in Dublin had done only a year before, but the bloody aftermath pressed the need for another kind of intervention. Relations between the governments were not derailed, and the process initiated by Lynch's speeches of 1970 continued. The taoiseach had reiterated these public statements throughout 1971, and, at a series of meetings with Heath and the Northern premier Brian Faulkner in September 1971, Ken Bloomfield had noted the lack of grandstanding from the South, and the tacit recognition by the British of an Irish dimension. These developments outlasted the frenzy of Bloody Sunday and its aftermath. By 1973 Heath's own views had moved very close to Lynch's, to judge by his meeting with the Foreign Relations Committee in Washington, DC, where he emphasized Britain's close and warm relations with the Republic and remarked that they must

decide in Northern Ireland whether unification should be sought by creating tension as the IRA and others believed, or (as the British government believed) by relieving it. The way forward should be by lessening the importance of the border. It should thereafter be possible to get on with the necessary arrangements such as raising the standard of living in the South through the Republic's membership of the European Community.

He had in fact offered Lynch joint enterprises in cross-border issues such as energy and transport.[47] The assumptions behind this speech are striking; fortunately for him, Ulster Unionists apparently did not hear about it.

By then plans were well afloat for a new Northern assembly and government, based upon power-sharing between Faulkner's Unionists and the three-year-old SDLP, dominated by John Hume, Gerry Fitt and Paddy Devlin. The last two represented varieties of Labour politics, though Devlin had a Republican activist past; Hume's credo was social-democratic Europeanism with a distinctly Catholic–nationalist tinge. In the heady days of August 1969 Fitt and Devlin had appealed for arms to defend the Catholic communities of Northern Ireland; three years of Provisional IRA tactics had precipitated them firmly in the opposite direction. Hume's trajectory towards the South was rather different. While his pronouncements of the mid 1960s indicated that his priorities were civil rights and a just society within the borders of Northern Ireland, the events of early 1972 had infused a greener tint. The widening popular base of the Provisionals also meant that the SDLP could ill afford to seem unsound on the national question. Hume's contacts with the Dublin government had been carefully nurtured, and he had briefed Eamonn Gallagher about plans for the formation of the SDLP from an early stage.[48] Thus an 'Irish Dimension' was heavily stressed in the constitutional blueprint that emerged in October 1972. The SDLP increasingly adverted to 'long-term reunification', sugared by the coating of imminent EEC membership of both countries. (This lay behind Heath's remarks in Washington a few months later.) By the time of the Northern Ireland elections of May and June 1973, the SDLP was a force to be reckoned with.

The replacement of Lynch's government by a Fine Gael–Labour coalition led by Liam Cosgrave and prominently featuring both Garret FitzGerald and Conor Cruise O'Brien made for a movement on Northern policy, though the outlines remained those suggested by mandarins from the Lynch regime. And ominously, while Dublin was alive to the dangers of pushing too hard on ultimate reunification, Hume was in favour of much more aggressive language. When the final meetings took place in December 1973, Whitelaw had been replaced by the pathetically ignorant Francis Pym, whom Sunningdale participants remember hanging around in corridors asking people what was going on. Hume carried much before him. It is now generally agreed that insistence upon a high-profile 'Council of Ireland' linking North and South was a bridge too far for the Northern majority and a decisive element in the sabotaging of the Sunningdale executive by industrial militancy in Northern Ireland during the summer of 1974. But a disastrously timed general election a month after the new power-sharing executive got under way had already demonstrated the over-whelming opposition of the Northern majority – and boosted the spectacular rise of Ian Paisley's Democratic Unionist Party.

What did all this mean for the South? The government of the Republic had accepted a Council of Ireland as their input; all things being equal it might seem an attractive halfway house to reunification, or at least an earnest of good intent. It certainly propelled them no further towards Belfast than most of them wanted to go. Garret FitzGerald has recorded the distinctly gingerly approach of Dublin diplomats towards the idea.[49] Seen as a whole, the Sunningdale Agreement could be presented by Republican irredentists as a sell-out – 'the greatest in our history', according to Neil Blaney.[50] Kevin Boland challenged the Irish government's recognition of Northern Ireland as unconstitutional, but the High Court ruled that this was merely 'a statement of policy' and had not changed the Republic's claim on the territory of the North as expressed in Articles 2 and 3 – another nail in Faulkner's coffin, and a mixed blessing for Cosgrave. In the oddly muted Dáil debates on the projected new arrangements Blaney continued to condemn the increasingly doomed Sunningdale settlement, while Fianna Fáil, as Clare O'Halloran has put it, tried 'to cobble together an anti-Sunningdale motion with a pro-Sunningdale amendment' to the 1949 Act declaring Ireland a republic.[51] Much of this was irrelevant posturing by now. But in terms of the South's apprehension of Northern realities, Articles 2 and 3 – and the use that Unionist intransigents made of them – were put into sharp perspective. And the whole episode led Conor Cruise O'Brien further and further away from the green side of the political spectrum. The celebrated but counter-productive broadcasting ban on Sinn Féin in 1975 was one result. Already, in November 1972, the entire RTÉ authority had been dismissed after broadcasting an interview with Mac Stíofáin, and much was made of the invasion of media rights. The years between the failure of the Sunningdale experiment in 1974 and the return of Jack Lynch to power in 1977 saw the North threaten life in the South in many ways: thirty-three citizens of the Republic were killed by UVF car bombs in Dublin and Monaghan on 17 May 1974, and IRA arms importations, kidnappings, bank robberies and assassinations cast an ominous shadow across normal life within the Republic. The climax was the murder of the new British ambassador, Christopher Ewart-Biggs, along with a member of his staff, by a bomb placed outside the gates of his official residence in County Dublin on 23 July 1976.

One of the less noticed achievements of the Provisionals was the expansion and change in function of the Irish Army. It doubled in size between 1969 and 1979, and shifted its emphasis to anti-subversive activity, learning from the publications of Brigadier Frank Kitson and assiduously attending counter-insurgency courses abroad. The kind of unreconstructed opinions so dramatically expressed by Captain James Kelly were also moderated among the rank and file.[52] Another unintended effect of the Provisionals' campaign was reflected in opinion polls, which showed partitionism gaining ground in the South in proportion as IRA violence increased.[53] With their ineffable solipsism, the Provisionals seemed incapable of realizing that their lethal tactics would not enhance the prospect of reunification to people south of the border. Jimmy Drumm's Bodenstown oration in 1977, cowritten by Gerry Adams and Danny Morrison, lamented the lack of

a positive tie-in with the mass of the Irish people who have little or no idea of the suffering in the North because of media censorship and the consolidation of conservatism throughout the country. We need to make a stand on economic issues and on the everyday struggles of people. The forging of the strong links between the republican movement and the workers of Ireland and radical trade unionism will create an irrepressible mass movement and will ensure mass support for the continuing armed struggle in the North.[54]

Delusional prophecy is par for the course at Tone's grave, and what the Provisional campaign had actually done for 'the everyday struggles of people' was increasingly clear to the South. But the underlying message was more significant: a realization that reunification was nowhere near, and that the war of national liberation had remained restricted to the North. One indication was Gerry Adams's fantastical presentation of the Dublin government as at once a 'Vichy-type' appendage of London and a collaborator 'offering Irish resources and Irish labour on a joint-partnership basis between Irish and American capital'.[55] By the late 1970s some of the rhetoric of the now defunct

Official IRA had been brazenly rediscovered by their supplanters, but it would prove no more sustaining for its new exponents. It would certainly not awaken sympathetic echoes among 'the masses' in the Republic. *Straight Left*, the autobiography of the future Labour Party leader Ruairi Quinn, describing his politicization as a young socialist architect in the late 1960s and early 1970s, betrays strikingly little interest in the North – so much so that he inadvertently gave his memoir exactly the same title chosen by the Northern Labour politician and SDLP founder Paddy Devlin a decade before.[56] As the British government tried to contain violence in Northern Ireland by a policy of 'Ulsterization', Provisional IRA rhetoric flailed around the indisputable but inadmissible fact of the Republic's indifference – an indifference firmly based on difference.

V

From the late 1970s too, official attitudes in the South began to look differently towards the North. It might be supposed that this was due to Lynch's successor as leader of Fianna Fáil in 1979. As we have seen, when the intended transference of power to George Colley was botched, Garret FitzGerald had raised the question of Haughey's 'flawed pedigree'. Fianna Fáil mountainy men affected to see this as arrant snobbery, but most people knew that FitzGerald meant the brazen performance in the Arms Trial, the sinister brother with IRA connections, the declared admiration for hardline Provos like John Kelly, the banknotes smuggled out in brown-paper parcels to buy guns on the Continent. Illegitimate parcels of banknotes would certainly feature during Haughey's ascendancy, tainting Fianna Fáil and acting as his nemesis in the end. In fact, by this stage of his career he was interested in money for its own sake, rather than for whom it could arm. But this was not yet apparent.

What seemed clear was that he wanted to steer Northern policy away from the line pioneered by his predecessor, who had accepted partition for the foreseeable future. The fact that FitzGerald had sustained close links to Lynch on Northern matters during the latter's last administration was further reason for Haughey to move ostentatiously in the opposite direction.[57] Much attention was paid to the new taoiseach's description of Northern Ireland as a 'failed political entity', to his unexpected 'special adviser' on the North, Martin Mansergh, and to his much touted meeting with Margaret Thatcher in December 1980, which produced another ringing but empty phrase about examining 'the totality of relationships within these islands'. The substance of all this seemed to vanish like fairy gold under the pressures of the next following year, as the floundering Provisionals were at last given the issue they needed to galvanize support in the Republic. This did not come from the recognition by 'the masses' that their everyday struggles could be ameliorated by socialism mediated through more Provo bombs. Rather, it came from an ancient mechanism of Irish nationalism: voluntary blood sacrifice.

The deaths on hunger strike of ten IRA prisoners in pursuit of 'political' status in the Maze prison during 1981, after a long and uniquely harrowing campaign, had a convulsive effect on political opinion in the Republic. It is widely described as a 'turning point' in attitudes towards the North. But the real turning point was in bringing electoral dividends to the Provisionals' politicial persona, Sinn Féin – to such an extent that the IRA leadership kept the strike going even when the strikers themselves had decided it had become counterproductive. The election of the dying hunger striker Bobby Sands to Westminster at the Fermanagh–South Tyrone by-election, after the SDLP failed to contest the seat, was, as a senior IRA man succinctly remarked, 'worth twenty bombs in England'.[58] In the Republic the phenomenon produced two Dáil seats for the Republicans in the 1981 election, and an outpouring of emotional rage at Thatcher's intransigence. However, just as with Bloody Sunday nine years before, the effect on general opinion in the South was cathartic but short-lived. The potent long-term effects were on the Republican movement in the North, where the possibilities and advantages of a political campaign in tandem with violence were suddenly and dramatically demonstrated. 'Many of the H-Block committees throughout the country became Sinn Féin *cumainn* overnight.'[59] In Danny Morrison's memorable phrase, the ballot paper in one hand and the Armalite in the other would signal a dual route to 'power in Ireland'. But as this policy was embraced, abstentionism was forgotten, and, as seats were contested by Sinn Féin for the Dáil and in local government, there was much less heard about Dublin as Vichy.

Further potential was promised by the way that 1981–2 saw power shifting between delicately poised coalitions in the Dáil. Haughey himself had taken a strident line on the North when he was in opposition, deriding 'wishy-washy talk of appeasing unionists and all that'; he had also taken a much friendlier line towards rabidly pro-IRA groups in America than had his Fine Gael rivals.[60] However, the insecurity of his position within his own party, the perilous state of the Irish economy and his own private agendas left little room for new thinking on the North. In any case, his interest in that volatile area of policy seemed curiously muted, considering his past. Between December 1982 and January 1987 the Fine Gael–Labour coalition under FitzGerald and Dick Spring possessed not only a secure majority but an extended opportunity to make a new approach. In some ways this might seem to veer away from the path laid down by Lynch in the 1970s; FitzGerald has been accused in some quarters of following the increasingly green line of John Hume, to the detriment of stability and realism in South–North relations.[61] This is to forget the immediate situation following the hunger strike, and the enhanced appeal of the Provisionals. It also does less than justice to FitzGerald's own approach to the Northern problem, less sulphurous than Haughey's but more analytical, more consistent and more progressive.

FitzGerald's confident upper-middle-class background represented not only the old Republican elite but also Ulster Protestant radicalism. Through his mother, Mabel, he had relatives entrenched in the comfortable Unionist bourgeoisie, and he was more familiar with Northern Ireland than most politicians in the Republic. An undeferential Catholic, he had in 1972 openly criticized priests 'who seemed ready to condone sectarian murder and denounce internment, but not the acts which provoke it'; as early as 1978 he had come out in favour of changing Articles 2 and 3.[62] He was also easily at home in government circles in London or Brussels, and found Haughey's visceral Anglophobia puzzling. FitzGerald, for instance, saw the potential of the British–Irish Association, a well-meaning voluntarist group promoting three-way dialogue between Britain, Northern Ireland and the Republic through annual off-the-record conferences on the post-war Königswinter model: Haughey believed, apparently sincerely, that they were a front for MI5.[63] Particularly in the late 1970s and early 1980s, these conferences enabled valuable contacts to be made and maintained between people who did not generally meet in public, though the process of bringing the two traditions together was not always easy. After one debate between suspicious DUP representatives and unbending Northern nationalists the current BIA chairman (a businessman with links in North and South) expostulated, 'It's like dealing with children. *Big, Mad Children*.' In this he probably reflected opinions that the mandarins in London and Dublin held in private, and that brought them closer together.

FitzGerald found Haughey's pronouncement that the North was 'a failed entity' both sterile and unrealistic. Fianna Fáil was strongly opposed to the attempt at 'rolling devolution' for the province drafted by James Prior as Conservative secretary of state for Northern Ireland in 1982, with advice from behind the scenes by the young Unionist legal academic David Trimble. This reflected a new degree of autonomy allowed to Northern Ireland ministers; Thatcher had kept a tight rein on Prior's predecessor Humphrey Atkins. However, she had been distinctly thrown off balance when the DUP burned her in effigy ('But they're *Unionists*!') and allowed Prior and the imaginative Lord Gowrie a freer hand. In Dublin, Fine Gael and Labour saw some potential in Prior's incremental approach to power-sharing in the North, devolving powers to an assembly in proportion as the principals managed to make it work. In fact, the chances of this halfway-house were wrecked by Hume's flinty opposition, and the pressure he brought to bear on Haughey's government before it fell.[64] (Hume's supposed power in Merrion Street was now an article of Unionist faith, contributing powerfully to his demonization.) The fact that rolling devolution was also abhorrent to integrationist Unionists and hardline Conservatives argues that there was something to be said for it. But, at the very least, the abortive initiative demonstrated the increasing convergence of thought between senior civil servants and politicians in London and Dublin. This was assiduously worked by FitzGerald, who, born to the political purple and moving easily between London and Dublin since childhood, found no difficulty in handling the English political *gratin*. His other tactic would be the cultivation of 'nationalism lite' through adopting the idea of a therapeutic talking shop in Dublin, the New Ireland Forum.

Before this, during his brief administration of 1981-2, FitzGerald departed spectacularly from accepted rhetoric when he announced in a radio interview that he fully understood Northern Unionists' reluctance for closer ties with a Republic whose tenor was implicitly sectarian, and declared the need for a 'crusade' to remove elements from Ireland's constitution that were by nature repugnant to Protestants. This broke a long-standing rule of political etiquette, up to this breached only by inveterate trouble-makers such as Sean O'Faolain, Hubert Butler, Owen Sheehy-Skeffington and Conor Cruise O'Brien. Most Protestants in the Republic preferred not to complain in public about the integration of Catholic social teaching into the laws of the land, protesting instead that they felt perfectly well treated in every other way. (Martin Mansergh, whose Protestant background was made much of by the Fianna Fáil public-relations machine, reproduced this line in a rather tightlipped response to FitzGerald's expansive declaration.) Moreover, even supposedly radical politicians like Seán MacBride displayed their patriotic credentials by cringing deference to bishops. This approach did not come easily to someone of FitzGerald's cosmopolitan, mildly bohemian background and intellectual Catholicism; he also knew exactly how priest-ridden traditional Irish politics appeared from a Northern perspective. Nor was he inclined to easy platitudes and wishful thinking about the North. His blood had run cold when the patrician British foreign secretary Lord Carrington had greeted him cheerfully with 'Well, Garret, how do we unite Ireland?'[65] FitzGerald, in fact, resourcefully enlisted Henry Kissinger to counsel the British against any idea of withdrawal from Northern Ireland. On the question of secularism in the South, FitzGerald also knew he was far in advance of most of his party, and he was canny enough to conceal his intentions from them before his broadcast. For all his chatty academic style, he never minded infuriating his colleagues, and he was effectively conducting a long-term campaign against remnants of the Cosgrave old guard. 'He is about as nice as you can be and get ahead in politics,' Conor Cruise O'Brien remarked about his old friend and rival at this time, 'but no nicer. There is steel under all that pretty wool.'[66]

VI

As it happened, 'Garret's Crusade' would be derailed by the pro-creation wars dealt with elsewhere in this book, when the issues of contraception and abortion invaded the political arena, which was convulsed by the 'Pro-Life' amendment campaign. But the initiative demonstrated, in September 1981, his sense that the North must be made to see that the South was capable of new thinking, and that the South must recognize in its turn that the North was inhabited by a million Protestant Unionists. Back in power in March 1983, Fitzgerald continued this strategy through the New Ireland Forum, but it did not work out quite as he expected. The forum was to meet in Dublin Castle and called for submissions from all parties and individuals interested or involved in the increasingly fashionable question of Irish identity – a word given added currency by FitzGerald in another of his interventions, the 1982 Dimbleby Lecture in London. Here he interpreted the antagonism in Northern Ireland as a clash of cultures – much as F. S. L. Lyons had done in *Culture and Anarchy in Ireland* three years before but with a less pessimistic forward projection. The Forum was to follow this through.

By the time it got under way the advance of Sinn Féin in the North had added both a new dimension and a new urgency. But the elements represented in Dublin Castle came overwhelmingly from a nationalist orientation. Very few Unionists felt the need to travel to Dublin and say their piece, and the idea of demonstrating the existence of Unionist identity to the Republic fell rather flat. Those nationalists who did go were often more interested in declaiming set-pieces than in debating ideas. FitzGerald had been determined that the Forum would represent all Irish parties; Haughey, out of power and temporarily positioning himself as a Kelly-green incorruptible, was equally determined to adhere to his 'failed entity' analysis. While FitzGerald's opening speech stressed the need for structures accommodating both 'Irish/Irish identity and British/Irish identity', Haughey's called for 'the withdrawal of the British military and political presence from Northern Ireland'. In a further reversion to pre-1970 verities, he directly contradicted Lynch's argument by stating that the Northern Ireland problem was neither the fault nor the responsibility of any element on the island of Ireland, but that of the British alone. In a swipe at his rival's constitutional crusade, he declared, 'We need apologise to nobody about the character or performance of our state, and we do not intend to do so.' This line continued throughout the deliberations leading up to the Forum Report: Martin Mansergh has revealingly recalled, 'my role behind the scenes was to act as a watchdog on successive drafts and submissions against the excesses of political revisionism.'[67]

The result would be a certain opacity of language in the eventual report of June 1984, and a tendency to dress up traditional reunification in a pluralist gloss. Haughey's insistence that a 'unitary state' was the only option, rather than the federal or joint-authority routes also prospected, is essentially reflected in the report's conclusions. Unity 'by consent' was not particularly reassuring for the few Unionists who took an interest. But the deliberations in Dublin Castle open a window into the state of Southern thinking about the North, at least among those who felt the need to participate. Much of the testament was unreconstructed, even from those who had been sidelined or bewildered by the previous decade's events. The idiosyncratic Desmond Fennell dismissed the Unionists as 'a minority ethnic group' without political rights. A Bela Lugosi performance by Seán MacBride, mouthing antique anti-partitionism, provided another star turn. Other fantasies included the idea that the joys of 'native culture' and speaking Irish would seduce 'intelligent Unionists' into discovering their true identity. But some voices raised uncomfortable issues: two economists, Charles Carter and Louden Ryan, crisply scotched both Haughey's idea that Britain would pay the financial cost of reunification and the more general delusion that the Republic could afford it. FitzGerald's opening remarks had stressed the need 'to secure the real consent and commitment of the South, a consent based on true awareness of the political and economic realities and not on a myth or bravado or chauvinism'. Not many submissions lived up to this. Clare O'Halloran's close examination of the Forum Report argues that it essentially gave new expression to the 'anti-partitionism' of the 1920s, and it is hard to disagree.

Therefore Sinn Féin, while not taking part, expressed pleasure at the outcome endorsing a 'unitary state'.[68] But, despite this, several of the submissions did indicate that a new rhetoric was needed towards Unionists; and FitzGerald rapidly tried to turn the report to his own purposes. Thatcher's apparently dismissive response notwithstanding, the year after the Forum Report saw the Anglo-Irish Agreement of 1985 redefining the interest of the South in the North. Years of Irish diplomatic spade-work in Washington bore fruit, as pressure was brought to bear on the prime minister from Ronald Reagan and Tip O'Neill.[69] The line that FitzGerald took on the South and the North was, in fact, distinctly different from the implication of the Forum Report, and he presented it passionately to Thatcher at Milan in June 1985, after several tortuous months trying to indicate the basis of an agreement between London and Dublin that would facilitate movement in Northern Ireland. The question of amending Articles 2 and 3 had hovered predominantly over early discussions, and one of the cards FitzGerald felt able to play was 'on our side, recognition of the status of Northern Ireland'; from the British, he wanted a commitment to reforms, especially regarding the police, that would make Northern Ireland work. At Milan, FitzGerald recalled in his informative and unbuttoned autobiography,

I began by telling her that she should understand that I was not seeking these things for the benefit of our people in the South; in fact our people did not want to be involved in the North. We had just had local elections in the South, and time and again people had come to us to say, 'Stop talking about Northern Ireland; we want tax down, we want unemployment cured, and we do not want to be involved in Northern Ireland.' This was the background against which I had initiated the current negotiation, because it seemed to me to be vital to break out of the cycle of violence in Northern Ireland, even if this involved taking risks.

I would tell her, I went on, how I saw the whole question. This business would never have started if the right thing had been done at the right time. In 1969, when the trouble had started, all the minority community had then wanted had been a right to be represented in Parliament as a constitutional opposition on the basis of equal rights. But there had been fierce opposition even to that minimal change from Unionists in Northern Ireland. Then in 1974 a British government – not hers – walked away from an agreement that had been made at Sunningdale, and things that could well have worked collapsed, again in the face of Unionist opposition. And even as late as 1982, if the ideas in relation to power-sharing that Jim Prior had canvassed and then dropped had gone ahead, things might have worked out.[70]

The contrast with Haughey's posture was striking: in FitzGerald's version the South cared little about reuniting with the North, and an internal solution was both possible and practicable. The message got through, and the Anglo-Irish Agreement of November 1985 was discreetly based on these iconoclastic assumptions – though public attention was focused instead on the introduction of a role for the Republic in guaranteeing the position of the Northern minority. Unionist fury was predictable, and helped FitzGerald to sell the agreement as a victory for Nationalism Lite. Haughey's opposition, based on opportunism and sour grapes, did not help his political credibility in the Republic. However, his adviser Martin Mansergh opposed the agreement on the grounds that it accepted British sovereignty over the North, and this was the line that Haughey argued in the Dáil and ordered the unfortunate Brian Lenihan to expound to sceptical Americans.

Committed irredentists could argue that the agreement signed at Hillsborough, in taking a step towards 'joint authority', indeed underwrote the existence of the Northern Ireland state. FitzGerald later reassured Thatcher, 'Nobody in the South said "This is a step towards a United Ireland"', though he was embarrassed when her literal-minded Northern Ireland secretary, Tom King, repeated this bluntly at a Brussels lunch.[71] Five years later one of the negotiators admitted that the agreement had been designed 'to protect the whole island from the IRA–Sinn Féin menace by means of two methods: through changes in security, the administration of justice and the prisons; and by some form of focus which would allow the minority to focus loyalty inside Northern Ireland rather than outside.'[72] In other words, joint authority was to work not merely as an alternative to reunification but as a bulwark against it. Sinn Féin saw the point, arguing that the agreement 'copper-fastened partition', and Bernadette Devlin McAliskey was just one irreconcilable who saw the agreement as an effort 'to eradicate Republicanism' north and south.[73] Garret

FitzGerald would have said that it was simply a process in redefining Republicanism; and in 1990 the Supreme Court decided that the agreement did not, in fact, constitute a climbdown from the 'constitutional imperative' of Articles 2 and 3. This was not entirely welcome news to its progenitors. But its underlying significance remained – as did the inescapable fact that it had been arranged between London and Dublin. John Hume was inevitably consulted, at a fairly late stage, but the Unionists were left out completely and presented with a fait accompli. The Big Mad Children were not to be allowed to spoil this meeting of grown-ups.

Haughey's insistence on opposing the agreement was not only wildly out of line with Irish public opinion; it also helped to precipitate the long-awaited split in Fianna Fáil. Only 52 per cent of the party's supporters backed the leader's line, and Desmond O'Malley seceded to form the Progressive Democrats. In some ways, the *démarche* at Hillsborough in November 1985 had a more drastic effect on politics in the South than in the North, where its declared objective of eroding support for Sinn Féin and bolstering the SDLP was not dramatically apparent. However, if Sinn Féin was not marginalized in the North, its effect was none the less contained within the Northern unit. This was clear in the 1987 election in the Republic, which returned Haughey to power – where he rapidly did a U-turn and supported the Hillsborough Agreement. Less than a year later Hume made the first overtures in what would become a continuing dialogue with Gerry Adams.[74]

The Sinn Féin Ard-Fheis of 1 November 1986 had announced the ending of the abstention principle. In a speech that announced the crossing of the Rubicon, Martin McGuinness said the movement must 'accept the reality of the fact that they were not at war with the government of the Republic' and that 'after sixty-five years of republican struggle, republican agitation, republican sacrifice and republican rhetoric, we have failed to convince a majority in the twenty-six counties that the republican movement has any significance to them.'[75] Despite the assurance that military attacks on 'the forces of occupation' would continue in the North (a promise murderously kept), an irrevocable admission had been made. The initiative remained with McGuinness and Adams, who hinted at further steps in *The Politics of Irish Freedom*, published in late 1986. Sinn Féin was on its way in from the cold – within the context of a partitioned island. The outcome of this, which must have been embarrassingly clear to Hume's colleagues as soon as he began talking to Adams, was that success would allow Sinn Féin to inherit the electoral position of the SDLP. Fitz-Gerald, much later, would call this a 'heroic act of self-abnegation' on the part of the SDLP.[76] Not all of the party faithful saw it that way.

As for Sinn Féin, after 1985 its standard rhetoric about Britain's strategic and economic interest in retaining control of Northern Ireland looked more threadbare than ever. Even Danny Morrison unguardedly admitted the huge drain that the province represented for the Treasury.[77] It continued to denounce the idea of devolved government envisaged by the agreement, but this too could be re-thought. The party's socially radical credentials, which had been given regular airings from the late 1970s, were also mothballed; by late 1986 Morrison was reassuring interviewers that it was 'not a Marxist organisation, and indeed many of its members and leaders, including Gerry Adams and Martin McGuinness, are committed Catholics'.[78] This was all starting to look familiar, and even predictable. And from 1986 they were no longer forbidden to take seats in the supposedly illegitimate Dáil. Like so many Republican purists before them, Sinn Féin under Adams's leadership prepared to segue into a 'slightly con-stitutional' status. The return to power of Haughey (and Mansergh) would make the process all the easier; in time, Adams's friend, the ubiquitous Father Alec Reid, would persuade the Irish government that a ceasefire could be negotiated as a preliminary to negotiations. But this would not mean that solutions would be canvassed in an all-Ireland context. And the extent to which the IRA would abandon violence, or at least restrict it to what Adams called the 'vastly prefer-able' targets provided by British army personnel, remained an impon-derable.[79] The carnage of 'ordinary people' on Remembrance Day 1987 in Enniskillen was a horrific reminder that this was not easily controllable.

In the South, partitionism was now respectable politics. Austin Currie, a founder of the SDLP and a member of the short-lived Sunningdale administration, effectively driven out of Northern politics by the Provisionals, followed the formal logic of Northern nationalism by going south and canvassing for a seat in the Dáil, warmly encouraged by FitzGerald and others. To his surprise he found immense hostility on the doorsteps of West Dublin, focused on his Northern antecedents.[80] Danny Morrison was beginning to realize the same thing. 'People of the Twenty-six Counties that don't want the Six Counties,' he told a Dublin journalist in 1988, '*let us know*. If they're telling us to fuck off, telling us they're happy with the state they've got and fuck 1916, then tell us. Because if they don't want us then I would have to look again at the situation.'[81] The decision to 'look again at the situation' would lead to the Good Friday Agreement ten years later; and it was initiated by the realization that the 1985 Anglo-Irish Agreement gave the Republic of Ireland exactly as much of a role in the North as it needed to save face, and no more.

VII

The political narrative of 1985 to 1998 shows the Northern policies of the Republic and the United Kingdom running more and more closely together. The Anglo-Irish Agreement allowed the Republic formally to recognize both the legitimacy of the Northern Ireland state and the impracticability of reunification. Articles 2 and 3, those treasured pieces of Republican family silver, were at last to be taken out and auctioned. This happened thirteen years later, when the Good Friday Agreement sealed the process by implicating Northern Republicans in the same recognition. The *Animal Farm* denouement of the story would see Martin McGuinness and his Sinn Féin colleagues taking office as ministers of HM the Queen in a devolved power-sharing government in Northern Ireland. Many inducements had to be offered to bring this about, and a great deal of unpleasant medicine swallowed by constitutionalists: the release of paramilitary killers on both sides, the glad-handing and glorification of Sinn Féin politicians and the effective euthanasia of the SDLP.

It also required an unshaken belief in the bona fides of Sinn Féin; a readiness to use language that could state one thing and implicitly promise quite another; a reliance on obscure connections and contacts between Republicans and Whitehall, not always made known to

Dublin (the canny Ken Bloomfield noted how much readier the British government was to 'talk to terrorists' than the Irish, but this was nothing new); and a belief that they could 'deliver' the hard men and harder women of the IRA. These requirements were successively embodied by John Major and Tony Blair in one jurisdiction, and Albert Reynolds and Bertie Ahern in the other. But the vital need was for a Unionist leader who bought into enough of the analysis to risk his own political skin.

David Trimble surprisingly emerged to take this role. Others played more easily predictable parts. Conor Cruise O'Brien, from the first revelations of the Hume–Adams initiative, issued Cassandra-like prophecies. On the opposite side of the political spectrum, the stridently unreconstructed Bernadette Devlin McAliskey fulminated against any signs of what she saw as a sell-out. By 1992 she was convinced that the Republic planned to give up its constitutional claim on the six counties of Northern Ireland. In the self-regarding style that had progressively alienated her political colleagues for nearly a quarter-century, she delivered a lecture in Dublin that September on her own political identity, which developed into a tirade against 'the South'. She told her surprised audience: '[In 1921] you bought your liberty with our slavery'; if the 'Free State' dared complete the process, the IRA would 'vent their wrath'. 'My national identity is not something for you to barter or trade or sell . . . I tell you, on the peril of all our mortal lives, don't you even try to put us out of this nation – or we'll leave you without a blade of grass.'[82] She was applauded by some visiting Irish-Americans, who were attending the lecture as part of the Yeats International Festival, but not by the more hard-nosed politicians in her audience. As both they and she knew, negotiations were under way that just over a year later would produce the Downing Street Declaration of December 1993 – a vital stage in cementing precisely the partitionist enterprise that McAliskey denounced so fervently. But her own speech unintentionally demonstrated just how far apart Southern and Northern nationalism had become.

Public rhetoric remained obdurate, but change was on the way. Sinn Féin's closely marshalled contributions to an important independent commission, the Citizens' Inquiry chaired by Torkel Opsahl, which sat in Northern Ireland during January and February 1993, did not deviate in public from its sacred texts: partition must end, and the British could end it. One observer said it was like listening to the Militant Tendency. In private, however, they let Opsahl's commissioners know that they were ready to explore another route.[83] The SDLP (or at least its leader-in-waiting Mark Durcan) was explicitly open to a 'shared Ireland' that might not be 'united' nor even 'federal'. One of the Unionist submissions put it more bluntly: 'If you picked up the phone today and offered [the North] to Albert Reynolds [then taoiseach], he'd emigrate.' This judgement was echoed, more cautiously, by Michael Farrell, once a PD firebrand, now a Dublin solicitor; he had been in Bernadette Devlin McAliskey's audience the previous September and had not applauded. Old moulds were being broken once again.[84]

Reynolds in Dublin and the similarly newly fledged Prime Minister John Major in London were both pragmatic self-made politicians, operating in the shadow of a charismatic predecessor's personality cult and determined to register a decisive political success. In early March 1993 Seán Duignan, the Fianna Fáil press secretary, was astonished when Reynolds suggested opening talks with the IRA and persuading it to lay down its arms in return for 'unity by consent' ('Doesn't sound like the IRA to me'). The reaction of Reynolds's coalition partner Dick Spring was equally sceptical: 'You're on your own, Albert.'[85] In May, Reynolds was the only Southern politician to welcome openly the revelation of Hume's talks with Adams. The Downing Street Declaration engineered by Reynolds and Major that December drew the outlines of a possible settlement for Northern Ireland, based on inducements to bring Republicans into the political process – including 'dynamic' institutions linking North and South. While this was superficially reassuring to Republicans, the real point was that any settlement would have to be endorsed by separate majorities in the North and the South, which entrenched the consent principle. To Republicans, it was hinted that the suggested framework held the promise of gradually diluting the border. To Unionists a different logic was presented, implying that the complete and 'permanent' cessation of Republican violence that would necessarily accompany the settlement would guarantee the future of a devolved North as long as its majority wanted: thus the declaration could be read as 'an Orange document in Green language'.[86] Further reassurance would come eight months later with the IRA's announcement of 'a complete cessation' of military operations on 31 August 1994, just as the declaration had hinted. But 'permanency' was not part of the IRA's promise.

Moreover, the way the ceasefire was sold to the faithful was less encouraging: Gerry Adams appeared in the Falls Road uneasily clutching a bouquet of flowers and a bottle of champagne, objects much less familiar to him than they would later become. He announced, without anything like his habitual certainty, that his community had fought through to victory. This almost audibly teeth-grinding presentation should be seen against the background of behind-the-scenes threats from Reynolds that, unless the IRA laid down its arms, he was prepared to go ahead with a separate deal for the North that might exclude Sinn Féin altogether. And the ceasefire thus celebrated was far from permanent. It would end traumatically with the Canary Wharf bombing of February 1996, when the IRA lost patience with what Republicans perceived as the Unionist drift of policy – in Dublin as well as London. The game was changing. Northern Republicans might be lured in from the cold, but what they were invited into was participation in the twenty-six-county state. As Sinn Féin began to pick up seats in local politics, and then the Dáil, as more Northerners were appointed to the Senate, as the mould-breaking President Mary Robinson (who before her election had opposed the Anglo-Irish Agreement because it ignored the Unionists) was replaced by the feel-good Northern nationalist Mary McAleese, the scenario feared by Republicans such as McAliskey seemed to be coming true. The rhetoric of 'two states, one nation' meant partitionism with a friendly face.

It was no coincidence that this became institutionalized in the same decade that saw the economic and social transformation of the South. In 1993 Fionnuala O Connor published her study of Northern Catholic consciousness, *In Search of a State*, and caught the moment when Northerners were realizing that the Republic was now embracing materialism, prosperity, secularism, modernity and sexual laxity, and deciding it was acceptable to feel indifferent towards the North. Two of her most prominent interviewees, Gerry Adams and the future president McAleese, inveighed against the Republic's 'revisionism' of their history, for destabilizing their worldview. Adams complained: 'What revisionism has done is tell people they can't be satisfied with what they come from ... the effect's like a family trauma, like discovering you've been adopted.' McAleese, who had moved to Dublin in the 1970s, lectured in law and briefly entered Fianna Fáil politics, had been shocked by Dublin ('it isn't the Republic'), historical revisionism ('it isn't Ireland') and above all by Conor Cruise O'Brien. 'If ever anyone was a culture shock, Conor Cruise O'Brien was to me. Here was this extraordinarily arrogant man, in the process of revising everything that I had known to be a given and a truth about Irish history.'[87]

To Southerners, of course, the 'arrogance' implicit in Adams's and McAleese's expectations was equally striking, and so was their reluctance to alter their inherited assumptions. Younger citizens of the Republic saw exactly the destabilization complained of by Adams and McAleese as liberation. By the mid 1990s, even the official party language regarding Northern Ireland had changed. In 1994 the policy statement of Democratic Left, the descendants of the old Official IRA via the Workers' Party, now en route to uniting with Labour, produced a formula that set in stone everything Bernadette McAliskey had denounced from the Peacock Theatre stage two years before.

The seventy years of separation from the South, the development of the welfare state, divergent social development North and South, and twenty-five years of terrorism have made Northern nationalists a people apart. They have potentially more in common with their fellow Northern Irish people than with their Southern neighbours. The primary objective of an Agreement should be to unite the people of Northern Ireland on the basis of peaceful coexistence by putting in place structures which will help develop a pluralist democracy.[88]

Jack Lynch had said exactly the same twenty-five years before. And a year later Fianna Fáil finally followed his lead by quietly amending the party's traditional aim 'to secure the unity and independence of Ireland as a Republic'. It now read: 'to secure in peace and agreement the unity of Ireland and its people'. By then the party's *éminence grise* on Northern affairs, Martin Mansergh, had been meeting Gerry Adams in private for at least two years, in the spirit of Hume's

Newspeak approach of 'uniting people rather than territories' – a phrase that had in fact been articulated by Lemass nearly thirty years before. Lemass, however, had spoken of the necessity to 'reunite Irish people as well as reuniting territory'.[89] Hume's version implicitly admitted that uniting 'territory' was now generally accepted as an archaic impossibility. It was up to the people.

Uniting 'people' often seemed equally unrealistic, especially when the IRA periodically decided to bomb them to extinction (Enniskillen, November 1987; London, April 1992; Warrington, March 1993; Shankill Road, October 1993). But the arguments presented by Mansergh to the Republican leadership through the 1990s offered inclusion on the basis of giving up their addiction to violence – which prevented (in Mansergh's words) 'combination [of Irish nationalists] for electoral or other purposes'.[90] What the other purposes were remained to be seen. Less obscurely, Sinn Féin was brought to see that Britain's supposed strategic and 'colonial' interest in Northern Ireland was another archaic delusion. This had been the case for decades, but it had not been in the IRA's interest to admit it. Finally Secretary of State Peter Brooke said it so specifically in a series of speeches during 1990 that it had to be taken on board. The British government had 'no selfish strategic or economic interest in Northern Ireland' and would happily accept unification by consent. From the 1994 ceasefire, Adams was also signed up to the statement 'we cannot resolve this problem without the participation and agreement of the Unionist people.' Private discussions steered by key figures from the Department of Foreign Affairs and the Department of the Taoiseach had, by the mid 1990s, helped to redefine a diluted Republicanism.[91] The 1993 Downing Street Declaration was really the public statement of private ambiguities – partly because several early drafts had been run past Sinn Féin, whose tortuous objections and rewordings prompted Mansergh's revisions.[92] The IRA Army Council, which conveniently included the Sinn Féin leaders Adams and McGuinness, had approved a green-tinged preliminary draft of June 1993, requiring the British government to act as 'persuaders for Irish unity' and to adopt a timetable for withdrawal, but this was clearly a non-starter; its only function had been to keep extreme Republicans notionally on board.

The effectiveness of this was not immediately obvious. In October

1993 an IRA bomb inflicted carnage on the Shankill Road (ten dead, fifty-seven injured); the bomber was killed too, and Gerry Adams ostentatiously acted as one of his pall-bearers. When the declaration emerged in December, Sinn Féin withheld its support: the endorsement of the majoritarian principle within Northern Ireland was a bridge too far. As the declaration had it, 'It is for the people of the island of Ireland alone, by agreement between the two parts respectively, to exercise their right of self-determination on the basis of consent, freely and concurrently given North and South, to bring about a united Ireland, if that is their wish.' Or not.

Even Mansergh felt that Sinn Féin's opposition to this principle left it 'riding two horses at the same time, in trying to reassure the wider leadership [sic] that this was still consistent with core demands'. He also admitted that a negotiated settlement that would 'fall considerably short of Irish unity' was now on the cards.[93] Domestication of the IRA continued in 1994, with the lifting of the broadcasting ban on Sinn Féin and the issuing of a US visa to Adams by the Clinton administration. The glamour of the American connection lured Republicans further into the establishment, as represented by the ambassador to Ireland, Jean Kennedy Smith, who argued for Adams's visa against the wishes of the entire State Department and her Anglophile London colleague Raymond Seitz. Meanwhile her nephew Joe Kennedy visited Belfast and presented an inflexibly Republican line to the few Unionists he met. Several Dublin diplomats must have winced at this. From the 1970s the high-fliers of the Department of Foreign Affairs – especially Seán Donlon and Michael Lillis – had devoted much time to re-educating Joe's Uncle Ted, a notoriously slow learner, in the realities of Northern Irish politics. Hume had been a key ally in deflecting influential Irish-Americans away from the fundraisers of NORAID and the Irish National Caucus, who sustained the IRA, and opening the ears of Capitol Hill to the SDLP instead.[94] Lillis had in fact drafted speeches on Ireland for former President Carter, and the Friends of Ireland organization had pushed financial support in the direction of constitutional nationalism and away from the IRA. But there had been a change. When in power in the 1980s, Haughey had favoured Mario Biaggi's far more militant Ad Hoc Committee for Irish Affairs and other fellow travellers, and done his best to have

Donlon moved. Hume's influence remained, but by the early 1990s there was a new dispensation in Washington, and in turn a new 'Irish-Americans for Clinton' group run by Niall O'Dowd and Bruce Morrison – who were closer to Sinn Féin than to the SDLP. The Kennedy family were successfully wooed, and reverted to type.

As this implies, the lauding of Adams in the USA was inevitably at Hume's expense. Though it caused some diplomatic difficulties between London and Dublin, the awakening of Clinton's interest in the Irish issue added to the leverage towards a ceasefire. Further negotiations included a US visa for the veteran IRA killer Joe Cahill, whose curriculum vitae caused even Clinton to blanch.[95] Once the ceasefire was in place, Reynolds could entertain Hume and Adams in Dublin; within weeks they would be testifying at yet another 'Forum', this time aimed at 'Peace and Reconciliation' rather than a 'New Ireland'. The post-ceasefire speeches written by Mansergh for Reynolds missed no chance to parallel the 1994 démarche with the acceptance by Fianna Fáil of democratic constitutional politics in 1926. The fact that the 1926 capitulation also marked the de facto acceptance of a partitioned Ireland was elaborately ignored. So was the uncomfortable fact that a necessary condition of ceasing violence was, in the view of the British government at least, the decommissioning of the IRA's arsenal. When Mansergh raised this with the Republican leadership, 'he was given a blank "no".'[96]

The Canary Wharf bomb that killed two people and ended the ceasefire on 9 February 1996 underlined this message; Albert Reynolds had been warned of such an eventuality by his Republican contacts two weeks in advance.[97] It also underlined the IRA's disapproval of the recent change of government in Dublin, now led by the Fine Gael taoiseach John Bruton. For his part, Bruton had been astonished to find out just how vague the arrangements for decommissioning weapons were.[98] The IRA further signified its disapproval of the American senator George Mitchell's proposal, a fortnight before Canary Wharf, of six basic principles for renouncing violence. Nor did it like John Major's insistence on an electoral mandate before the next round of talks opened. Most aggrieving of all was the final report of the Forum for Peace and Reconciliation, which was issued from Dublin at just this time and reaffirmed the necessity of majoritarian consent in the North as an underpinning for any settlement. Republican sensitivities were, however, slightly soothed by the changed political landscape from mid 1997, when Fianna Fáil's Bertie Ahern ascended to power in the Republic, and Tony Blair became prime minister in Britain. This reinvigorated the negotiations that culminated in the Good Friday Agreement of 1998.

It had been an edgy business so far, and clarity of expression had been an early casualty. By now, in the words of the disillusioned Brian Lynch (government spokesman on Northern Ireland a decade earlier),

The peace process was remarkable for its paradoxical combination of precision and vagueness. For this purpose an anti-language was developed, one that by use excavated itself of meaning – after a while it was hard to distinguish between code and cod. Saying not much in this anti-language required a great deal to be said, ambiguously and at length, but with the simplicity of a phrase-book and the repetitiveness of an advertising campaign.[99]

This was one of Hume's chief bequests. Following the second IRA ceasefire in July 1997, the much written about peace process required acceptance of a series of blank cheques and open-ended promises on decommissioning in order to keep the ball rolling. But equally striking was the rate of advance on Articles 2 and 3. As late as November 1997, at a debate in West Belfast, Mansergh said that the question of deleting them 'simply does not exist';[100] the infuriated Unionist reaction was rapidly absorbed by Ahern, and Mansergh was set to drafting alternatives, to the discomfiture of Sinn Féin. The new versions abandoned the territorial claim, affirmed the principle of consent and enshrined the agreeably woolly statement that 'every person born in the island of Ireland' was 'entitled to be part of the Irish nation', and that 'the Irish nation cherishes its special affinity with people of Irish ancestry living abroad who share its cultural identity and heritage' (but not, presumably, if they don't). In these reformulations the spirit of Lemass was felt, yet again, from beyond the grave; in his brief retirement he had sat on the unproductive Committee on the Constitution and recommended a more conciliatory version of Article 3.[101] From their side the British adapted the assertion of sovereignty over Northern Ireland in the 1920 Government of Ireland Act. The future of the province was to be left to its inhabitants. Thus the 'consent' principle permitted both governments to disengage themselves from embarrassing inherited positions.

Sweeping cross-border institutions were held out as a quid pro quo for Republicans, but at Trimble's behest these were significantly reduced in what the Unionist leader boasted was 'a ritual humiliation' for Ahern.[102] Six 'implementation bodies' were to oversee inland waterways, food safety, trade and business development, special EU programmes, the Irish and Ulster Scots languages, and 'aquacultural' matters. (Bobby Sands's sister would later remark grimly that her brother had not died for a cross-border tourist authority.) The much thornier issues of policing arrangements, arms decommissioning and demilitarization were to be left for the future. Blair's vacuous promises to 'exclude from the government of Northern Ireland those who use or threaten violence' and to keep prisoners in jail 'unless violence is given up for good' were taken as read. Many people supported the agreement with crossed fingers and what has been described as 'a combination of willed hopefulness and desperate weariness'.[103] Its real heft lay in the recognition of a partitioned island by Sinn Féin, and the fact that the referendum on abandoning Articles 2 and 3 was endorsed by 96 per cent of those voting in the Republic. In the North about the same proportion of Catholics voted to support the agreement – but only 55 per cent of Protestants. The ensuing summer would see an outbreak of violence around the Orange marches of mid July, which had been escalating for several years. 'What seemed implied by the confrontations over parades', reflected the acute commentator Malachi O'Doherty, 'was that Northern Ireland was a society that would be tearing itself apart anyway, even if the bombers and gunmen stayed at home.'[104] That was certainly how it looked from the South.

And not all the bombers were staying at home. A month later saw the massacre of thirty-one people in Omagh by dissident Republicans calling themselves the 'Real IRA'. Political opposition came from the '32-County Sovereignty Movement', led by Bobby Sands's sister and her husband. To most Southern opinion, they might as well have been called the Flat Earth Movement, but they represented the purist Republicanism that would not, in Gerry Adams's words, go away. He himself continued his breathtaking balancing act, declaring after the Omagh outrage that even if he had any information about its perpetrators, he would not cooperate with the RUC. The new devolved government briefly functioned in 2000–2001; observers from the South were assured on visits to Stormont that ministers of different parties got on very well, but they could not help noticing that the difficult issues of policing and decommissioning 'were not being discussed at all'.[105] The IRA at peace continued to pull off bank robberies, administer punishment beatings, run rackets, keep fraternal contact with international terrorist organizations and complain of being 'demonized'. Sinn Féin's protestations that it was uninvolved in any of this were given as much credence as they deserved. 'Loyalist' paramilitaries conducted themselves similarly but with far fewer resources. When IRA violence had trickled over the border, such as the murder of Garda Jerry McCabe during a Limerick bank robbery in 1996, local opinion was uniformly denunciatory, and the long-running question of releasing McCabe's killers under the Good Friday amnesty became a test case. Northerners noted, with some bitterness, that this sensitivity did not extend to deaths within their jurisdiction.

And if Northern hatreds continued, they now represented the kind of reality from which the Good Friday Agreement allowed twenty-six-county nationalism to detach itself. 'Joint authority', which had loomed into the sphere of government policy in the 1980s and retained a shadowy existence in the Maryfield secretariat set up under the 1985 Anglo-Irish Agreement, had receded again. So had the prospect of 'saving the SDLP'. But the halting progress of the new devolved government, and its eventual suspension amid recriminations about arms decommissioning, was of little interest to Southern opinion. Much of Fianna Fáil's rhetoric, and all of Sinn Féin's, continued to invoke reunification by degrees. But after Good Friday 1998 the Republic could retire from its role as sundered mother to the orphaned North, just as the British adjured the role of adoptive father. The Big Mad Children could be left to wreck the nursery by themselves – or to repair it.

Looking back in 1998, Malachi O'Doherty decided that uncompromising Republicanism and its appeasement had posed exactly the wrong answer to Northern Ireland's problems: had, in fact, made

things worse. A number of authorities have indicated the same conclusion, implicitly or explicitly. It was hard to accept, at the turn of
the twenty-first century, that the six north-eastern counties were a
better place to live in than thirty-odd years before.[106] It could be
argued that at the core of the peace process lay a recognition of the
intricate Balkanization of local political culture in Northern Ireland,
and that the two communities were now more divided than ever –
though not all analysts agree.[107] If there is truth in this gloomy analysis,
obdurate Unionism has to share the blame with uncompromising
Republicanism: if the post-1969 reforms had been pressed ahead in a
spirit of cooperation, if the language of pluralism had been discovered
earlier, if Trimble had not been the first Unionist leader to say publicly
that the province had been 'a cold house for Catholics', alienation
might not have taken such a deep hold of the ghettoes. In this process,
the British Army also played a decisive and ignoble part. So did the
readiness of both Labour and Conservative governments to sacrifice
continuity in Northern Ireland policy to the dictates of narrow majorities in the House of Commons. There was nothing inevitable about
the sorry catalogue of ineptness, bullying, pusillanimity, political
gangsterism and inadequate leadership that accompanied Northern
Ireland's thirty-year nightmare from 1968 to 1998.[108]

But the past was the past, and by 1998 two results were obvious.
One was a degree of institutionalized separateness between the communities that was formally, if implicitly, recognized in the Good
Friday protocols. 'Power-sharing', floated periodically as a recipe for
isolating the extremes, was now the mechanism whereby the extreme
parties were supposed to work together.[109] The other outcome has
been the subject of this chapter: the growth of an equally institutionalized partitionism, seen from the South. The border had not
floated away like a redundant sticking plaster. Jack Lynch's prophecy
in 1970 that the IRA would find violence 'was not advancing their
cause but rather retarding it' was proved true.[110] The Republic and
the UK emerged from the 'peace process' closer than ever (as both
Garret FitzGerald and David Trimble, for their different purposes,
ironically pointed out[111]). In 1969 the Irish minister for external affairs
had been told by a junior minister at the Foreign Office that the North
was none of his business; within twenty years the language of joint

authority was an accepted lingua franca between London and Dublin; ten years on from that, both governments were devoutly praying for the restoration of devolved government, based on the acceptance of an intrinsically divided community. Northern rituals, whether they were Orange marches, triumphalist Sinn Féin Ard-Fheiseanna, or mawkish testaments by ex-bombers, seemed correspondingly more and more alien.

One compensating response was the discovery of a neo-nationalist rhetoric that stayed firmly fixed on the twenty-six-county unit – inspired in part by the need to compete with Sinn Féin, whose progress in twenty-six-county politics continued apace. This was based on saying very little about reunification and a great deal about corruption, social conditions and cultural nationalism. The ninetieth anniversary of the 1916 Rising was therefore celebrated with aggressive government backing, reinstating in 2006 the military parade abandoned by the Fine Gael–Labour government of 1973. The official cult fusing Pearse's blood sacrifice and Christian iconography was proclaimed once more with gusto, particularly by President McAleese. Once again, no one mentioned the uncomfortable fact that the 1916 rebellion, while indubitably the founding event of the twenty-six-county state, had also started a process that put paid to any possibility of an autonomous Ireland that might include the North. In that same year, 1916 memorabilia were auctioned for huge prices in a Dublin sale room while Sinn Féin protesters stood dolefully outside.

It was none the less considered safe, and even desirable, to stress cultural difference from Britain and to glow with pride in the liberation struggle of nearly a century before – particularly as the IRA's traditional liberationist strategies were, for the moment, tactfully in abeyance in the North. There was ample room to exercise what Arthur Koestler christened 'the political libido', allowing the insecure self to identify with nation, tribe, church or party: 'when this unconscious tendency towards identification produces pleasurable results, these are willingly admitted to the conscious self [and thus] every American feels satisfaction about the War of Independence as if he had fought it.'[112] A similar impulse to neo-nationalist identification, now that the North was out of the way, was reinforced by the commodification of Irish history. In 2002 the Hollywood star Colin Farrell, from the comfortable middle-class suburb of Castleknock, introduced the readers of *American Way* to 'My Dublin'. They were counselled to stay at the Shelbourne Hotel, 'where a lot of the 1916 Easter Rising, when Ireland was won as a free state, was fought literally from the bedrooms you'd be staying in; it's got a great old Dublin ambience.' On, then, to visit 'the most famous building in Dublin, the General Post Office. It's where a lot of the 1916 Easter Rising was fought.' He concluded, unnecessarily, 'I've been accused of promoting the Irish cliché. But it's a part of who we are.'[113] 'Who we are' clearly stopped short at the border.

In the same year the magazine *VIP*, a home-grown Irish version of *Hello!*, profiled Gerry Adams and his lifestyle 'in his home town of Belfast' – taking pride of place on the cover above 'the Mount Charles family in magnificent Slane Castle' and an Irish model just appointed 'the new face of Wonderbra'. The key quote from Adams, unironically flagged across the cover, ran: 'Those of us who've come through 30 years and are still standing have a lot to be thankful for.'[114] Not all his constituents would have agreed. But it chimed perfectly with the sense of relief felt in the Republic, once the North was firmly relegated to a perpetual aspiration. It also reflected Celtic Tiger priorities as well as style. It had often been assumed that prosperity in the South would erode Unionist fears about joining a backward state. By the 1990s the Republic was far outstripping Northern Ireland in GDP and GNP;[115] as it achieved undreamt of prosperity, the North lurched into economic stasis. But not only did the Unionists decline a ride on the back of the Celtic Tiger; in a poignant role reversal the newly rich Republic evinced little desire for reunion with an ailing, unprofitable and expensive backwater. 'John Bull's Political Slum' had become an economic slum as well, and Southerners did not want to cross the tracks. By 2007 the plutocratic Irish government could throw money at the problem instead, providing a large contribution to the financial package aimed at persuading Ian Paisley to enter devolved government with Sinn Féin. Last-ditch Northern Republicans continued to preach the holy writ that all the handouts, agreements and amendments of the peace process would never deliver 'the ultimate aim of the Irish nation'.[116] But the irreconcilables preferred not to follow up the implication that there might be something deluded about the 'ultimate aim', or that the 'Irish nation' now required some redefinition. The South had long since arrived at these conclusions. The unintended achievement of thirty years of Republican strategy was to entrench the border more deeply than ever before.

5

How the Short Stories
Became Novels

I

The post-sixties era that saw economic bust and boom, social upheaval and political rollercoaster rides in the Republic, as well as near-revolutionary conflagration in the North, were remarkable in other ways too. Again as in the French Third Republic, political crisis and social disorientation were counterpointed by cultural achievements that suggested a dramatic development in confidence and innovation. For the Irish to conquer the English-speaking world through literature was, of course, nothing new; the motor of twentieth-century modernism in poetry, fiction and drama was driven by the Irish engineers Shaw, O'Casey, Joyce, Yeats and Beckett. But from about 1970 Irish cultural achievement came into focus once more. This time production happened within Ireland, by artists based at home – though they were addressing a global audience that owed much to the diaspora and its continuing connection with the homeland, enabled by the communications revolution. The talent and ambition of Irish musicians and writers were equally striking. In literature particularly, the inhibitions imposed by the achievements of the great early innovators seemed to lift, or to be converted into, an enabling example. The scale changed; the 'classic' Irish short story, revolving around an emblematic or epiphanic episode, was replaced by the expansive, teeming world of the novel.

Much of the story of Ireland in the late twentieth century concerned the breaking down of boundaries in notions of Irishness, and in identity politics, manifested through globalization, feminization, and other changes in economics, politics and religion. Woven through these questions has been another kind of expansion: the altering, popularizing and extending of forms of Irish cultural expression, most strikingly in music and literature. These phenomena have intersected with Irish politics and economics, sometimes in unexpected ways. There is, for instance, a strange echo from the cascade of events that led to the revelations about politics and corrupt finance inescapably connected with the career of Charles Haughey. On that February morning in 1992 in Orlando, Florida, when Ben Dunne was removed by the police from his Grand Cypress Hotel balcony in a state of disarray, there was another Irishman staying on the seventeenth floor, who was not part of the millionaire's entourage. He had, in fact, brought his own, though he was alone when he was spotted leaving the hotel by one of the call girls who had been summoned by Dunne the night before. 'One of the strangest things of that very strange morning', she later recalled, 'was that leaving the hotel I saw Bono of U2 walking past me. I've always been a fan but it hardly seemed the time to introduce myself, and besides, he looked very grim.'[1]

There is something symbolic about this bizarre coincidence, occurring at a moment when Ireland was about to become 'globalized'. And there is something symbolic about Bono, the new-model Irish cultural icon, invariably disguised in American Stetson, shades and cowboy boots, occupying an international space while representing a new-Irish intersection of money, art and politics. This was a trail blazed earlier by the remarkable Bob Geldof; students of the phenomenon might also like to meditate upon the cut-off career of the late Phil Lynott, or the pretensions of Shane MacGowan. There is, perhaps, another kind of political dimension available to Irish public figures than that adorned by the satraps of Fianna Fáil, and it may in the future be occupied by Bono and Geldof. U2 in particular, while owing much of their appeal to a smart combination of transatlantic stadium-rock values, iconic images of mythic Americana and the adoption of (equally Americanized) Protestant-evangelical modes, have branded themselves with a new kind of Irish patriotism. For a group hailed since 1987 and *The Joshua Tree* as 'the greatest rock band in the world', manipulation of Irishness has had a distinct significance.

Their success intersects suggestively with the ancient image of the Irish as entertainers, exploited so effectively in the Victorian theatre or mid-twentieth-century Hollywood. In the late twentieth century Irishness became fashionable on a level unknown since the cultural renaissance at the turn of the twentieth century. Much of this cult status concerned (as it did a hundred years before) the theory that the Irish had access to special reserves of soul. There has been a reversion to the social characteristics supposedly stamped out by the 'Devotional Revolution' of the mid nineteenth century: the Bacchanalian 'patterns' and the three-day fair are back with us, in the guise of rock festivals and summer schools commemorating writers in their localities (or some of them). In the film *Titanic* the Irish below decks are found expressing real emotion through music and dance, in contrast to the gilded dummies above. There is an interesting linkage here to the historiographical fashion, at first American but rapidly popular on this side of the Atlantic, for referring to the Irish as 'black' or 'ex-black': as in 'how the Irish became white'.[2] The description clearly has come to mean something other than negritude. The Irish are, apparently, virtually 'black' (despite any 'false consciousness' they may attempt for themselves) because they were victims, economically and historically; because they play good music from a distinctive and original native tradition, and possess natural rhythm; because they are not English; because they have a permanent moral advantage; because they are fashionable; and because right-on social historians want to work on them as a subject. All this effortlessly outweighs any evidence that the Irish might actually have seen themselves as white.

This indicates something about the transformation of Ireland over the last thirty years – which has been in many ways a transformation of cultural expectations, based not only on a new confidence in the wider world but also on the rejection of some old authoritarian formations, as well as the manipulation of certain new-found identities. The prevalence of second-generation Irish musicians in British popular music became striking from the 1980s – for Shane MacGowan, John Lydon ('Johnny Rotten'), Morrissey, Hazel O'Connor, Liam and Noel Gallagher, Elvis Costello and many others an assertion of Irish 'roots' conferred authenticity, rebelliousness and entitlement, as social critics as well as subversive musicians. Lydon, even in his Sex Pistols days, none the less showed what he had learnt from holidays with his Macroom relations. 'Patriotism', he told a Dublin interviewer in 1979, 'is a dangerous weapon', going on to scoff at the idea that Irish immigrants were ever treated as badly as blacks and declaring that a return to the homeland would serve no purpose for children of the diaspora like himself.[3] Within the island of Ireland, by the dawning of the twenty-first century there was another phenomenon to be considered: the large-scale immigration of people seeking asylum or jobs, who came not just from Eastern Europe or the Philippines but from Africa. Metaphor was replaced with reality as the country witnessed the establishment of communities of young Irish people who were *actually* black, and who were beginning to develop a musical and cultural style using a mixture of traditions. While this was more obvious in the clubs of northside Dublin than mass-market music, African rhythms with an Irish accent became increasingly audible. It is an illustration of how immigration may prove to be one of the defining characteristics of Irishness in the twenty-first century, just as emigration did in the twentieth.

The potency of popular music has not been missed by politicians, especially of Bertie Ahern's generation. Assertions that 'internationally the Irish nation is perceived very much through the medium of its music' are matched by photo-opportunities with local rock celebrities and strategic appearances at concerts and festivals.[4] The celebrated photographs of Bono flanked by John Hume and an appalled-looking David Trimble had been anticipated by Garret FitzGerald, who, sharp for his purposes, aligned himself with Bono and U2 in a well-publicized visit to a recording session as long ago as 1982: photographs of the 'two garrulous national heroes' were widely broadcast the week before FitzGerald was elected taoiseach.[5] The music magazine *Hot Press*, founded in 1977, was soon carrying long *Rolling Stone*-inspired interviews with politicians and public figures, tempting Haughey, among others, to some fatal indiscretions in a celebrated piece by John Waters.[6] The journal also showcased the causes of homosexual law reform and the introduction of divorce. U2 and Bob Geldof used their status to manipulate political power with increasing confidence – generally addressing world rather than Irish issues. (The odd exception was the 'Self-Aid' concert of 1986, an attempt to confront the current Irish economic crisis by raising money for Irish poverty; it was just as well that the IDA was lining up other potential rescuers around the corner.) Simultaneously, less sophisticated (and completely politically unaware) phenomena such as Boyzone, Westlife and other Irish boy-bands were repackaging a version of the 'showbands' followed by their grandparents' generation. This might be seen as a 'return of the repressed', though at least one analyst has freighted the boy-band with more meaning. Not only do they 'play a crucial role in authenticating the Celtic Tiger economy and its concomitant cultural superstructure', but 'the eroticised band and its continued success replace the love of the country – the feminised nation that was the untouchable love object of the romantic nationalist balladeers'.[7] This may be carrying the tune a little far. But the fact remains that for a country with a tiny record industry, Ireland's influence in the cultural export of music is extraordinary; in the first year of the new century Irish popular musicians sold over fifty-six million albums.[8]

This raises several questions about the way Ireland has been 'marketed' to the world at large over the last generation, especially through music and literature. International styles and modes have been smoothly assumed by many of the most successful practitioners in both fields, but the taste for a distinctively 'Irish' tone, derived from familiar tradition, has been effectively exploited too – perhaps most obviously in the school of *Riverdance* spectaculars. The cultural implications of this have been plumbed by many analysts. It takes us into odd territory, such as that of 'liberation psychology' enthusiastically advanced by some sociologists and applied liberally to the Irish psyche.[9] And it raises the question of the part played by new-look culture in the marketing of the New Ireland. Sunil Khilnani has written incisively about 'Branding India' through the use of 'soft power': the use of seductive popular media images that often disguise or evade questions of hard economic influence.[10] Ireland's international image has been similarly packaged. 'Missing the Industrial Revolution was the best thing that ever happened to Ireland,' announced the IDA, in advertisements aimed at attracting new investment: user-friendly microelectronics would flourish in a landscape of green fields and rainbows, uncorrupted by redundant nineteenth-century factory plant. This also usefully differentiated the peaceful Republic from the dangerous (and grimy) North. It was paralleled in terms of cultural production by a new soft language of 'feelings rather than facts' –

as in the bestselling reflections of John O'Donoghue, sold as Celtic spirituality, or in the (also bestselling) anti-modernist polemics of journalists who recall an imagined Ireland of the 1950s, whether or not they have actually experienced it. This lost domain is presented as a more authentically Irish place, based entirely on a catalogue of abstract concepts such as kindliness, gentleness, innocence and spiritual communion. Mysticism, in fact, is never very far away. So is class resentment and anti-urban bile, but these feelings are not framed in such un-Irish terms; instead, they are situated in a catch-all notion of 'colonialism' and a resentment of 'outside' influences, whether from 'England', America or Europe.

All this has a very strong resonance with the arguments advanced by some Irish-Irelanders a hundred years ago, and suggests that echoes from earlier eras come through the rhetoric of supposedly postmodern Ireland. For the Mystical Tendency, Ireland must find its way back to some mysterious collectivity based on communion with the land, mediated by shaman figures who range from the journalist John Healy to the musicians Bono and Shane MacGowan.[11] The word 'magic' recurs. So does another echo from the last Celtic revival: the emphasis on the urban–rural divide, with authenticity located firmly beyond the metropolis. The demonization of 'Dublin 4' by journalists of an essentialist bent has its origins in the fulminations against 'Rathmines' by D. P. Moran in his *Philosophy of Irish Ireland* in the early 1900s. Moran's generation have long been the subject of close study; the historian of contemporary Ireland will in turn have to look seriously at the figures who have come to be identified with the newly fashionable Irish culture at the turn of the twenty-first century. With Ireland prominent on the world stage, to an extent even greater than the cultural revival of a century before, the regular paralleling of Seamus Heaney and W. B. Yeats is no accident. There are other, less obvious figures who have occupied the world stage and expressed something about Ireland – for instance Bob Geldof, a quintessential New Irishman in that he combines being a successful business mogul and a gifted writer with the vocations of rock star and global campaigner. Geldof's Irish roots bear an instructive comparison to Heaney's a generation before: fathers figure largely, but the rural idyll remembered by those Northern poets who grew up in the 1940s (cruelly dubbed 'the pre-electric men' by Colm Tóibín) is replaced by adolescent angst in 1960s Dun Laoghaire. Geldof's autobiography deserves close reading, unlike many of the genre. He presents the Dublin of that era as a Joycean centre of paralysis, and what fuels his youthful rebellion is boredom with a prevalent conservatism. But the story he is telling suggests another, countering theme: that in fact his native city was open to an array of outside cultural influences that gave him, and his musical colleagues, both the materials and the audience to begin a popular music phenomenon. In interviews he announced refreshingly, 'Let me tell you I'm not ashamed of being middle class, in fact middle-class morality suits me fine', but his autobiography underplays his cosmopolitan and sophisticated ancestral background: Belgian entrepreneurs who created one of Dublin's legendary restaurants.[12] Similar evasions apply to the background of the band in general, two of whom were from creative sectors of the Protestant middle class. Geldof's return from Canada in 1975 was the catalyst; when he refers to the Boom Town Rats' first punk intervention as the equivalent of 'Luther nailing his theses on the church door',[13] he may be making a characteristically mordant joke on a number of levels, though the creative interaction of popular music in Dublin and the socio-political developments of the 1960s were already well established.[14] And even though he produced an album called *A Tonic for the Troops* in 1978, the North does not feature. It had its own experimental musical scene, memorably in Derry with the come-and-go phenomenon of the Undertones, and its own world-class troubadour in Van Morrison. Partitionism ruled in this as in less rarefied spheres.

But Geldof dominates, as the late-twentieth-century Irish icon who achieved global status by using his formidable abilities and influence to attack global issues: and his articulacy, sharply focused analysis and effective political interventions contrast dramatically with the woolliness and mysticism of so many of his contemporaries, just as his music contrasts with the Celtic fantasies of the world-conquering Enya, who started out as a traditional Irish singer with a family group. The 'Celticization' of Irish popular music began in the fusion experiments of the 1970s and earlier. Modes of traditional music were 'revised' from the late 1960s in the folk-rock movement. Horslips' album *The Book of Invasions* used not only a title from medieval Gaelic literature but the musical phrasing of Seán Ó Riada. At first their enterprise was – as the music critic Bill Graham put it – to act as 'interpreters . . . translating for an audience whose experience of their Irish identity doesn't conform to the value-system ordained by their education or Radio Éireann'.[15] But this took hold, and even the gritty and urban Phil Lynott transposed folk elements into some of his most successful songs. By the end of the 1970s Planxty and their imitators had established modes whereby Irish music could be defined for a new era, a period that also saw the infusion of a political element (usually Republicanism Lite). U2 defined themselves differently, sharply distancing themselves from NORAID supporters on their American tours: Bono famously threw back a proffered tricolour at a New Jersey audience while singing 'Sunday Bloody Sunday', shouting 'All I see is fucking red.'[16] The politics faded, Horslips entered history, but by the twenty-first century Enya became the most-played musician in the world, conquering the air waves in every muzak situation from sitting in a plane before take-off to pushing a trolley around a shopping mall. Finally, her ethereal adaptability provided the soundtrack for the most frequent televised replay of the World Trade Center's apocalyptic detonation. Irishness had gone global once more.

The phenomenon of popular Irish music in the wider world relied upon its exploitation of a post-modern notion of 'Celticism' (though the concept remains problematic for ethnologists and prehistorians). Thus Van Morrison's world success came through exploitation of *this* note, rather than the edgy Belfast fusion of blues music and baroque Dylanism that made his Irish name. Modern Irish cultural modes, however, remain closely intertwined with American influences, batted back and forth across the Atlantic with bewildering ease. Bill Whelan and Michael Flatley's world-conquering *Riverdance* stage show in the 1990s eradicated the solemn liturgy imposed on traditional Irish dance by de Valera's cultural commissars, substituting the razzle-dazzle of Busby Berkeley and Broadway hoofers.[17] (The succeeding shows, *Lord of the Dance* and *Celtic Tiger*, pursued another American tradition, by plundering Irish history to dredge up the deepest levels of kitsch.) The influence of American soul music in Ireland has been profound, as has the effect of deracinated gospel modes; here again the effect of Protestant revivalism on U2's cultural formation represents a less expected variety of Irishness. Singers like Mary Black have hit another kind of jackpot by updating showband sentimentality and selling it back to the Americans. Black's own words present a practised spiel of psychobabble, which would not be out of place in an IDA advertisement luring foreign investors to make money in Ireland.

There is a purity about Irish music, a purity which modern people of the middle generation yearn for and which they have lost somewhere between their own childhood and the place they are now. I think that people today long for melodies, sweet melodies. And since they often can't find them in modern, international music, they turn to Irish music instead.[18]

'Sweet melodies' might not be immediately associated with the Pogues, playing on expatriate Irishness and showing a near-genius for travesty; but, like *Riverdance* and its successors, they have used this mode to repel modernity, divide consciousness (or suspend disbelief) in their listeners and conquer. Shane MacGowan declares a wish to have joined the IRA in its glory days of the 1970s, retails a skewed version of Irish history, writes off Shaw and Yeats as 'not really Irish' (i.e., Protestant) and finally celebrates the Irish as 'the best race in the world'.[19] Some of us may feel that we have been here before.

I I

All these aspects of the musical revolution, like other transformations over the last thirty years of the twentieth century, are inseparably linked with the marketing of Irishness. By 1998 Ireland's music industry was presented by An Bord Tráchtála (dealing with Irish exports) as one of the magnets attracting tourists to the country, cited by up to 80 per cent of incomers as a primary reason for their visit.[20] The history of Irish tourism, in its many aspects, is an under-researched story, too often retailed simply as institutional history.[21] Bord Fáilte (the Tourist Board) counts for a great deal more than that. The way Ireland has been sold over the last thirty years is part of modern Irish culture and has rebounded upon the island itself in the shape of pre-ordained and received images of history-as-kitsch, existing alongside the real achievements of Irish high culture in the late twentieth century. Thus the astonishingly fabricated notion of the Irish pub, created from Singapore (where there are three) to San Francisco, drawing from a literal storehouse of catalogued bric-à-brac that would never be seen in an Irish pub in Ireland but that can be ordered on from the chosen franchiser and installed: churns, whiskey jars, clay pipes, scythes, horse collars, old-style Bakelite telephones, pre-kilometre road signs, along with fake foodstuffs packaged in 1950s wrappings. The company that provides these, 'Interiors Trading Company', of Finglas, deals in salvage and reproduction – the latter, it seems, taking over from the former. Part of the interior is a fantasy on an eighteenth-century cottage, part on a rural grocery store: supposedly totemic objects are stacked up haphazardly in a homage to history as bricolage, summoning up a nostalgia for something that never was. Four different companies operate franchises for Irish pubs worldwide, dictating basic design layouts: the 'Victorian', the 'Cottage', the 'Gaelic'. The last, significantly, is conceived of as 'evoking Irish history'. These places exist in Abu Dhabi, Reykjavik and Shanghai, an empire embracing more than forty-two countries. Now they are starting to appear in Ireland as well.[22]

The synthesized Irish pub is almost too ready a metaphor, and should be seen against a developing exploitation of Irish imagery since the 1960s. In that decade, tourist imagery was monopolized by the brilliantly coloured images of John Hinde's postcards (now much analysed by cultural historians, and marvellously mocked by the montages of the artist Seán Hillen). But from the late 1960s, when so much began, advertising agencies were given a new brief on selling Ireland: a country where the past sustained a continuing dimension, in the sense that privilege still awaited the modern tourist ready to step out of time. In full-page advertisements in the new colour supplements, country-house lawns and silver tea services replaced bog roads as the promised Ireland at the end of an Aer Lingus flight. Accommodation was either in a castle or a simple but perfect farmhouse: either way, unobtrusive service and splendid food was guaranteed. Horses also seemed magically omnipresent and available. This was made all the more explicit for American visitors. 'The hills are as green as they've always been. Life is as quiet as it ever was. And time has a way of standing still. Let Pan-Am take you there.' Pan-Am has gone the way of several American corporate giants invited into Ireland, but the hype lingers on. There was, confusingly, a deliberate intention (according to an account executive at the firm that repackaged Ireland from the late 1960s) also to prove that Ireland was actually luxurious.[23] And it was going to prove that antiquity could mean fun: 'Ireland: the Ancient Birthplace of Good Times'. And, following time-honoured tradition, it was going to rerun historical images. The principal campaign was to revolve around two themes, 'Invaders' and 'Humour'. Ireland, seductively portrayed, had been found 'irresistible' by 'the Vikings – the Normans – the Saxons'. 'So think what a grand time we'd show you. Especially since you'd be the only ones of the lot we actually invited.' The follow-up advertisements stress what was not yet called 'the craic'. But that, of course, was to come.

The notion of at least one misguided commentator that Ireland's modern tourist identity is the result of colonizing images 'projected onto an Irish screen by English visitors . . . [teaching] Irish people habits of silence and subservience' is hilariously wide of the mark.[24] Ireland, in fact, has been hailed as one of the first countries to consciously and professionally manage its brand image.[25] Government spending on tourism, frequently attacked as inadequate up to the 1960s, increased exponentially from the 1970s. Even as early as 1965 joint tourist initiatives featured high on the Lemass–O'Neill agenda. Larger and larger grants were made available for tourist accommodation, which shot up from £30 million in 1983, while development funds increased from £4.75 million to £14 million.[26] This was encouraged by flurries of market research. The 1988 *Programme for National Recovery* mounted a major offensive, with tax incentives, grants and EU support. By 1993, £770 million had been invested over five years, an amount nearly equalled over the next five-year period. While a considerable proportion came from EU regional funds, it also represented a high government priority. Bord Fáilte's 'Brand Ireland' campaign in the 1990s (which alone swallowed up £30 million) merely formalized something that had been invented a generation before: the presentation of Ireland as a combination of friendly people, beautiful scenery and a leisurely pace of life.

The tourist marketing organizations of countries as diverse as

Greece, New Zealand and Spain have taken note and followed suit in terms of redefining their country's public personality and pushing it upmarket. And Bord Fáilte's campaigns succeeded, bringing profitable tourism to a degree not yet envisaged in the late 1960s. By the mid 1990s the growth in Irish tourism was twice that of the OECD average, creating an income that had trebled since the mid eighties.[27] After being shuttled around between various government departments, the 'industry' had its own ministry from 1977. Though it would be variously linked over the next thirty years to Transport, Sport and the Arts, it clearly outranked all. Although part of the profits generated came from selling fantasy to well-off escapists, the real profits came not from sectors who stayed in castles or rode to hounds but from those who followed the kind of tourist trail established long before, and were drawn by long-existent family ties, a sort of chain-emigration-in-reverse. This syndrome was recognized in the 1990s by a series of cloying 'Welcome Home' initiatives, greeting bemused arriving tourists as if they were all returned emigrants. None the less, the lure of a re-created history and a sophisticated cultural 'package' remains potently seductive. A 1995 Bord Fáilte market-research report asserted that Ireland was seen among Continental Europeans as 'a saved country and culture undisturbed by European history – a mythical island – a real and authentic destination that could offer escapism and freedom', and a similar survey seven years later suggested that this still held good. The chief expert in the field has robustly described the image of Ireland created by the Literary Revival as a 'great brand vision' that, whatever its lack of reality, has remained for marketing purposes a self-fulfilling prophecy.[28] This was cleverly combined with a kind of salvage ethnography – the presentation of Ireland as the location of exoticism and purity on the western edge of Europe.

Accordingly, a certain amount of sanitizing was observed early on. Bord Fáilte was displeased by the American Muriel Rukeyser's account of the annual three-day Puck Fair at Killorglin, County Kerry, published in 1965 and roundly called *The Orgy*. Once bitten, the government's magazine *Ireland of the Welcomes* cautioned a writer on the same subject: 'only stress those aspects of Puck Fair which are universally acceptable as attractions.'[29] From the late 1960s more 'acceptable' festivals were highlighted instead: oysters in Galway, films in Cork, opera in Wexford, theatre in Dublin and Irish womanhood (genteelly known as 'Roses') in Tralee. In 1970 the Dublin tourist authorities began turning St Patrick's Day into a week-long 'festival', much influenced by American ideas.[30] Meanwhile, as has been rather sourly pointed out, 'The Hidden Ireland' has changed its meaning. A phrase coined by Daniel Corkery in 1924 to describe the life of the oppressed and dispossessed Gaelic intellectuals in eighteenth-century Ireland now supplies the title of a lavish booklet advertising 'accommodation in private heritage homes'.[31]

Yet the associated emblems have a way of declaring their own independent and subversive life. Though the horse continued to be a kind of ur-symbol of Irishness, by the end of the twentieth century this had taken a new twist. Hundreds of the animals roamed the sink housing estates of Dublin's perimeter (at least until the Dáil passed the Control of Horses Act, 1996), creating new urban myths such as the horse stuck in the lift in the film *Into the West*. This, however, was as contrary to the marketed images of Ireland in the USA as the controversy over the participation of Irish gay organizations in the New York St Patrick's Day Parade. These contraventions have their place in any analysis of how Irish images and stereotypes were marketed and adapted in the later twentieth century. Similarly, by an enormous irony, the use of an idealized elite view of the Irish past, in the new-look tourism offensive mounted by Bord Fáilte and Aer Lingus from the late 1960s, coincided with the beginning of an era that would see an assault on the actual historical fabric of Ireland's environmental and architectural heritage by the forces of 'development' and new money. The archaic Ireland that foreigners were being tempted to revisit was in considerable danger of destruction.

The re-formation in 1958 of the Irish Georgian Society was followed by the development of An Taisce (founded in 1948 as a 'National Trust for Ireland' but without a statutory role), and the eventual creation of An Foras Forbartha (the National Institute for Planning Board) and Dúchas, an organization for protection of the historic environment. Though the last two were conceived of as organizations to protect national heritage, much of the impetus was voluntarist. Decisive intervention finally came from protest movements started by the academic and student communities, as Dublin's streetscapes were toppled by 1960s and 1970s development, and provincial architecture sacrificed to road schemes and developing agribusiness. And here too we encounter the uses of history as rhetoric, with Kevin Boland declaring that preservationist societies were the preserve of 'the idle rich and belted earls', and that the eighteenth-century terraces of Hume Street and their like represented colonial oppression and should be eradicated.[32] Charles Haughey was equally prepared to profit from land development, but none the less determined to live in a Georgian mansion designed by James Gandon. Haughey's ideas about Dublin's preservation tended to vary; he was sympathetic to the campaign to try to stop a dual-carriageway through the Liberties and, as one of Ahern's best Malapropisms had it, deserves the credit for 'turning Temple Bar into Dublin's West Bank'.[33] The vicissitudes of preservation, and the casual attitude to architectural and archaeological heritage, remain a fascinating and often depressing barometer of Irish attitudes to the past. Thirty years on the party of Haughey and Boland axed An Foras Forbartha, turned Dúchas into a powerless 'advisory' body under another name and pioneered a 'one-stop' development process to drastically curtail the examination of planning applications and force through large-scale road schemes. Meanwhile illegal structures in places of outstanding beauty were either tacitly allowed to stand or retrospectively legalized. From the 1970s Bord Fáilte joined forces with An Taisce to produce a series of reports suggesting the use of vernacular styles in building, and the preservation of sensitive sites and location, but they fell on stony ground – or on earth already being ripped open by the teeth of the ubiquitous 'digger'. Most symbolically of all, by the early twenty-first century the green light was given to a huge motorway exchange within 1,000 metres of the Hill of Tara, carving a corridor through 141 archaeological sites.[34] Against an outcry from academics and scholars that rapidly became international, the Department of the Environment's chief archaeologist maintained the Panglossian line that 'it could be argued that the M3 will be a monument of major significance in the future and be seen as a continuation of the pattern of route development through the valley'.[35] The notion of continuity in Irish history can be put to some very special uses indeed.

Another kind of continuity was discernible in the number of local landowners and consortia set to make fortunes from the scheme, and in their political connections to the various authorities responsible. In a despairing state-of-the-environment survey by Frank McDonald and James Nix, photograph succeeds photograph showing grinning local councillors whose family farmland has fortuitously been rezoned for light industrial development or a 'retail outlet village', while unplanned suburban sprawl and one-off concrete haciendas invade the countryside still resolutely presented as Arcadia by Bord Fáilte and the IDA. Eamon Ó Cuiv, minister for community, rural and Gaeltacht affairs, was able to produce another useful Celticist argument, stating that his 'vision of rural Ireland is a populated countryside' and advocating 'the Celtic plan of dispersed settlement' rather than 'forcing people' into towns and villages. Moreover, people with 'local connections' should effectively be allowed to build where they like, a principle enshrined by a Kerry councillor as his people's 'God-given right to build on their own land'. Attempts to raise issues of historical artefacts, groundwater, sewage systems, car reliance, vernacular housing and noise pollution were written off as elitism, snobbery and – worse – 'a fundamental lack of perspective on what life is about'.[36] Plans for decentralization of government services, and attempts to establish Limerick, Cork or Waterford as alternative metropolitan foci, were abandoned or came to grief in clientelist politicking, as the population figures for Dublin headed towards 40 per cent of the state as a whole. Meanwhile, especially from the 1970s, the abuse of the coastal environment continued, with ribbon development of single dwellings. An attempt in the 1990s to impose guidelines on clustered building, and to encourage vernacular modes in house design, has been tacitly abandoned.

But there remain the consolations of historical symbolism as 'branding'. The names of the house models in a guide called 'Plan-A-Home Ireland' are redolent of a history that never was.[37] 'Inishfree' [sic] actually has a thatched roof; 'Inishlacken' 'seamlessly juxtaposes a modern fully glazed sun lounge to a traditional style cottage'; 'Sherkin', 'Inishboffin', 'Rathlin', 'Inishdooey', 'Little Skellig', even 'Saint Macdara' nod towards history and geography in their names but never in their aesthetics. This is reminiscent of the way that, over the last generation, Irish people have been taught to read their own history through folk parks and heritage centres. These may become all that is left. After decades of caution about exploiting Ireland's astonishingly well-preserved but fragile historic sites and buildings, the 1960s ushered in a new approach. These often stemmed from what Eric Zuelow has called the 'late-night epiphanies' of the Minister, Erskine Childers, prone to firing off post-prandial letters at odd hours to his taoiseach, Seán Lemass, envisioning a missionary museum at Glendalough or a folk park at Muckross. Despite the tight-fistedness of the Department of Finance, and the sardonicism of Lemass, the latter project actually came to pass and became an enduring success. As with the transformation of Kilmainham Jail into a museum, local enthusiasm and voluntary effort had much to do with the outcome. But in the next generation the ambitious and sophisticated developments at Newgrange or the 1798 Centre at Enniscorthy relied on more affluent sources from the government and the EU, following consciously evolved policies pioneered by Bord Fáilte from the late 1980s. The part that the commemoration boom in the 1990s played in the political construction of history deserves remembering here.[38] Iconography and memory have become new subjects of analysis, as well as new buzz words; in a sense this is simply the contemporary version of that ancient Irish discourse of shaping history to immediate purposes. In the Ireland of the Celtic Tiger, this has taken new and vivid forms, linked to the advances of media technology and the popularity of public spectacle – often at the expense of historical evidence and analysis. Meanwhile the actual historical environment is too often desecrated or buried under a folk park. Just as the Celtic Tiger began to roar, this was foreseen in Dermot Bolger's visionary 1990 novel *The Journey Home* by one of the disaffected protagonists drifting through the lost city, alternately suburb and slum.

I can see it, Cait . . . a city ringed by golf clubs. Exclusive restaurants between the green canals, sporadic insurrections still in the shanty towns. The crowd of youth not dispersed by water cannon but by the bored cameraman finally screwing the cover over the lens. Out here electric fences will hum in the evenings, crackling when a stray dog stumbles against them. In the white pillar beside the solid wooden gates an intercom will wait for messages.

Motorists gliding silently through the woodlands, the drone of French and Dutch over the car telephones.

And the chosen million Irish left: red-haired girls bringing menus to diners in the converted castles, at one end of the scale; at the other, middle-ranking civil servants who will close their eyes at night, knowing that once we could have stood up as equals, not been bought out like children by the quick lure of grants.[39]

III

All these developments are preserved and crystallized in the Irish fiction of the era since 1970; and that fiction was itself transforming. In 1985 Colm Tóibín noted that Irish history was traditionally seen as a linkage of short stories, emblematizing bravery, tragedy and romance but providing no continuity and no legacy. 'How can the novel flourish in such a world? The novel explores psychology, sociology, the individual consciousness; the novel finds a form and a language for these explorations. We require an accepted world for the novel to flourish, a shared sense of time and place.'[40] He went on to examine the tradition of experiment, fracture and evasion in Irish fiction: the only contemporary Irish novelists to succeed did so, he asserted, 'in a manner that was experimental, personal and innovative'. Tóibín instanced Francis Stuart, Aidan Higgins, Sebastian Barry, John Banville and John McGahern, who worked with strategies derived from Joyce, Flann O'Brien and Beckett – and in the process denied themselves an audience, which did not, in any case, exist in Ireland.

There was no audience here for such books. It was not just that Ireland did not offer a shelter between history and destiny for the novelists to pitch their tents, thus causing them to write at one remove from what was happening. But there was no-one to read the books, no set of educated, curious, open-minded literate people. It should not be assumed that censorship did not deeply affect what was written and in what style it was written during this period. The result was a tradition of the novel that was clever, inventive and self-obsessed.

Tóibín's essay called on Irish writers to explore themes taken up, for their own countries, by African and South American novelists:

Displacement, cultural deprivation, violence, post-colonial deracination and all the other things that were put in train the moment the white man came raiding down the valley have become the material for a great tradition in fiction. A fiction in which the country itself, Ireland, South Africa, Peru, Nigeria, lurks between the lines, nagging at the characters, a strange and insistent protagonist. It is a fiction which we have yet to explore seriously in Ireland.

The way in which Tóibín would make Ireland, and Irish history, feature in his own fiction was characteristically subtle and did not, as it turned out, directly follow his own prescription. He was then finishing his own first novel, *The South*, long in the making and an astonishingly assured debut. Tóibín used an unlikely and in some ways dislikable central character to express the confinement and repression of Irish artistic life before the 1960s. A woman artist from a vaguely snobbish provincial Protestant background leaves her husband and child to become a painter in Spain, returning at the novel's end to recognition in an Ireland whose cultural and psychological boundaries are cautiously widening. Irish antipathies, memories and repressions are counterpointed against a portrait of rural Catalonia in the same era; but 'the South' also implicitly stands for the twenty-six-county state that she has left.

When in 1990 the novel was published, to considerable acclaim, Tóibín was already well known as a journalist; he had been a crusading editor of *Magill* in the 1980s and had in 1987 published an intense and subtle account of a walk along the Irish border, from Derry to Carlingford Lough, undertaken in 1986. The Anglo-Irish Agreement was then very recent history, and so were a number of terrible sectarian murders perpetrated in the terrain he was traversing. The characteristic combination of intensity and detachment that Tóibín brought to his observations on the people and places he encountered was later criticized by some of his cruder critics, but at this remove *Walking Along the Border* (later republished as *Bad Blood*) stands (like Dervla Murphy's *A Place Apart* fifteen years earlier) as a key testament to cultural difference as well as a profound recognition of the subterranean pull of violence in the Irish historical current. Tóibín's view is essentially 'Southern', and his negotiation of the local cultures in the disputed land he travels already suggests the kind of novelist he would become.

So did his more conventional investigative journalism. On *Magill* he was responsible for some major features researching the Irish state and its power structures. One of these pieces concerned the judiciary; in a series of meticulously researched articles he presented the backgrounds, politics and legal philosophies of the men who both practised and made the law in Ireland's courts, and analysed the importance of the Supreme Court in setting precedents and responding to constitutional challenges.[41] The links to his second novel are clear. In 1992 he published *The Heather Blazing*, a slow-burning study of a middle-aged Irish judge coping with changing mores in the society around him and within his own family. The most haunting passages carry him back to his Wexford youth, lived against a background of devout Catholicism, heartfelt Fianna Fáil values and early bereavement. It is a matchless evocation of small-town life in the 1940s, seen through the eyes of a sensitive and conventional boy who will be more imprisoned by it than he knows. Over all hangs the memory of lived history, in the form of the 1798 Rising (invoked in the novel's title) and the later Troubles of 1919–22, imbibed through the memories of his parents' generation and atmospherically conveyed in the treatment of the 1951 general election. Later, as a judge, he would advise the Irish government of 1972 how to combat the revived IRA with non-jury courts. 'The north, he argued, must be presented as a different society, a place apart.'[42] The political and emotional inconsistencies of one man's life stand for the state. While Tóibín's later fiction extended his canvas audaciously, the themes of repression, memory and inherited politics would survive; and so would Ireland as a 'strange and insistent protagonist'.

Meanwhile, the call to reflect the new Ireland in a new way was taken up by other writers, notably Dermot Bolger, whose importance both as entrepreneur and writer was decisive. Bolger's small presses, Raven Arts and New Island, were responsible for presenting the work of his generation to an Irish audience, while his own novels such as *The Woman's Daughter* (1987), *The Journey Home* (1990) and *A*

Second Life (1994) confronted the dislocations of the new Irish urban existence, and the ghosts of memory with the weapons and insights of Dublin counter-culture. In the inner suburbs of North Dublin, Bolger declared, there existed a world

neither country nor city – these streets possessed no place in the school books and poems we learnt at our wooden desks … This aspect of Irish life, despite being an everyday reality for an increasingly large percentage of the population, was almost totally absent from Irish writing until recently … It is only in the post-1968 generation that the confidence to remain true to ordinary modern urban experience around them finally begins to be displayed.[43]

This was not before time. Well into the 1970s, to judge by the intermittently brilliant pages of journals like *Crane Bag*, the preoccupation continued with Yeats, Beckett, Joyce and O'Brien, and interviews were sought abroad with Marcuse, Ricœur and Chomsky, even as a different local world grew and hardened beneath the surface. Similarly, the world of pastoral remained dominant in Irish fiction and poetry. Cultural critics such as the influential Richard Kearney (a founder of *Crane Bag*) astutely noted the conflict between tradition and modernity early on; and those, such as Bolger, who self-consciously asserted new directions would sometimes attract attack as 'liberal post-nationalists', enmeshed in their own variety of self-deception and waging 'a war against the past'.[44] Certainly while drugs, alienation and unemployment ravage Bolger's characters, they are also – most specifically in *The Journey Home* – the victims of power structures erected by the winners of Irish history. It was inevitable that Irish writers would exploit the post-modern collage, the stew of skewed references, manifested in the liberalization of Irish culture and the breakdown of traditional barriers; but, in doing so, they have also exploited traditional modes of Irish remembering. In this, both Tóibín and Bolger stand for a new direction in Irish fiction.

Anthony Giddens has described identity as founded upon 'the capacity to keep a certain narrative going'.[45] Examinations of identity have kept Irish cultural commentary in business over the last thirty years, while the narratives of Irish life have changed dramatically, often by incorporating sexual confession as transmitted by the mass media. Novelists inevitably profited by this. There is even a case for arguing that the transformations of the late twentieth century actually enabled the Irish novel formally to transcend the inhibitions that had restricted it until then. By the dawning of the twenty-first century, as George O'Brien has it, 'the Irish novel – long the poor relation of our literary family, the resort of exiles, eccentrics and other misfits including the not infrequent crawthumper; occasion of the censor's official repression for its representations of resistance to repression, official and otherwise; by virtue of formal insecurity and thematic ambivalence the very image of a quaking sod – is now the elephant in the room.'[46] This was not an exaggeration. Up to the 1970s it seemed that the Irish excelled at the Chekhovian short story. The tradition of Sean O'Faolain and Frank O'Connor was sustained by Mary Lavin, Bryan MacMahon and others. When Hubert Butler was writing short stories in the 1940s, his friend Sean O'Faolain pressed him to try a longer form of fiction, in which he could combine objectivity and pride about the world he came from. 'Most people writing about your world are objective as to its comic aspects but not the other; or the other, and not objective. It needs a Gogol. Are you dotty enough to be a Gogol? I wish you were!'[47] By the 1960s there was still no resident Irish Gogol. Oddly, to produce a sustained stream of achieved novels, it seemed that an Irish writer had to live largely somewhere else, like Joyce Cary, Kate O'Brien, Brian Moore, William Trevor and Elizabeth Bowen, while domestic products like John Broderick somehow withered on the vine; Edna O'Brien started in Ireland, in the 1960s, but left, after shocking Charles Haughey. The practical issues of the Censorship Board, and the structures of the publishing industry, provide some practical explanations, but there also seems to have been a certain question of psychological reluctance. Sean O'Faolain summed it up by claiming that there was no such thing as the Irish novel.[48]

From the 1970s this changed. To take only high-profile examples from the Republic, John Banville, Colm Tóibín, Anne Enright, Roddy Doyle, Patrick McCabe and Eoin McNamee have each produced an œuvre that has gained international recognition and shows no sign of slackening; Banville, Doyle and Tóibín are regulars on the major prize shortlists, and others will follow them. In Northern Ireland, Robert

McLiam Wilson and Glenn Patterson are equally confident and equally prolific, while the less well-known David Park has produced perhaps the most accomplished and haunting fiction about public and private violence in the North. McLiam Wilson imagines Belfast itself as a novel, much as Bolger had done earlier for Dublin. 'The city's surface is thick with its living citizens. Its earth is sown with its many dead. The city is a repository of novels, of stories, present tense, past tense or future. The city is a novel.'[49] But a violent past is not in itself a condition of creativity, and the conditions out of which the great Northern literary renaissance began, most obviously in poetry, constitute another question. It is worth pointing out that, in the cases of Derek Mahon, Michael Longley, Seamus Heaney, Tom Paulin, Paul Muldoon and others, the conditioning and background to their work is by no means bounded by living in the six counties of Northern Ireland, and that with several of them experience of life in the Republic plays a large part.

With Heaney, the borders have been extended more widely still. The title of the collection that conferred his unique authority was *North*, and its publication in 1975 has been hailed as a defining moment in modern poetic development, like Eliot's publication of *Prufrock*. From this point on, the way that 'the North' could be written about was changed. The controlled violence of Heaney's language can still shock and sometimes jar. Though his favourite methods and metaphors continued to evoke the underground and the implicit, there was no doubt that he was conveying the way violence and cultural antipathies are encoded into society. A later, greater work, *Station Island*, extended the themes of historical haunting but also proclaimed artistic commitment and the ambiguities of independence. By the time of his Nobel Prize in 1995 Heaney had attained with apparent effortlessness an international status: occupying chairs at Harvard and Oxford, looking as closely to Mandelstam and Milosz as to Kavanagh and MacNeice, and recolonizing English poetry with a phenomenal version of *Beowulf*. Along the way he had inherited Yeats's ability to relate the personal to the political, and to discipline experience into formal shape, without becoming an 'official' voice. His authority within Irish culture rested partly on the range and scale of his work; but, unlike Yeats's, it existed against the background of an extraordinary period of achievement by other Irish poets, most of whose work is neither inhibited by nor imitative of his own formidable authority. This is particularly true of his contemporaries Michael Longley and Derek Mahon, strikingly confident and original in their own work and achieving international recognition in their own right, but it applies to the younger generation as well.

North and South, the achievement of Irish literature over a concentrated period since the sixties has been generally noted but never very convincingly explained. Believers in 'liberation psychology' explain Irish creativity as an offshoot of 'systems of domination such as colonialism, where there are so few opportunities in political and economic spheres . . . creativity offers a vehicle for self-expression and advancement'; but this is related, predictably, to 'carnival and coded ballads', not to reverent reviews in the *New York Review of Books* or appearances on the major literary prize lists.[50] The liberationists also employ the popular argument that 'the loss of the native language and the experiences of poverty and anti-Irish racism compounded the traumas of famine and prevented survivors from healing or expressing their grief and other emotions', but it is not clear where this fits in with creative fluency; and indeed the whole question of 'memory suppression' in this area has been comprehensively scouted by scholars such as Cormac Ó Gráda and Niall Ó Ciosáin.[51]

Historians might prefer to look at developments in education at second and third level since the 1960s (North and South); the relaxation of censorship; perhaps too the passing of a generation since the deaths of Joyce and Yeats, who in their respective disciplines had left such extraordinary and inhibiting legacies (Austin Clarke compared it to growing up under the shadow of a huge oak tree). The arrival of a distinct and conscious feminist presence in literary criticism and literary production after 1970 is also vitally important.[52] The confidence, originality and bravura of the new Irish writing is undeniable. None the less, as Joe Cleary has sharply pointed out, the style, subject and setting of Irish literature can be 'modernized' without disturbing established narrative codes (the great success of Martin McDonagh's pastiche plays about Irish violence are just one example).[53] And what is still striking is the power and suggestiveness of historical themes in the creative literature – dramatic as well as fictional and poetic – that has poured out of Ireland over the last thirty-odd years. Even in the work of apparent traditionalists such as John McGahern, Jennifer Johnston and William Trevor, past Irish politics play a subtle but unmistakable part both in the destinies and the psychology of their protagonists. Starting with *A Star Called Henry*, Roddy Doyle alternated his colourful imagined world of 'Barrytown' (working-class North Dublin again) with novels about Irish history. Sebastian Barry's plays and novels are beginning to look like a sustained meditation on the Irish past as seen through the experience of pariahs and out-groups (emigrant navvies, island Protestant sects, ex-policemen in the Free State, transvestite colonial medical officers). John Banville began his glittering literary career by parodying the Big House memoirs of the turn of the century, swerved into the fictionalized histories of transgressive European intellectuals and scientists, and then set himself to the Ireland of GUBU, founding one of his most brilliant novels on the murder scandal that helped bring down Haughey's government and creating a sinister Conradian character sustained through successive books. This last group of novels moves the action to a particular kind of surreal landscape that may be christened Banvilleland but sometimes has odd echoes of Iris Murdoch territory – a novelist who latterly has herself been claimed as 'Irish'. Eoin McNamee uses dark corners of recent Ulster history to produce *film noir* novels like *Resurrection Man*, *The Blue Tango* and *The Ultras*. Anne Enright moved from a surreal take on modern suburban Dublin (*The Portable Virgin*, *The Wig My Father Wore*) to a meditation on the life of the nineteenth-century Irish adventuress Eliza Lynch: her forte remains the secret sexual histories encoded within families. Emma Donoghue has similarly looted eighteenth-century history for her recent work, after coming to attention as the fictional chronicler of Irish lesbian liberation. Colm Tóibín and Dermot Bolger, as has been seen, have consciously set themselves the task of redefining the connections between present crisis and imagined past. Irish novelists in the last generation have claimed attention for their experimentation, their confidence, their readiness to extend boundaries of gender and nation (McLiam Wilson's *Eureka Street* does this in a highly deliberate way, patterned against the political breakthroughs and realignments of the late 1990s). But history remains the preoccupation.

Something of the same holds true for Irish drama, which has asserted a presence abroad unparalleled since the Abbey's first flush a hundred years ago, and in their variety, authority and originality the playwrights of the late twentieth century have equalled their predecessors. But the overarching theme remains history and its negotiations. This is strikingly true of the most famous plays of the last thirty years: Brian Friel's *Translations*, Sebastian Barry's *The Steward of Christendom* and Frank McGuinness's *Observe the Sons of Ulster Marching towards the Somme*. These should be seen as only part of each playwright's achievement: Barry's early *Prayers of Sherkin* was a revelation to other writers, especially Tóibín, and Friel's greatest play, *Faith Healer*, is neither political nor obviously historical, though it deals – like much of Tom Murphy's remarkable œuvre – with displacement and loss against an abandoned Irish background. The protagonist of Murphy's 1985 masterpiece *Bailegangaire* has stayed in 'traditional' Ireland, which she herself (an old woman storyteller) represents; but the windows of her cottage are raked by the headlights of endless traffic, and a Japanese computer plant is closing down in her village. Much in the late-twentieth-century Irish dramatic renaissance paid deliberate homage to the achievements of a century before, especially the work of Synge. Contemporary Irish history is less obviously appealing as a theme, apart from Barry's controversial *Hinterland* of 2002, which used the theme of Charles Haughey's disgraced last years as the framework for a meditation on fame, corruption and family. Barry's eerie capturing of what Fintan O'Toole called Haughey's 'absurd grandiosity and half-comic savagery' caught the public attention far more than the Shakespearean echoes infused by the playwright: 'GUBU Roi', remarked one literate Dublin wit. In another echo back to the Literary Revival, the debate staged in the auditorium after the opening performance recalled the furies aroused by *The Plough and the Stars* or *The Playboy of the Western World*.

A preoccupation with the past was less obvious in Irish film. Neil Jordan's *Michael Collins*, which used past history to suggestive contemporary effect at the time of the peace process, became in itself a kind of cultural phenomenon – in Ireland at least. Jordan was the most prominent and prolific director of his generation, and his work reached a belated apogee in the age of the Celtic Tiger. The two Oscars won by actors in Jim Sheridan's *My Left Foot* in 1990 inaugurated a decade when films made in Ireland by Irish directors finally predominated over those that simply used the country as a location, with bit parts played by actors recruited from the Abbey. The success of Jordan, Sheridan and Thaddeus O'Sullivan in Britain and the USA was accompanied by a proliferation of new young directors in Ireland itself, often using the dissonances and dislocations of modern Irish life to produce richly original and parodic interpretations. This direction had been signalled earlier by directors like Bob Quinn, Kieran Hickey, Joe Comerford, Cathal Black and Pat Murphy, who had started out in harder times. None of these developments would have been possible without state aid. An Bord Scannán (the Irish Film Board) was formally established in 1981 and then promptly cut back in the economic crisis of the mid eighties. Revived in 1993 with a far larger budget, it was further stimulated by tax breaks luring foreign film producers to Ireland. As Irish actors and directors became established and even famous, the whole subject of Irish film created an academic industry on the model, if not the scale, of those that have formed like coral reefs around Irish literature and drama. It may prove in time more alluring to students than either of these predecessors.

Analysing what has mediated and enabled this wave of successful and internationally acclaimed creativity should be a question for future historians, as it is a question for historians of the Irish Literary Revival exactly a century before. As with that revival, the roots may be seen to stretch further back than generally thought; and, as with that revival, the simple nuts-and-bolts facts of educational opportunity, publishing mechanics (and economics), circles of literary influence and international accessibility all play their part. So do devoted individual entrepreneurs like Dermot Bolger, who first put people like McNamee and Fintan O'Toole between hard covers. So, vitally, did Haughey's introduction of generous tax-free incomes to artists and even – in the form of Aosdána – a salaried academy for the elite. But it must also be noted that, just as a hundred years ago, the major literary market remains London. For all the growth of small Irish publishing houses since the 1980s, there has not been a commensurate increase in, for instance, the profession of literary agents or heavyweight reviewing outlets. Here too the historical parallel with the world Yeats knew is very striking. The difference is that the productivity is taking place within Ireland, while the phenomenon of the expatriate writer has dwindled. Or returned to base: J. M. McNeill published two brilliant studies of the twilight life of the London-Irish (*Open Cut* and *Duffy is Dead*) before returning to live in Ireland and write – of course – historical novels.

Where the Irish language fitted in to all this remains a matter of dispute. The Language Freedom Movement, founded in 1966, was much reviled by traditionalists but insisted on airing the arguments against the traditional policy of compulsory Irish in schools, and the traditional doublethink. In 1988 a Bord na Gaeilge report squarely admitted the divisiveness of the old approach:

The changes in the nature and structure of our society over the last quarter of a century have been so dramatic that the previous mobilising rhetorics do not operate in the same way, or as effectively in the past. The ways in which earlier understandings became incorporated into Irish national life have not turned out to have been entirely beneficial to the language. They have encouraged a widening gap between the symbolic significance attached to Irish as an official emblem of national identity, and its use as a richly expressive vernacular in everyday life.[54]

But by then another sign of divergence between North and South was that over the same period the nationalist symbolism and commitment bound up in speaking Irish had been reinforced in Northern Ireland, with the development of a Gaeltacht and Irish-speaking schools in West Belfast. Irish-speaking had been established as a lingua franca of revived Republicanism, most potently within prison communities ('the Jailtacht'). The 1998 Good Friday Agreement laid heavy emphasis on encouraging and promoting the Irish language, much as the Free State had done in the 1920s and perhaps for similar reasons: to emphasize that a continuing link to Britain need not impede a sense of Gaelic cultural identity. Simultaneously, pursuing 'parity of esteem', the Unionist community was presented with a bewildering range of incentives to communicate through Ulster Scots or Ullans.

South of the border, the recognition that the old ways had not worked led to a more relaxed attitude towards the 'first national language'. Cultural activities through the medium of Irish continued to be earmarked for generous funding, and film was one of the areas that benefited hugely. The poets Máire Mac an tSaoi and Nuala Ní Dhomhnaill achieved considerable and deserved *réclame*, though their audience was transformed when they published in simultaneous English translation. Ní Dhomhnaill herself has attacked, with elegant ferocity, the official attitudes behind the patriarchal *Gaeilgeoir* mentality and the exclusiveness of the traditional policy of 'compulsion' in education.[55] In the next generation the poems of Cathal Ó Searcaigh have also reached a wide audience, despite – or because of – the unabashedly homosexual nature of many of his lyrics. All this reflects a deliberate effort to stress the language as a vehicle for change and modernity. The obvious failure of the old-style models of Gaelicization led to some rethinking from the 1970s. The statistics of those actually using the Irish language, as opposed to claiming some proficiency in it, carried on plunging downwards, fuelled by the resentment of those who had been forced to learn it at school in order to pass examinations; as late as 2006 a bilingual writer who decided to travel around Ireland speaking only Irish was taken aback to find himself shunned as 'a footsoldier of the Irish Taliban'.[56] Where he found cause for hope was in the relaxed attitude of the younger generation who were attending the 'Gaeilscoileanna', Irish-speaking schools voluntarily set up to cope with an educational system cracking apart under the stresses of urban expansion and rural depopulation. Here, a hybridized text-speak Irish was evolving among the young; there is also some evidence that learning Irish socializes immigrant children by putting them on a level with their equally ignorant native-born peers.

The creation in 1996 of a lavishly funded special television channel supposedly devoted to programmes in the Irish language (though in practice heavily reliant on subtitles and bilingualism) also made a difference, which was apparent by the turn of the new century. Making short films in the Irish language under the 'Oscailt' scheme, and creating media jobs west of the Shannon, conferred a much needed cachet and glamour on speaking Irish, though also arousing considerable resentment in terms of expenditure and clientelism. By 2003 alone TG4 cost RTÉ nearly €12 million a year, while the Irish-language station's annual grant was approximately €24 million; it received 19 per cent of all public money spent on broadcasting in the

Republic. The creation of the new channel was itself seen by one supportive commentator as a move 'from revival and restoration to preservation and consolation'.[57] How long the everyday practice of speaking Irish would be kept up by alumni of the Gaeilscoileanna, or by those who migrated from TG4 to the more luxuriant pastures of RTÉ in Dublin, remained to be seen. Globalization and Anglo-American popular culture do not seem to set a favourable climate for Irish-language revival, especially as possession of the English language has played such a large part in Ireland's economic success. But immigration, modernization and secularization, along with a revolution in communications, may have helped a modest revival in the 1990s, simply by eroding the old pietistic attitude to the 'first national language'. Whether the designation of Irish as a recognized European language, or the aspirational statements about parity of esteem in the Good Friday Agreement, will make a difference to many people outside the lucrative translation industry is less certain.

Despite the changed conditions of the 1990s, many of the arguments about preserving and enabling the language are similar to those aired a hundred years before. In that first Celtic Revival too there was a danger of what Edna Longley has called 'ethnic boosterism' at the expense of the European and international aspects of the literary revival. The idea of marketing recurs; and it is worth bearing in mind Joep Leerssen's brilliant coinage of 'auto-exoticism' for the Irish ability effortlessly to see themselves as 'other' and endlessly analyse their uniqueness. This might be applied to many aspects of the post-modern cultural consciousness that supposedly characterizes the new Ireland. International academic criticism of the Irish literary phenomenon, as Edna Longley has also remarked, emphasizes individual talent rather than tradition, and thus may miss a number of important clues (including historical ones).[58] Nor is the construction of Irish literature immune from the tendrils of the heritage industry: while one can applaud the devoted reconstruction of the house on Ussher's Island that inspired Joyce's 'The Dead', there is less consensus about selling tasteful mementoes, including a snow-globe that, with one shake, gives you snow becoming 'general all over Ireland'.[59]

IV

In his influential study *Inventing Ireland*, published in 1995, Declan Kiberd observed: 'the century which is about to end is once again dominated by the debate with which it began: how to distinguish what is good in nationalism from what is bad.'[60] A consideration of the shifts and rearticulations in Irish culture over the last thirty years would not be complete – or accurate – if it simply gave the impression of the breaking down of barriers and the opening up of new perspectives and the forgetting of traditional limitations. All this has happened in various areas of cultural (and even academic) endeavour, but, by a countering tendency, certain old formations have been maintained and even reaffirmed. 'Ownership' of Irish history has re-emerged in some recent controversies, for instance the debate sparked by Tom Dunne's assessment of the 1798 bicentenary celebrations and his memoir *Rebellions*, which fused personal, local and national histories in a peculiarly potent way.[61] The politics of historical commemoration have become a subject for historical commentary in themselves, along with the dangers of projecting imported concepts from psychotherapy and 'liberation psychology' such as 'collective memory' and 'post-stress trauma' on to the historical experience of past centuries. This can lead to crudely airbrushed views that come to resemble exactly the kind of black-and-white, green-and-orange versions from which the Irish supposedly have been trying to liberate themselves. The conclusion that Irish historiography could profit from a close study of the history of hatred might not be to everyone's taste.[62] But the experience of the last thirty years, within the academy as well as on the streets, might be adduced in evidence.

Indeed, some recent studies of the creation and articulation of Irish national identity have indicated that, even in the brave new world of late-twentieth-century Ireland, the battles over historical interpretation stand for a wider alignment of opposing forces. Originally, from the 1970s a conflict between traditionalists and modernizers was discernible; in the words of O'Mahony and Delanty, there has now appeared a third and very diffuse movement . . . composed of a growing number who identify with a neo-nationalism that compensates for the ennui of what they experience as a standardisation of cultural identities and who espouse a new commitment to national peculiarity. The combination of traditionalist national identity constructs, and neo-nationalist ones, ensures the continuing potency of inclusive, communitarian symbolisation in moral and political discourse. Communitarian symbolisation such as appeals to Irish tradition remains more powerful than liberal or social-democratic symbolisation as a resource for the symbolic 'packaging' of successful political messages.[63]

Other scholars have also interrogated the interventions of 'post-nationalists' and 'liberal culturalists' in contemporary Ireland and wondered whether this has amounted to a dilution or a transmutation of traditional nationalism. Tom Garvin, for one, argues that old-style formulations have been replaced by 'an equally nationalist paradigm which is entrepreneurial, open to the outside world, agnostic on cultural matters and eventually on religious matters as well'.[64] The self-righteous Ireland Institute, set up in 1997 by, among others, Declan Kiberd, Edna O'Brien, the painter Robert Ballagh and the Australian novelist Thomas Kenneally, declared an intention 'to nurture writing which tackles the revisionist and anti-nationalist stance'; it was apparently galvanized by what its founders perceived as the inadequate response to the eightieth anniversary of the 1916 Rising the year before.[65] National opinion remained unconcerned, and by the time the ninetieth anniversary came along, the Ireland Institute had faded, while (as we have seen in the last chapter) the Fianna Fáil government of the day was involved in a concerted effort to prevent the newly domesticated Sinn Féin from taking over the cause of 1916 commemorations altogether.

By then too the uncomplicated cause of 'anti-revisionism' had been replaced by a more fashionable-sounding 'post-revisionism' among some historians and (more especially) cultural-studies pundits. But from time to time the underlying arguments, together with the oddly querulous tone of some of the critiques levelled at writers such as Tóibín, Barry and Bolger, suggest that post-revisionism amounts to something rather like nationalism with footnotes. It is certainly fed by the movement of roots-discovery among people of Irish stock born and living abroad, where the recent vogue for identity politics sometimes goes with a curious brand of late-nineteenth-century racial essentialism, as well as unreconstructed Anglophobia. All this has recently and hilariously been expressed in the American Tom Hayden's testament of Irish rediscovery, *Irish on the Inside*, which reads like an update of Flann O'Brien's parody *An Béal Bocht* (*The Poor Mouth*). On the basis of one set of Irish great-grandparents, he traces to his Irish descent the victimization imposed even on a middle-class son of Detroit who married Jane Fonda. 'I internalized WASP standards of sexual attraction, and was controlled by them. I was sexually colonized. The rejection of Irish Catholics was an indication of unconscious self-hate.' His attempts to come to grips with the mother country on trips 'home' resemble a terminally bewildered Candide. Visiting South Armagh around the same time as Colm Tóibín's border walk, Hayden is told by the 'captive minority' of local Republicans that the Irish think of Cuchulainn 'the way you Americans think of the Founding Fathers'. Buoyed up by born-again nationalism, he is utterly foxed by John Hume's refusal to embrace the MacBride principles (which laid down religiously defined quotas for job recruitment by American firms in Northern Ireland). The partitionist outcome of the peace process throws him further off balance. To Hayden's essentialist belief, even his fellow countrymen Tom Foley and Tip O'Neill were 'cases of internalized infatuation with the coloniser', which may explain the mystery – as does the 'self-hating Irishness' epitomized by Fintan O'Toole or Garret FitzGerald. As so often, the refuge from bewilderment is mysticism. The 'Irish' (actually American-Irish) must 'join the renewal of spirituality, including Catholic spirituality, by identifying with the religious dissenters, liberation theologists, goddesses and nature traditions, and the deeply creation-centered spirituality of Brigid and Columkille that infuses the original Irish character.'[66]

Political tourism and reinvented Irishness were much in vogue by the 1980s, and not just from across the Atlantic. In 1985 the Australian writer Vincent Buckley published an account under the ominous (and ungrammatical) title *Memory Ireland*. Buckley came to live in Ireland in 1981 and, like Hayden later on, received a shock. As he saw it, the country was being 'asked to lose its national memory by

a kind of policy, in which politicians of almost all parties, ecclesi-
astics of all religions, media operators and revisionist historians cooperate to create (and let us hope they do not need to enforce, for if
they need to, they will) a new sense of corporate identity'.[67] Living
unhappily in a cottage outside Dublin, with juggernauts thundering
past, and ignored by unfriendly locals, Buckley's experience in the
early 1980s spiralled downwards into paranoia about the ancient
enemy. As the book goes on, he asserts that Britain was responsible for
deliberately fomenting bovine tuberculosis in Ireland, besides turning
Ireland into

a testing and dumping ground for British junk products, including TV programmes and tabloid newspapers with their racist intolerance. As the stuff
pours into the country, it is sent around by a middle class that grew into
degeneracy as if born to it. The Irish, the perfect complement to their ancient
tormentors: choleric, agreeable, envious and promiscuous with ideas, where
the English are spiteful, reserved, self-satisfied and formalistic . . .[68]

Once again the links back to the turn of the twentieth century are
striking, carrying clarion echoes of the better-written polemic of D. P.
Moran nearly a century before. Buckley's book was published by
Penguin and sold extremely well; it was oddly popular with some
members of the Department of Foreign Affairs. Even more intri-
guingly, it predicted syndromes that were about to surface in Irish
historiography. One was the idea of a unique linkage between past
and present in Ireland, mediated by 'group memory'. Another was the
notion that this set up continuing resonances that could not be
accessed by the usual tools of historical inquiry, especially when they
allegedly had been blunted by an attempt at impartiality.

Along with an emphasis on the superior powers of empathy, touchy-
feely history was on the way. By the 1990s *Irish Times* readers were
following the columnist John Waters's entertaining attacks on what
he saw as the demonization of de Valera's Ireland by a cabal of
un-Irish liberals resident in 'Dublin 4'. Waters's thesis was advanced
under various covers, including an emotional evocation of the voice
of the late sports commentator Michael O'Hehir. This phenomenon,
Waters told his *Irish Times* readers,

is perhaps the last evocation truly capable of protecting those 'pre-modern' decades from the strange false memory syndrome afflicting social and political analysis in Ireland. His voice transcended history, fiction, propaganda, because it was full of life.

We are blessed that it remains on tape for us to hear again, a truth capsule to use as an antidote to the cultural disinformation with which we are besieged. It is not what he said that matters, but the way he said it, which evokes in us all a truthful memory of what it was really like at that time. That voice may remain the most useful commentary on those years because it was not possible to hear it and remember those times for anything other than what they were: less prosperous, certainly, less enlightened, possibly, but kinder, more ethical and far less brutalizing than the age in which we now live.[69]

For John Waters, born in 1955, 'those times' made up a comparatively short part of his life; but they can be accessed only by 'truthful memory' rather than by 'social and political analysis'. There is a connection here to the spiritualized, mystical white-goddess view of Irish identity invoked by Tom Hayden, which became popular around the same time and in which an imaginary history replaces religion. Thus John O'Donoghue, author of a bestselling book on 'Celtic spirituality' called *Anam Cara*:

It is time to take back the power and reawaken our sense of critical participation in our own culture. Many of the functionaries are merely adept custodians of the gateways. They are proficient in the legality of membership and convention. But they can tell little of the landscape that lies beyond the entrance. They do not seem to know of the mountains or where the wells are hidden . . . Imagine scholarship which would engage the disciplines of history, psychology and theology in an analysis of the deeper psychological structures of our present culture. In which the disciplines of philosophy and literary criticism would excavate the terrain where the narrative mythologies and discursive questioning engage.[70]

Unfortunately, this kind of 'scholarship' is already here, though it has not led us very far into the mountains or any nearer to finding the wells. After the upheavals and reconsiderations of the last thirty years, too much cultural analysis in Ireland seems either to wander down the track of mellifluous waffle or to fall back on crude old cowboys-and-Indians history, especially as crafted for tourists. The actor Colin Farrell's instructions to American visitors might be instanced once again – or the imaginative facility 'Rebel Dublin Tours', 'guided by individuals with a university background in history' who offer the 1798 tour, the 1916 tour and the 'Rebel Women' tour as an instant route to the glamorous parts of Irish history.[71]

The options of Irishness at the end of the twentieth century reflect a great dislocation. Looking at the new motorway encircling Dublin, the cultural commentator Ann Marie Hourihane caustically pronounced: 'History is finished here. Now we are going to live like everybody else.'[72] But it is not that simple. On the one hand, you can assert ownership of the Rebel Tour, like Colin Farrell – or, indeed, like the self-proclaimed 'croppy' impresarios of the 1798 celebrations. On the other, you can explore the more mystical side of memory, though you may end up at a fairly similar destination. Or you can use history for your immediate interests, like the youthful horse-owners of the Dublin housing estates who instantly interpreted the Control of Horses Act (1996) in terms of the eighteenth-century Penal Laws. 'Under a fiver wasn't it, it couldn't be a value over five pound or you paid a fine – yes they'd take it from you.'[73] In a brilliant time-loop, the Dublin 'Corpo' becomes the Georgian Ascendancy. Meanwhile, despite Hourihane's assertion, history goes on happening, though recently it seems to have gone into fast-forward mode – or transformation.

Thus the shape-changing in Irish culture over the years of the Celtic Tiger has affected various intellectual fashions, and been faithfully reflected in the advertising and marketing industries. One analyst of Irish themes in American advertising has noted from the mid 1980s 'the devolution of male virility' in the Colgate-Palmolive ads for 'Irish Spring' deodorant soap: 'Seán', the brand's spokesman and the chief character in the storyline, has become progressively feminized over the years of the campaign, distinctly swapping an authoritative Irish masculinity, based on 'the labourer', for a more nebulous image of the Irish New Man.[74] Fiction, again, may provide a prophetic guide. Perhaps the transformations in McLiam Wilson's Belfast novel *Eureka Street*, in which the ceasefires enable characters to change their appearance, their political orientation and their erotic direction, are becoming actual rather than metaphorical. One could instance the other life of UDA hard man Sammy Duddy, who maintained alternative existences as poet, cartoonist and drag artist – in which capacity he was known in the 1970s as 'the Dolly Parton of Belfast' until his commander ordered him to drop his voice, grow a moustache and cease operations forthwith. As *The Times* put it, 'to the outside world he is the face of Northern Ireland's most vicious loyalist terrorist group. But to his friends he will always be Samantha.'[75]

If for politicians and even for terrorists the accepted mode at the end of the twentieth century was transfiguration, creative writers saw it first. In November 1993, towards the end of his legendary five-year stint as Oxford's professor of poetry, Seamus Heaney delivered a sombre lecture reflecting on identity, Irishness and bilocation. He cast back to the 1981 hunger strikes (when he had also been in Oxford) and forward to the current discontents, a year before the IRA ceasefire and in the wake of the Shankill Road bombing. Referring to the 'exacerbations and entrapments' of Northern Ireland's politics, he dwelt on the negotiations of cultural identity practised by MacNeice, Hewitt and, unusually, himself, and ended with one of his own visionary poems from *Seeing Things*, dealing with the intersection and overlap between the worlds of the quotidian and the miraculous.[76] A decade and a half of seismic change later, his fellow poet, the pyrotechnical wunderkind Paul Muldoon, looked back on Irish transformations. Muldoon's own multiple existence allowed him to serve not only as Heaney's successor at Oxford and a Pulitzer-winning elegist and lyricist but as the songwriter for what he describes as a 'three-car-garage band'. It is in this persona that he has written rock songs, alternating an astonishing range of references to popular Americana with attacks on the motorway threatening the Hill of Tara or the cuisine of smart Cork restaurants; while free-association from an old Irish word for hillside rebel produced his 'Rapparee Rap'.

> Now the Rapparees have taken up daylight robbery
> And all the former outsiders are into inside jobbery
> And the disease seems less acute than chronic
> When the surface-to-airs are superchthonic

As corporal punishment and General de Chastelain
Have launched right into Amhrán na bhFiann
And the little black numbers are coming to the crunch
And Paddy's almost as pleased as punch
To know a kidney punch is a form of backslap
And the clapped-out pony's not hitched to the claptrap
And we know fine well we needed those new kneecaps
Now we're doing the Rapparee Rap[77]

Conclusion:
The Strange Death of Romantic Ireland

The fourth episode of *Back to Methuselah*, George Bernard Shaw's 1921 play cycle dealing with evolution, religion, history and the future, opens on a pier jutting into the Atlantic off the Galway Burren in the year 3000. The region is the home of a colony of extremely long-lived people who possess many of the secrets of life. Visitors come from the more short-living 'Eastern Island' to consult the Galway oracle, but exposure brings the risk of dying from the killer disease 'discouragement'. In their efforts to 'acquire mental flexibility', one of the natives remarks, 'intercourse with us puts too great a strain on them.' The Galwegians have ruthlessly adapted their own human – or post-human – nature and live by codes of strict realism. The visiting protagonist in 'The Tragedy of an Elderly Gentleman' is interrogated by an alarming child-woman, and comes face to face with the insufficiencies of his culture and his creed. Finally, like the Fianna hero Oisín when he returned to Ireland from the Land of the Ever Young, he dies when he touches the oracle's hand. Past meets Future in the mythic west of Ireland.

Shaw was well aware of the mercilessly realistic side of Irish nature, prepared to exploit the past with one hand and jettison it with the other; he also shared his fellow countrymen's clear-eyed apprehension of the advantages of being situated between England and America, and their need to try to profit from both. In *Back to Methuselah* the Elderly Gentleman recounts to his interlocutor a Shavian (or Old Testament) version of the St Patrick story. By the end of the twentieth century all the Irish had emigrated to spread nationalism in other countries, which they did so successfully that all national grievances were met. Having 'lost their political faculties by disuse except that of nationalist agitation, and owed their position as the most interesting race on earth solely to their suffering', they were left wandering in the wilderness until counselled by an English archbishop to recolonize their own country. After they landed in Galway, however, the young repudiated the stony landscape, and subsequently all sense of Irishness, preferring to return to England. Thus the Irish race 'vanished from human knowledge', leaving the world 'a tame, dull place'. The long-lived and modern-minded native is unimpressed. 'What a ridiculous thing to call them Irish because they live in Ireland! You might as well call them Airish because they live in air. They must be just the same as other people.'[1]

It is tempting to think that Shaw intended 'The Tragedy of an Elderly Gentleman' to prophesy a specific, if satirical, Irish future, as well as provide a general metaphor for the forces of Creative Evolution. But in the late twentieth century the Irish chose a different course than that of evangelizing nationalism to the four corners of the globe. Instead, over the last thirty years surveyed in this book, Ireland itself was in many ways transformed, modernized and globalized; in matters such as fertility and marriage patterns, sexual attitudes, the tabloidization of the newspapers and fast-food culture, the Republic has joined the mainstream of the Western world since 1970. But 'the Irish race' did not vanish from the face of the earth. Returning to the two strains of interpretation outlined in my first chapter ('Boosters and Begrudgers'), the 'Boosters' like to emphasize that Creative Evolution has been a two-way process:

The end to introspection, the turning outwards to the world and the new self-confidence which are the results of both the Celtic Tiger experience and the involvement in Europe have had other remarkable effects. Our cultural influence extends through the whole world in many different forms. This process has been called the hibernicisation of Europe but it is fair now to talk about the hibernicisation of the world. Our music, dance, films, pubs, literature, theatre, athletes are everywhere.[2]

Ambitions for world domination may be left for the future. But it is undeniable that with luck has come confidence. Another Irish playwright of the diaspora, Eugene O'Neill, created in *Long Day's Journey into Night* the character of James Tyrone, who ruined his talent by playing one role over and over again until he could do nothing else; O'Neill intended this syndrome to be emblematic of the Irish in general.[3] One of the profound changes of attitude experienced by the Irish in the late twentieth century was the realization that they could play many roles, and that history did not dictate a determinist and stereotypical fate. In this, as in other ways, Charles James Haughey stood for something larger than himself when he declared in 1982, 'I don't intend to be a prisoner of my past.'[4]

Invoking Haughey reminds us that the story is one of shade as well as light. The rate of breakneck change experienced by Ireland has strained the social as well as the political fabric, and has been, as suggested earlier, paralleled in previous eras of Irish history that often ended in some great and traumatic upheaval. The last thirty years within Ireland might be seen as a pattern of interconnected crises, much in the manner that George Dangerfield diagnosed for Britain before the First World War. Dangerfield called his study of a political and social culture transformed under stress from several directions *The Strange Death of Liberal England*. Also on the eve of the First World War, W. B. Yeats's 'September 1913' declared 'Romantic Ireland's dead and gone.' But the Easter Rising three years later enforced a reconsideration, and from 1922 the new Irish state deliberately reinforced many of the traditional belief-systems that underpinned Romantic Ireland. From the 1960s, however, this came under unmanageable stress. A Yeatsian echo was picked up by John Montague in 1963 when his poem 'The Siege of Mullingar' sensed with poetic prescience a change of mood.

> At the Fleadh Ceoil in Mullingar
> There were two sounds, the breaking
> Of glass, and the background pulse
> Of music. Young girls roamed
> The streets with eager faces,
> Shoving for men. Bottles in
> Hand, they rowed out a song:
> *Puritan Ireland's dead and gone,*
> *A myth of O'Connor and O'Faolain.*[5]

Puritan Ireland fought hard for survival, as we have seen, but it went in the end. If Romantic Ireland is also dead and gone, what has replaced puritanism and romanticism? The changes dealt with in this book suggest some answers. As always, they may not be the kind of changes expected by the pre-Tiger age. Where change was forecast, in Northern Ireland, it too came in unexpected ways and only after the acceptance of large elements of the status quo. Meanwhile the Republic transformed itself with very little ostensible reference to the Northern developments. In so doing, it drove home the message of how deep the border had become in the first fifty years of its existence (a message eventually recognized by Sinn Féin). Yet at the same time the Northern crisis, viewed from the South with a strange mixture of apathy, guilt and apprehension, may have helped condition or even direct some of the changes in the South. The ways in which the North came South during the period of the Troubles were often subtle and not always predictable. The Field Day group set up by Northern writers declared that it wanted to create and sponsor works inhabiting a 'Fifth Province' of cultural endeavour. This imaginative mantra was quickly adopted by Mary Robinson and others eager to break out of the old moulds, and Field Day's enterprise marked one of the more influential innovations in the politics of culture – though it was more successful in stimulating brilliant interventions in drama and poetry than in levering Irish cultural discourse out of the old binary oppositions and *ad hominem* attacks. None the less, if approaches both to Catholicism and to Protestantism changed south of the border from 1970 to 2000, so did traditional approaches to Republicanism, nationalism and the Irish identity altogether.

The part played in this by the Northern crisis is a complex question, which also requires consideration of so-called 'post-revisionism' in Irish cultural debates; indeed, what I have called the 'Begrudger' response to Celtic Tigerism bears a certain affinity to post-revisionism. Both seem to use 'liberal' as a term of abuse, and both sometimes gesture back to the verities of old-style Fianna Fáil politics. The question of historical 'revisionism' in general, and the uses made of the Irish past over the last thirty years, have been amply dealt with elsewhere. But the operations and manipulations of Irish memory are at the centre of much of what Ireland has made of itself during this very period. Examples include Tom Parlon ingeniously invoking Parnell against the planning restrictions, or Shane MacGowan's historically incoherent but culturally influential expatriate glamorization of the IRA, or the Famine memorial incongruously planted right outside the gleaming new Financial Services Agency in Dublin. History is there to be used, as shamelessly as Irish literature. It would be gratifying to declare an open season on politicians who sententiously intone, from Heaney's *Cure at Troy*, the new cliché for the 1990s: 'Let Hope and History Rhyme.' If such an assonance is contrived – for the best of reasons – it usually requires some radical massaging of the record. In terms of a utilitarian approach to Irish history, it is more instructive to remember a less guarded remark of Ahern, self-confessed foe of 'the revisionists': 'we can't change the past, but we can try to clean it up.'[6]

There are more sophisticated arguments that can tend to equally dubious conclusions. One of them concerns a recurrent hostility to 'liberalism', and indeed the idea (shared by both the Catholic *ancien régime* and the post-revisionist Begrudgers) that liberalism or even pluralism are somehow un-Irish. Isaiah Berlin, again, argued not only that pluralism is a necessary component of freedom but (more troublingly) that equality and freedom frequently conflict, and a civilized polity involves balancing these competing demands against each other. The destabilizing pressures of Irish history since 1970, which included political subversion, financial corruption, the challenge of immigration and a sometimes spectacularly unequal prosperity, have presented the Irish state with a series of challenges, often impressively surmounted. In the end it is hard not to side with the Boosters rather than the Begrudgers, and to recognize that in several spheres, not just the economic, a certain amount of good luck was maximized by good management.

Berlin also liked to quote Kant's argument that a single, scientifically organized system of government by reason was impossible: 'out of the crooked timber of humanity no straight thing was ever made.' Ireland over the last thirty years presents an engrossing picture of humanity in a state of change – if also of more kinds of crookedness than one. To look at it as a historian of the future is an enlightening process. 'Why do you short-livers persist in making up silly stories about the world and trying to act as if they were true?' the post-Irish realist asks Shaw's Elderly Gentleman. The pragmatic new Ireland has shown a similar tendency, like America, to live aggressively in the present. As Ahern pointed out, this is better than living in the past. But understanding the future requires an expanded sense of what has just happened, and a map of the landscape receding so bewilderingly behind us.

Notes

INTRODUCTION: CULTURE AND ANARCHY IN IRELAND C. 1970-2000

1. Will Hanafin, *De Little Book of Bertie* (Dublin, 2001), p. 20.

2. Isaiah Berlin, *Flourishing: Letters 1928-1946*, ed. H. Hardy (London, 2004), pp. 633-4.

3. O. MacDonagh, *States of Mind: A Study of Anglo-Irish Conflict 1780-1980* (London, 1983).

4. 'Carleton: Novelist of the Folk' in *Thomas Davis: Essays and Poems* (anonymously edited, Dublin, 1845), p. 110.

5. *Culture and Anarchy in Ireland 1890-1939* (Oxford, 1982).

6. J. J. Lee, 'Centralization and Community' in J. J. Lee (ed.), *Ireland: Towards a Sense of Place* (Cork, 1985), p. 84.

7. Ellen Hazelkorn and Colum Murphy, 'The Cultural Economy of Dublin' in Mary P. Corcoran and Michel Peillon (eds.), *Ireland Unbound: A Turn of the Century Chronicle* (Institute of Public Administration, Dublin, 2002), p. 127.

8. Colum Kenny, *Moments That Changed Us* (Dublin, 2005), p. 171.

9. Hazelkorn and Murphy, 'Cultural Economy of Dublin', pp. 124, 132.

10. http://www.forfas.ie/ncc (3 Oct. 2006).

11. As reported in the *Irish Independent*, 18 Nov. 2004.

12. Seán Ó Riain, 'The Flexible Developmental State: Globalization, Information Technology and the "Celtic Tiger"' in *Politics and Society*, 28:2, pp. 157-93; Peadar Kirby, *The Celtic Tiger in Distress: Growth with Inequality in Ireland* (London, 2002), p. 97.

13. Lyons, *Culture and Anarchy*, p. 177.

CHAPTER 1: THE MIRACLE OF LOAVES AND FISHES

1. 'Selling Tara: Buying Florida', a lecture at the University of Connecticut, Oct. 2006.

2. Tom Garvin, *Preventing the Future: Why was Ireland So Poor for So Long?* (Dublin, 2004), Chapter 4.

3. The most perceptive overview at this stage was Cormac Ó Gráda's article 'Is the Celtic Tiger a Paper Tiger?', *Quarterly Economic Commentary* (Spring 2002), pp. 51–62. Also see Kieran Allen, 'Neither Boston nor Berlin: Class Polarization and Neo-liberalism in the Irish Republic' in Colin Coulter and Steve Coleman (eds.), *The End of Irish History? Critical Reflections on the Celtic Tiger* (Manchester, 2003), p. 56 (for the Maurice O'Connell quote), and Peter Clinch, Frank Convery and Brendan Walsh, *After the Celtic Tiger: Challenges Ahead* (Dublin, 2002), p. 11.

4. Rory O'Donnell, 'Reinventing Ireland: From Sovereignty to Partnership', Jean Monnet Inaugural Lecture, University College Dublin, 29 Apr. 1999 (my thanks to Rory O'Donnell for a copy of this lecture). Also see Rory O'Donnell, 'The New Ireland in the New Europe' in Rory O'Donnell (ed.), *Europe: The Irish Experience* (Dublin, 2000), pp. 187–213.

5. *The Times Literary Supplement*, 23 Jan. 2004, p. 5.

6. Foreword to Jim Hourihane (ed.), *Ireland and the European Union: The First Thirty Years 1973–2002* (Dublin, 2004), p. xii.

7. Peadar Kirby, *The Celtic Tiger in Distress: Growth with Inequality in Ireland* (London, 2002); Clinch, Convery and Walsh, *After the Celtic Tiger*; Peadar Kirby, Luke Gibbons and Michael Cronin (eds.), *Reinventing Ireland: Culture, Society and the Global Economy* (London, 2002); Kieran Allen, *The Celtic Tiger: The Myth of Social Partnership in Ireland* (Manchester, 2000); Fintan O'Toole, *After the Ball* (Dublin, 2003).

8. A clear and interesting treatment of these two measurements is given in Patrick Honohan and Brendan Walsh, 'Catching Up with the Leaders: The Irish Hare' in *Brookings Papers on Economic Activity*, vol. 1 (Washington, DC, 2002), pp. 42–6. For a coherent account of this from a Begrudger angle, see Elizabeth Cullen, 'Unprecedented Growth, but for Whose Benefit?' in Richard Douthwaite and John Jopling (eds.), *Growth, the Celtic Cancer: Why the Global Economy Damages Our Health and Society, Feasta Review*, No. 2 (Dublin, 2004).

9. Kieran Allen, *Celtic Tiger*, p. 193.

10. David Byrne in Jim Hourihane, *Ireland and the European Union*, p. xii.

11. Denis O'Hearn, 'Macroeconomic Policy in the Celtic Tiger: A Critical Reassessment' in Coulter and Coleman, *The End of Irish History?*, p. 35.

12. O'Hearn, 'Macroeconomic Policy', p. 38; also Michael J. O'Sullivan, *Ireland and the Global Question* (Cork, 2006), p. 75.

13. Paper to Statistical and Social Inquiry Society of Ireland, 26 Oct. 2000, quoted in Clinch, Convery and Walsh, *After the Celtic Tiger*, p. 31.

14. O'Sullivan, *Ireland and the Global Question*, p. 77. Tom Garvin argues that GNP figures conceal discrepancies and give an over-gloomy picture of Irish prosperity before the boom: *Preventing the Future*, pp. 118–19.

15. Quoted in ibid., p. 113.

16. Kirby, *Celtic Tiger in Distress*, p. 141.

17. See B. Nolan and T. Smeeding, 'Ireland's Income Distribution: A Comparative Perspective', *Review of Income and Wealth*, Series 51, No. 4 (Dec. 2005), pp. 537–60.

18. Clinch, Convery and Walsh, *After the Celtic Tiger*, pp. 31ff.

19. *Magill*, Vol. 3, No. 7 (Apr. 1980).

20. Quoted in Garvin, *Preventing the Future*, pp. 38–9. See Chapter 4 in ibid. for a coruscating discussion of educational policy in independent Ireland.

21. Ibid., p. 249. *Investment in Education* is discussed in ibid., pp. 152ff.

22. Seán O'Connor, 'Post-primary Education Now and in the Future', *Studies* (Autumn 1968), pp. 233–51.

23. In 1978 more than two thirds of the fifteen-to-nineteen-year-old cohort had left school at or before fifteen. Statistics were even more drastic in areas of inner-city North Dublin.

24. O'Sullivan, *Ireland and the Global Question*, p. 63, for comparative figures, which puts Ireland's educational spending ninth out of fifteen peer countries.

25. For figures, and a rather sceptical view of the economic returns on investment in education, see Ó Gráda, 'Celtic Tiger', p. 54.

26. O'Sullivan, *Ireland and the Global Question*, p. 112.

27. Ibid., p. 111; Cullen in Douthwaite and Jopling, *Growth*, p. 36.

28. Clinch, Convery and Walsh, *After the Celtic Tiger*, p. 74.

29. O'Sullivan, *Ireland and the Global Question*, p. 115.

30. Niamh Hardiman, *Pay, Politics and Economic Performance in Ireland 1970–1987* (Oxford, 1988), p. 165. Also see *Magill*, Vol. 2, No. 2 (Nov. 1978).

31. It was a surge of post-oil-crisis inflation in 1975, for instance, that led the government to introduce a supplementary budget that tried to reduce the escalating cost of living – and was introduced on condition that the current National Wage Agreement terms were revised downwards, an important innovation. Hardiman, *Pay, Politics and Economic Performance*, p. 59.

32. By 1975 borrowing levels were at 16 per cent of GNP, more than twice

the proportion in the UK: ibid., p. 59. At the end of that year Cosgrave went on television to appeal for a national wage freeze.

33. *Magill*, Vol. 2, No. 3 (Dec. 1978), for an interview promising 'full employment by 1983' while admitting inflation might reach more than 7 per cent (it would in fact be 10 per cent); he also promised a growth rate of 7 per cent and reduced borrowing. A Green Paper of June 1978 had similarly promised full employment – if consensual policies were adhered to. This was much derided (Hardiman, *Pay, Politics and Economic Performance*, p. 73). O'Donoghue in a more sober frame of mind can be found issuing warnings for his successors after Haughey dropped him; *Magill*, Vol. 3, No. 5 (Feb. 1980).

34. See *Magill*, Vol. 2, No. 9 (June 1979). He may have meant Matt Merrigan, who opposed it, though his union – the Amalgamated Transport and General Workers' Union – eventually went against him and endorsed it.

35. See *Magill*, Vol. 3, No. 9 (June 1980), and Vol. 4, No. 8 (May 1981).

36. Hardiman, *Pay, Politics and Economic Performance*, p. 119.

37. Ruadhrí Roberts, quoted in ibid., p. 146, n. 26.

38. Honohan and Walsh, 'The Irish Hare', p. 30, for a striking graph.

39. *Magill*, Vol. 4, No. 1 (Oct. 1980). See also table showing shift in nature of exports in Hardiman, *Pay, Politics and Economic Performance*, p. 40.

40. See O'Sullivan, *Ireland and the Global Question*, esp. Chapter 4, and Ó Gráda, 'Celtic Tiger'.

41. Jim Hourihane, *Ireland and the European Union*, pp. 100–101.

42. J. R. Hill (ed.), *A New History of Ireland. Volume 5: Ireland 1921–1989* (Oxford, 2003), p. 361.

43. Garret FitzGerald, 'The Economics of EU Membership' in Jim Hourihane, *Ireland and the European Union*, pp. 79–80; also Garret FitzGerald, *All in a Life: An Autobiography* (London, 1991), Chapters 5 and 6.

44. Anthony Foley and Michael Mulreany, *The Single European Market and the Irish Economy* (Institute of Public Administration, Dublin, 1990), pp. 398ff.

45. See *Magill*, Vol. 1, No. 3 (Dec. 1978).

46. 11 per cent in favour, 18 per cent against, 66 per cent abstentions and spoilt votes.

47. Catharyn Costello, 'Irish and European Law' in Jim Hourihane, *Ireland and the European Union*, pp. 30–35; also see Diarmuid Rossa Phelan, *Revolt or Revolution: The Constitutional Boundaries of the European Community* (Dublin, 1997).

48. Ethel Crowley, *Land Matters: Power Struggles in Rural Ireland* (Dublin, 2006), p. 23.

49. For an interesting analysis, see Hilary Tovey, 'Milking the Farmer? Modernization and Marginalization in Irish Dairy Farming' in Mary Kelly, Liam O'Dowd and James Wickham (eds.), *Power, Conflict and Inequality* (Dublin, 1982), pp. 68–89.

50. Crowley, *Land Matters*, p. 29.

51. *Magill*, Vol. 2, No. 7 (Apr. 1979), for article by Brian Trench on PAYE and the tax revolt.

52. See Bryan Fanning and Tony McNamara (eds.), *Ireland Develops: Administration and Social Policy 1953–2003* (Institute of Public Administration, Dublin, 2003), pp. 111ff, on the creation of powerful farmers' unions. Also see *Magill*, Vol. 3, No. 1 (Oct. 1979), on the politics of the IFA. The movement against the 2 per cent sales levy was led by representatives of smaller farmers from the west. Irish representatives were also beginning to involve themselves in European agricultural organizations. But by the end of the century the IFA was seen as monopolized by the rich producers ('the Irish Friesian Association').

53. Reported in *Magill*, Vol. 2, No. 3 (Dec. 1978).

54. *Magill*, Vol. 2, No. 7 (Apr. 1979).

55. Tovey, 'Milking the Farmer?', p. 89.

56. Crowley, *Land Matters*, p. 30.

57. For figures see Liam Gallagher, Eleanor Doyle and Eoin O'Leary, 'Creating the Celtic Tiger and Sustaining Economic Growth: A Business Perspective' in *Quarterly Economic Commentary* (Spring 2002), pp. 64–5.

58. See Honohan and Walsh, 'The Irish Hare', pp. 5–6; and for top companies, Gallagher, Doyle and O'Leary, 'Creating the Celtic Tiger', p. 66 – a fascinating table.

59. Honohan and Walsh, 'The Irish Hare', p. 46.

60. Quoted in Michael Cronin, 'Speed Limits: Ireland, Globalization and the War Against Time' in Kirby, Gibbons and Cronin, *Reinventing Ireland*, p. 60.

61. Crowley, *Land Matters*, p. 203.

62. Jim Hourihane, *Ireland and the European Union*, p. 41.

63. The A. T. Kearney Foreign Policy magazine globalization index – discussed in O'Sullivan, *Ireland and the Global Question*, p. 34. Also see Coleman and Coulter, *The End of Irish History?*, pp. 110ff, and O'Toole, *After the Ball*, pp. 4ff.

64. *Ireland and the Global Question*, Chapter 7.

65. Fintan O'Toole, *The Ex-Isle of Erin* (Dublin, 1997), p. 12.

66. Coleman and Coulter, *The End of Irish History?*, pp. 19ff and 37ff.

67. In February 1979 *Management Today* published a list of the top fifty firms in Britain and Ireland, in terms of profits growth; there was only one

Irish company, the Smurfit Group, at no. 3 (its profits having risen eighty-fold between 1969 and 1979). Ten years later the picture would be very different. Twenty-five years later, there were several Irish billionaires on the *Forbes* list of the 200 richest people in the world.

68. *Autobiographies* (London, 1955), p. 135.

69. Cronin, 'Speed Limits', p. 57.

70. See Padraic White's informative first-hand chapters in Ray MacSharry and Padraic White, *The Making of the Celtic Tiger: The Inside Story of Ireland's Boom Economy* (Cork, 2000), Chapters 9–13; and Garvin, *Preventing the Future*, pp. 170ff.

71. Garvin, *Preventing the Future*, p. 185.

72. Gallagher, Doyle and O'Leary, 'Creating the Celtic Tiger', p. 68.

73. *Magill*, Vol. 1, No. 10 (July 1979).

74. Kieran Allen, *Celtic Tiger*, pp. 20 (for Adams), 26.

75. Cormac Ó Gráda, *A Rocky Road: The Irish Economy since the 1920s* (Manchester, 1997), pp. 54–5.

76. *Magill*, Vol. 2, No. 8 (May 1979).

77. As with the Glenburn clothing manufacture plant, which closed factories in the summer of 1979, only a year after getting an IDA grant (it had received £237,000 of a projected £499,000).

78. See *Magill*, Vol. 3, No. 2 (Nov. 1979), for annoyance expressed by Eoin O'Sullivan, chief of the IDA's North American operations, at the 'vociferous, emotional very local minority' of environmentalists making trouble for potential investors.

79. *Magill*, Vol. 3, No. 4 (Jan. 1980).

80. Gallagher, Doyle and O'Leary, 'Creating the Celtic Tiger', p. 69, quoting Michael O'Sullivan, 'Industrial Development: A New Beginning?' in J. W. O'Hagan (ed.), *The Economy of Ireland* (Dublin, 2000).

81. Fanning and McNamara, *Ireland Develops*, pp. 55ff, for the view that by 1982 all the infrastructural changes had been put in place, though some constraints still persist.

82. See Steve Loyal, 'Welcome to the Celtic Tiger: Racism, Immigration and the State' in Coulter and Coleman, *The End of Irish History?*, pp. 74–94.

83. www.cso.ie.

84. See Honohan and Walsh, 'The Irish Hare', pp. 19–20.

85. Foley and Mulreany, *The Single European Market*; see also Raymond Crotty, *Ireland in Crisis: A Study in Capitalist Colonial Undevelopment* (Dingle, 1986).

86. Clinch, Convery and Walsh, *After the Celtic Tiger*, pp. 24–7 for a useful summary.

87. See Joe Durkan in *Magill*, Vol. 3, No. 11 (Oct. 1979), for a treatment of the variation and unreliability of economic statistics released by government departments like Planning and Finance.

88. 'Celtic Tiger', p. 56.

89. Patrick Lynch in 1959, quoted by Ronan Fanning, 'The Genesis of Economic Development' in John F. McCarthy (ed.), *Planning Ireland's Future: The Legacy of T. K. Whitaker* (Dublin, 1990), p. 78.

CHAPTER 2: HOW THE CATHOLICS
BECAME PROTESTANTS

1. See, for example, Tom Inglis, *Moral Monopoly: The Rise and Fall of the Catholic Church in Modern Ireland* (2nd ed., 1998), pp. 248–9.

2. Ibid., p. 255.

3. Ibid., p. 253.

4. Father John Kelly, quoted in Louise Fuller, *Irish Catholicism since 1950: The Undoing of a Culture* (Dublin, 2004), p. 61.

5. See Robert Savage, *Irish Television: The Political and Social Origins* (Cork, 1996), pp. 155–7.

6. Quoted in Colum Kenny, *Moments That Changed Us* (Dublin, 2005), p. 230.

7. John Cooney, *John Charles McQuaid: Ruler of Catholic Ireland* (Dublin, 1999), pp. 357, 369.

8. James S. Donnelly, Jr, 'The Troubled Contemporary Irish Catholic Church' in Brendan Bradshaw and Dáire Keogh (eds.), *Christianity in Ireland: Revisiting the Story* (Cambridge, 2004), p. 274.

9. See Daithi Ó Corráin, *Rendering to God and Caesar: The Irish Churches and the Two States of Ireland 1949–1973* (Manchester, 2006).

10. *Ireland in the World: Further Reflections* (Dublin, 2005), p. 230.

11. See Progress Report (1975) reprinted in Bryan Fanning and Tony McNamara (eds.), *Ireland Develops: Administrative and Social Policy 1953– 2003* (Institute of Public Administration, Dublin, 2003), pp. 240ff.

12. Diarmaid Ferriter, *Mothers, Maidens and Myth: A History of the Irish Countrywomen's Association* (Dublin, 1994); Hilda Tweedy, *A Link in the Chain: The Story of the Irish Housewives' Association 1942–1992* (Dublin, 1992); Maria Luddy, 'Women and Politics in Nineteenth-century Ireland' in Mary O'Dowd and Maryann Gialanella Valiulis (eds.), *Women and Irish History* (Dublin, 1997); Linda Connolly, *The Irish Women's Movement from Revolution to Devolution* (London, 2002).

13. Connolly, *The Irish Women's Movement*, pp. 94–5 and 98ff, for the report that emerged.

14. Mary Holland in *Magill*, Vol. 1, No. 2 (Nov. 1977).

15. See Michael O'Connell, *Changed Utterly: Ireland and the New Irish Psyche* (Dublin, 2001), p. 150. As late as 2000 women's pay lagged 15 per cent behind that of men.

16. Yvonne Galligan, *Women and Politics in Contemporary Ireland: From the Margins to the Mainstream* (London, 1998), p. 51.

17. Ann Marie Hourihane, *She Moves through the Boom* (Dublin, 2000), p. 37.

18. *Irish Times*, 15 Apr. 1971.

19. *Magill*, Vol. 1, No. 1 (Oct. 1977) and Vol. 1, No. 12 (Sept. 1978).

20. Kenny, *Moments That Changed Us*, p. 6; see also Galligan, *Women and Politics*, pp. 150–52.

21. Cooney, *McQuaid*, p. 348.

22. See *Magill*, Vol. 2, No. 4 (Jan. 1979).

23. For a contemporary reaction from an American, see Elizabeth Shannon, *Up in the Park: The Diary of the Wife of the American Ambassador to Ireland 1977–1981* (Dublin, 1983), pp. 173ff.

24. Quoted in *Magill*, Vol. 2, No. 8 (May 1979).

25. 4 May 1971; quoted in Anne Stopper, *Mondays at Gaj's: The Story of the Irish Women's Liberation Movement* (Dublin, 2006), p. 174.

26. *Magill*, Vol. 2, No. 9 (June 1979).

27. Colin Coulter and Steve Coleman (eds.), *The End of Irish History? Critical Reflections on the Celtic Tiger* (Manchester, 2003), p. 99.

28. Tom Hesketh, *The Second Partitioning of Ireland: The Abortion Referendum of 1983* (Dublin, 1990).

29. See Inglis, *Moral Monopoly*, pp. 88ff, 220–21.

30. Attended by Máirín de Búrca, Mary Maher, Margaret Gaj, Máire Woods and Máirín Johnson. At a further meeting in Mary Maher's flat they were joined by Mary Kenny, Mary McCutcheon, Mary Anderson, Nell McCafferty, June Levine and Nuala Fennell – all journalists. See Pat Brennan's useful survey in *Magill*, Vol. 2, No. 7 (Apr. 1979). There is much valuable material in Angela Bourke, Siobhán Kilfeather, Maria Luddy, Margaret Mac Curtain, Geraldine Meaney, Máirín Ní Dhonnchadha, Mary O'Dowd, Clair Wills (eds.), *The Field Day Anthology of Irish Writing. Volume 5: Irish Women's Writing and Traditions* (Cork, 2002), pp. 177–315.

31. Galligan, *Women and Politics*, pp. 103–4, particularly on the Judicial Separation and Family Law Reform Act (1989).

32. Stopper, *Monday at Gaj's*, p. 129.

33. Partly reprinted in *Field Day Anthology. Volume 5*, pp. 220ff; in full in

Mark Patrick Hederman and Richard Kearney (eds.), *The Crane Bag Book of Irish Studies* (Dublin, 1982), pp. 573–8.

34. Basil Chubb, *Government and Politics of Ireland* (London, 1994), p. 221.

35. Galligan gives 34 per cent in July 1996, but a decade later see *Irish Independent*, 7 Jan. 2007, for a much smaller proportion.

36. Though their numbers did not reflect the number of women barristers and solicitors: see Galligan, *Women and Politics*, pp. 43, 60.

37. Stopper, *Mondays at Gaj's*, pp. 58–9, 76.

38. Galligan, *Women and Politics*, pp. 52, 55, 57.

39. Cooney, *McQuaid*, p. 392.

40. *New History of Ireland. Volume 5*, pp. 368–9.

41. *Magill*, Vol. 1, No. 9 (June 1978).

42. Kieran Rose, *Diverse Communities: The Evolution of Lesbian and Gay Politics in Ireland* (Cork, 1994), p. 2.

43. Stopper, *Mondays at Gaj's*, pp. 164–5.

44. Cooney, *McQuaid*, pp. 358, 360, 385.

45. J. P. Mackey and Enda McDonagh (eds.), *Religion and Politics in Ireland at the Turn of the Millennium: Essays in Honour of Garret FitzGerald on the Occasion of His Seventy-fifth Birthday* (Dublin, 2003), p. 254.

46. Marcus Tanner, *Ireland's Holy Wars: The Struggle for a National Soul 1500–2000* (London, 2001), p. 402; the nuncio was Alibrandi. Conway's complaints about FitzGerald were made to Con Cremin; see *Irish Times*, 30 Dec. 2006, quoting papers released under the thirty-year rule.

47. Mackey and McDonagh, *Religion and Politics in Ireland*, p. 259.

48. See *Field Day Anthology. Volume 5*, pp. 229ff. In 2000 the Republic had a (second) woman president, a woman tánaiste, three women cabinet ministers and three women junior ministers. Two small parties had women leaders and two large parties women deputy leaders. Yet women accounted for only 12 per cent of the seats in the Dáil, ranking very low in world terms. Local government figures were not much better, with 16 per cent.

49. John Fulton, *The Tragedy of Belief: Division, Politics and Religion in Ireland* (Oxford, 1991), pp. 161, 166–7.

50. See p. 14 for this piece by Seán O'Connor, associate secretary of the Department of Education: it is reprinted in Robert Bell, Gerald Fowler and Ken Little (eds.), *Education in Great Britain and Ireland* (London, 1973). Cooney, *McQuaid*, pp. 396–7, for McQuaid's role.

51. See Horgan, 'Education in the Republic of Ireland' in Bell, Fowler and Little, *Education in Great Britain and Ireland*, pp. 35–41.

52. See *Education Times*, 4 July 1975, reporting a Dáil speech the preceding week.

53. Mackey and McDonagh, *Religion and Politics in Ireland*, p. 146.

54. Galligan, *Women and Politics*, p. 83.

55. Incisively analysed in Fuller, *Irish Catholicism since 1950*, pp. 168ff.

56. *Education Times*, 13 Sept. 1973, for the leaking of the report and much commentary.

57. See Richard O'Leary, 'The President's Communion' in Eamonn Slater and Michel Peillon (eds.), *Memories of the Present: A Sociological Chronicle of Ireland 1997–1998* (Dublin, 2000), pp. 145–54.

58. Fulton, *Tragedy of Belief*, pp. 194–5.

59. An unpublished letter; my thanks to Rob Tobin and Julia Crampton.

60. Inglis, *Moral Monopoly*, p. 206.

61. Donnelly, 'Troubled Contemporary Irish Catholic Church', pp. 283–4.

62. Ibid., p. 285.

63. Tanner, *Ireland's Holy Wars*, p. 412.

64. My thanks to Rob Tobin and Julia Crampton.

65. Tanner, *Ireland's Holy Wars*, p. 391.

66. Quoted in Marianne Elliott, *The Catholics of Ulster: A History* (London, 2001), p. 475.

67. See, for instance, Lionel Pilkington, 'Religion and the Celtic Tiger' in Peader Kirby, Luke Gibbons and Michael Cronin (eds.), *Reinventing Ireland: Culture, Society and the Global Economy* (London, 2002), pp. 124–42. This elaborately attempts to argue that the Church of Ireland in the Republic does not deserve its reputation for liberalism – basing his argument on the grounds of the annual Drumcree demonstrations. (He is also critical of the use of Patrick Kavanagh's poem about the 1940s, *The Great Hunger*, in a Protestant service in Tuam Cathedral, which Dr Pilkington perceives as an insult to the Famine dead.) But see Martin Maguire, '"Our People": The Church of Ireland and the Culture of Community in Dublin since Disestablishment' in R. Gillespie and W. G. Neely (eds.), *The Laity and the Church of Ireland 1000–2000* (Dublin, 2003), p. 283. On p. 302 Maguire emphasizes Southern Protestant revulsion at Drumcree.

68. Tanner, *Ireland's Holy Wars*, p. 422.

69. Ibid., p. 425. See also Kenneth Milne, 'The Protestant Church in Independent Ireland' in Mackey and McDonagh, *Religion and Politics in Ireland*, pp. 64–83.

70. For which he was roasted by Archbishop Connell: see Inglis, *Moral Monopoly*, p. 223.

71. *Sunday Independent*, 24 Aug. 2003.

72. Mackey and McDonagh, *Religion and Politics in Ireland*, pp. 250–51.

73. See FitzGerald in ibid., pp. 251–2. Using the 1991 census, he states that

since 1926 the proportion of Protestants engaged in better-paid non-agricultural employment (commerce, insurance, finance, management, administration and the professions) had risen from 32 per cent to 39 per cent. And though non-Catholics were less than 5 per cent of the population, they were over-represented three to four times among aircraft pilots, writers, journalists, actors, musicians, and lecturers and professors. They were two to three times over-represented among government administrators, industrial designers, farm managers, ships' officers, insurance brokers, insurance, architects and technologists, as well as in films, broadcasting and business and professional purposes. There was a similar disproportion in ownership of farms over fifty acres; 17.5 per cent of the largest farms were in Protestant ownership.

74. Hubert Butler, *In the Land of Nod* (Dublin, 1996), p. 116.

75. J. P. O'Carroll in Fulton, *Tragedy of Belief*, p. 167.

76. Mary Kenny, *Goodbye to Catholic Ireland* (rev. ed., London, 2000), p. 329.

77. It should none the less be noted that the Irish priesthood had traditionally been the product of a society that was notably chaste: 'priestly purity would not endure if the people were not chaste', an Irish Jesuit remarked in 1957 (Mary Kenny, *Goodbye to Catholic Ireland*, p. 315). The cases that came to light in the 1990s had occurred from the 1960s, and may reflect changes in sexual morality in society at large.

78. D. Vincent Twomey, *The End of Irish Catholicism?* (Dublin, 2003).

79. Tanner, *Ireland's Holy Wars*, p. 408.

80. *Kenny Live*, RTÉ, 17 Nov. 1996.

81. Stopper, *Mondays at Gaj's*, p. 188, quoting Nell McCafferty.

82. Tanner, *Ireland's Holy Wars*, p. 392.

83. Maria Power, *From Ecumenism to Community Relations: Inter-Church Relationships in Northern Ireland 1980–2005* (Dublin, 2007), Chapter 1.

84. See ibid., Chapter 2 and conclusion. Small-scale community initiatives on the Corrymeela model seem to have worked best, but they may be preaching to the converted.

85. Patrick O'Mahony and Gerard Delanty, *Rethinking Irish History: Nationalism, Identity and Ideology* (Basingstoke, 2001), p. 168.

86. See Peter Shirlow and Brendan Murtagh, *Belfast: Segregation, Violence and the City* (London, 2000), and Peter Shirlow, 'Northern Ireland: A Reminder from the Present' in Coulter and Coleman, *The End of Irish History?*, pp. 192–207.

87. FitzGerald, *Ireland in the World: Further Reflections*, pp. 232–3; also see Galligan, *Women and Politics*, pp. 27ff, and Michael J. O'Sullivan, *Ireland and the Global Question* (Cork, 2006), pp. 114ff.

88. See O'Connell, *Changed Utterly*, pp. 47–51.

89. Mary Kenny, *Goodbye to Catholic Ireland*, p. 308.

CHAPTER 3: FIANNA FÁIL AND IRISH POLITICS IN THE LATE TWENTIETH CENTURY

1. Justin O'Brien, *The Arms Trial* (Dublin, 2000), p. 103.

2. Bruce Arnold, *Jack Lynch: Hero in Crisis* (Dublin, 2001), pp. 64ff.

3. T. Ryle Dwyer, *Fallen Idol: Haughey's Controversial Career* (Cork, 1997), p. 11.

4. See especially Colm Keena, *Haughey's Millions: Charlie's Money Trail* (Dublin, 2001), pp. 34ff.

5. Patrick Gallagher, quoted in the *Irish Times*, 16 Mar. 2006. For Kevin Boland, see Stephen Collins, *The Power Game: Ireland under Fianna Fáil* (2nd ed., Dublin, 2001), p. 40.

6. Arnold, *Jack Lynch*, pp. 81ff, and Brian Feeney, *Sinn Féin: A Hundred Turbulent Years* (Dublin, 2002), pp. 252–4.

7. Collins, *Power Game*, p. 43. The Lynch family allegiance in the early twentieth century, interestingly, was originally to the maverick William O'Brien – a figure celebrated for venturing into new policy departures and crossing party lines.

8. This version, first retailed by Vincent Browne in *Magill*, Vol. 3, No. 8 (Nov. 1980), has been confirmed by Blaney and others since. Haughey, Blaney, Boland, Gibbons, Lenihan and Flanagan applied pressure.

9. Collins, *Power Game*, p. 107.

10. Arnold, *Jack Lynch*, p. 210.

11. *Magill*, Vol. 2, No. 3 (Dec. 1978), Vol. 2, No. 6 (Mar. 1979), on the government's falsification of figures; Vol. 3, No. 5 (Feb. 1980), for a long article by O'Donoghue (now on back benches) warning about the future and the need to cut spending. Scathing analysis by the ESRI showed how near they came to requiring an international bail-out.

12. Arnold, *Jack Lynch*, p. 223.

13. Collins, *Power Game*, p. 106. When *Magill* resoundingly broke this taboo in Nov. 1980, Haughey's fury knew no bounds.

14. Keena, *Haughey's Millions*, pp. 69–70.

15. 11 Dec. 1979 in ibid., p. 77.

16. Collins, *Power Game*, pp. 126–7.

17. Keena, *Haughey's Millions*, pp. 216–17.

18. Reproduced in *Magill* [second series] (July–Aug. 2006).

19. Collins, *Power Game*, p. 182.

20. Sam Smyth, *Thanks a Million, Big Fella* (Dublin, 1997), p. 139.

21. The proposed farm levy was opposed by the Farmers' Union in 1979, arguing that the EMS in 1978 had eroded the favourable currency balance that had helped exports, and that changes in EEC subsidies to cope with overproduction also disadvantaged them.

22. Collins, *Power Game*, p. 155.

23. Conor Brady, *Up with the Times* (Dublin, 2001), pp. 6–10.

24. Ray MacSharry and Padraic White, *The Making of the Celtic Tiger: The Inside Story of Ireland's Boom Economy* (Dublin, 2000), p. 51.

25. As retraced by the Moriarty Tribunal: see Keena, *Haughey's Millions*, pp. 201–11.

26. Keena, *Haughey's Millions*, pp. 214–15; also ibid., pp. 97, 224, for other examples of the Revenue Commissioners' indulgence.

27. See articles in *Magill*, Vol. 4, No. 10, (June 1981), and Vol. 4, No. 12 (Sept. 1981).

28. *Magill*, Vol. 2, No. 12 (Sept. 1979).

29. A statement of 1998, quoted in the *Irish Times*, 16 Mar. 2006.

30. See Frank Dunlop, *Yes, Taoiseach: Irish Politics from Behind Closed Doors* (Dublin, 2004).

31. Paul Cullen, *With a Little Help from My Friends: Planning Corruption in Ireland* (Dublin, 2002), p. 244.

32. For Gogarty's and Ray Burke's evidence (about Century Radio as well as land deals) and some very revealing appendices, see *The Second Interim Report of the Tribunal of Inquiry into Certain Planning Matters and Payments* [the Flood Tribunal] (Stationery Office, Dublin, 2002), especially pp. 73–151. The Moriarty Tribunal reported in December 2006; for lengthy quotations, and responses from those involved, see *Irish Times*, 20 Dec. 2006.

33. Quoted in Lawrence Stone, 'R. H. Tawney', *Past and Present*, No. 21 (Apr. 1962), p. 76.

34. Neil Collins and Mary O'Shea, *Understanding Corruption in Irish Politics* (Cork, 2000), pp. 68–9.

35. Cullen, *With a Little Help*, pp. 206–11, 223–31, 271–2.

36. *Sunday Independent*, 19 Mar. 2006.

37. On the day of the election Haughey received a total of €200,000 from Mark Kavanagh, Michael Smurfit and Larry Goodman, very little of which ended up with Fianna Fáil. It was also at this time that Ray Burke allegedly received £30,000 from James Gogarty, and Pádraig Flynn £50,000 from Tom Gilmartin.

38. Keena, *Haughey's Millions*, pp. 247–9.

39. *Dáil Debates*, 31 Oct. 1990, cols. 585–6; Collins, *Power Game*, pp. 211–12.

40. 'Curiously named', as the second report of the Flood Tribunal put it (*The Second Interim Report of the Tribunal of Inquiry into Certain Planning Matters and Payments* (Stationery Office, Dublin, 2002).

41. O'Brien, *Arms Trial*, p. 60.

42. Niamh Hardiman, *Pay, Politics and Economic Performance in Ireland 1970–1987* (Oxford, 1988), p. 210.

43. *Irish Times*, 6 Nov. 1992 (Dáil Report).

44. Conor Brady, quoted in Fergus Finlay, *Snakes and Ladders* (Dublin, 1998), p. 211.

45. *Magill*, Vol. 3, No. 6 (Mar. 1980), for an ironic profile.

46. Ryle Dwyer, *Fallen Idol*, p. 19.

47. Kate O'Brien, *My Ireland* (London, 1962), p. 122.

CHAPTER 4: THE SOUTH AND THE NORTH

1. *Irish Times*, 17 June 2006.

2. See above, pp. 70–71; also Justin O'Brien, *The Arms Trial* (Dublin, 2000), an impressively full and judicious account.

3. Hubert Butler, *Grandmother and Wolfe Tone* (Dublin, 1990), p. 21.

4. For example, Henry Patterson, *Ireland since 1939: The Persistence of Conflict* (Dublin, 2006), p. 12.

5. See Clare O'Halloran, *Partition and the Limits of Irish Nationalism: An Ideology under Stress* (Dublin, 1987), for de Valera's speech; for his earlier view, *Private Sessions of the Second Dáil* (State Paper Office, Dublin, 1972), debate of 22 Aug. 1922, quoted by Conor Cruise O'Brien, *States of Ireland* (London, 1972), pp. 275–6.

6. Seán Mac Stíofáin, *Revolutionary in Ireland* (Edinburgh, 1975), pp. 154–5; Liam de Paor, *Divided Ulster* (2nd ed., Harmondsworth, 1971), p. 153.

7. See Geoffrey Warner, 'Putting Pressure on O'Neill: The Wilson Government and Northern Ireland 1964–1969', *Irish Studies Review*, Vol. 13, No. 1 (Feb. 2005), pp. 13–31, and a reply by Gary Peatling, 'Unionist Divisions, the Onset of the Northern Ireland Conflict and "Pressures on O'Neill" Reconsidered', ibid., Vol. 15, No. 1 (Feb. 2007).

8. *Sunday Times*, 3 July 1966; discussed in Peter Rose, *How the Troubles Came to Northern Ireland* (Basingstoke, 2000), pp. 45–7.

9. Patterson, *Ireland since 1939*, p. 157.

10. For changing DFA approach, Paul Bew, Henry Patterson, Peter Teague,

Between War and Peace: The Political Future of Northern Ireland (London, 1997), pp. 31–3; for Agnew, Austin Currie, *All Hell Will Break Loose* (Dublin, 2004), p. 77.

11. Recollection of Lord Gowrie, presenting the 2003 Ewart-Biggs Memorial Prize.

12. De Paor, *Divided Ireland*, p. 130. Barrington's 1988 judgment in the McGimpsey case, affirmed by the Supreme Court in 1990, and his hard line on extradition requests for paramilitaries suggest an underlying anti-partitionism.

13. Letter to Ambassador John Molloy in London, 23 Mar. 1962, National Archives of Ireland (hereafter NAI) 305/14/363, Part 2; my thanks to Daithi Ó Corráin.

14. Patterson, *Ireland since 1939*, p. 200.

15. See Peter MacLoughlin, ' "It's a united Ireland or nothing"? John Hume and the Idea of Irish Unity 1964–1972' in *Irish Political Studies*, Vol. 21, No. 2 (June 2006), pp. 157–80.

16. Kenneth Bloomfield, *Stormont in Crisis* (Belfast, 1994), pp. 80–81.

17. Henry Patterson, *The Politics of Illusion: Republicanism and Socialism in Modern Ireland* (London, 1988), p. 202.

18. Patterson, *Ireland since 1939*, p. 207. Cf. Roy Johnston, *Century of Endeavour: A Biographical and Autobiographical View of the Twentieth Century in Ireland* (Dublin, 2003), p. 242: 'After Burntollet Civil Rights became a crypto-nationalist issue.'

19. Johnston, *Century of Endeavour*, p. 283, for Tomás Mac Giolla in *United Irishman*, Jan. 1969. The editor of the *United Irishman*, Seamus Ó Tuathail, was also devoted to 'the issue of all-Ireland sporting organisations in the cycling context' (ibid., p. 282).

20. Ibid., p. 261.

21. Ibid., p. 280; also see Mac Stíofáin, *Revolutionary in Ireland*, pp. 107–8.

22. Tom Pocock in the *Evening Standard*, 14 Oct. 1969, quoted in Johnston, *Century of Endeavour*, p. 273.

23. *Observer*, 3 May 1970.

24. Thomas Hennessey, *Northern Ireland: The Origins of the Troubles* (Dublin, 2005), pp. 368–9.

25. 23 Aug. 1969; quoted in Patterson, *Ireland since 1939*, p. 184.

26. O'Brien, *The Arms Trial*, for a full treatment; using the Peter Berry diaries and recollections published in *Magill*, Aug.–Dec. 1980. Also see NAI 2001/42/1 for long reports by Eamonn Gallagher, 21 and 31 Dec. 1970, detailing how the trustees of the fund were squeezed out in favour of the Belfast IRA man John Kelly. According to the *Irish Times*, 13 May 1970 (reporting a

press conference of the 'Northern Defence Association' on 12 May), another senior IRA figure, Seán Keenan of Derry, had several meetings about this with Fianna Fáil figures.

27. *Magill*, Vol. 4, No. 3 (Dec. 1980); the intermediary was allegedly a reluctant Des O'Malley.

28. Discussed in detail from government records now available in Hennessey, *Northern Ireland: The Origins of the Troubles*, Chapter 9.

29. *Economist*, 6 June 1970.

30. For the 'more plural society', an interview in *Belfast Telegraph*, 17 July 1970. For Sheehy-Skeffington's support, a letter of 5 June 1970 in NAI 2001/6/518; for Browne's, a report in the *Irish Press*, 6 May 1970. There is evidence that de Valera and Maurice Moynihan also backed his actions very strongly (my thanks to John-Paul McCarthy for this).

31. Warner, 'Putting Pressure on O'Neill', p. 25.

32. Patterson, *Ireland since 1939*, p. 178.

33. *States of Ireland*, pp. 233ff.

34. Text of speech in NAI 2001/6/513.

35. *Irish Press*, 18 May 1970.

36. Draft in NAI 2001/6/516. As delivered, quoted in O'Brien, *Arms Trial*, pp. 170–72.

37. NAI 2001/6/517. Hillery, interestingly, took a 'greener' line, and publicly declared friendship for Haughey, then awaiting trial (press conference 8 July 1970).

38. Memo in ibid., laid before cabinet on 8 Sept. 1970. See also Frank Dunlop, *Yes, Taoiseach: Irish Politics from Behind Closed Doors* (Dublin, 2004), pp. 53ff.

39. NAI 2001/6/519; report of 1 Dec. 1970.

40. Richard English, *Armed Struggle: The History of the IRA* (London, 2003), pp. 121, 123.

41. Brian Lynch, *Pity for the Wicked* (Dublin, 2005), p. 22.

42. Patterson, *Ireland since 1939*, p. 226.

43. Eamonn Gallagher, again: NAI 2001/43/1278.

44. The articles were by R. G. Geary and began on 20 July 1970. At the first meeting of the IDU on 18 June 1970, Hillery forecast a three-stage process to reunification 'covering perhaps a generation'. Eamonn Gallagher was far less sunny. Around this time Lynch was constantly needled in the Dáil about his Northern policy by Michael O'Leary, Garret FitzGerald, Conor Cruise O'Brien and others, but gave little away in public: see, for example, *Dáil Debates*, Vol. 246, No. 9, cols. 1601–3 (14 May 1970).

45. *States of Ireland*, p. 277.

46. For his IRA career at this stage, see English, *Armed Struggle*, p. 110.

47. Meeting of 1 Feb. 1973, reported in NAI 2004/7/302.

48. NAI 2001/6/513.

49. Garret FitzGerald, *All in a Life: An Autobiography* (London, 1991), p. 203. He has since emphasized the reluctance of the Irish government to give the Council much of a role.

50. O'Halloran, *Partition and the Limits of Irish Nationalism*, p. 190.

51. Ibid., p. 192.

52. See a long investigation in *Magill*, Vol. 2, No. 8 (May 1979). 143 officers had attended counter-insurgency courses abroad, and the defence estimates had doubled 1970–75. In the emergency legislation after Ewart-Biggs's assassination the army was given the right to search and arrest.

53. See Tom Garvin, 'The North and the Rest: The Politics of the Republic of Ireland' in Charles Townshend (ed.), *Consensus in Ireland: Approaches and Recessions* (Oxford, 1988), p. 107, quoting surveys of 1970, 1974 and 1976 by Irish Marketing Surveys and the Market Research Bureau of Ireland.

54. Patterson, *Politics of Illusion*, pp. 161–2.

55. Ibid., p. 166.

56. Ruairi Quinn, *Straight Left: A Journey in Politics* (2005). H-Block candidates are mentioned incidentally but the North enters his political conspectus only post-1981.

57. See *All in a Life*, p. 331.

58. Brian Feeney, *Sinn Féin: A Hundred Turbulent Years* (Dublin, 2002), p. 291. For the leadership and the strikers, see Richard O'Rawe, *Blanketmen* (Dublin, 2005).

59. O'Rawe, *Blanketmen*, p. 238.

60. *All in a Life*, pp. 350, 412; also a profile by Olivia O'Leary in *Magill*, Vol. 5, No. 3 (3 Dec. 1981).

61. See, for instance, Brian Lynch's introduction to *Pity for the Wicked*, and various statements of Conor Cruise O'Brien.

62. Interview in *Magill*, Vol. 1, No. 4 (Jan. 1978); *Irish Times*, 4 Jan. 1972, reporting a seminar at Maynooth organized by the Association of Irish Priests.

63. Currie, *All Hell*, p. 338.

64. This was confirmed in a lecture by Martin Mansergh to the UCC Law Society, 4 Feb. 1999; my thanks to John-Paul McCarthy.

65. Reminiscence at TCD seminar, June 2006.

66. *Magill*, Vol. 4, No. 10 (June 1981). *All in a Life*, p. 105, is bracingly frank about the rifts he caused within Fine Gael. See ibid., p. 255, for the enlistment of Kissinger.

67. 'The Peace Process: A Personal Account', lecture to UCC Law Society, 4 Feb. 1999.

68. Alex Maskey, quoted in Gerard Murray, *John Hume and the SDLP: Impact and Survival in Northern Ireland* (Dublin, 1991), p. 138.

69. Thatcher visited Washington in Dec. 1984; Reagan had been in Ireland earlier in the year and approved of the forum. See also FitzGerald, *All in a Life*, pp. 520ff.

70. *All in a Life*, pp. 547–8.

71. Ibid., pp. 571–2.

72. Fionnuala O Connor, *In Search of a State: Catholics in Northern Ireland* (Belfast, 1993), p. 255.

73. Malachi O'Doherty, *The Trouble with Guns: Republican Strategy and the IRA* (Belfast, 1998), p. 209; Alex Maskey in Murray, *John Hume*, p. 171.

74. Though there had been meetings in 1980–81 (Murray, *John Hume*, pp. 109–10), 1988 saw the beginnings of the process: Patterson, *Politics of Illusion*, pp. 186–7.

75. Quoted in Feeney, *Sinn Féin*, p. 332.

76. *Irish Times*, 23 Nov. 2002.

77. Patterson, *Politics of Illusion*, p. 182.

78. Ibid., p. 185.

79. Ibid., p. 192.

80. Currie, *All Hell*, pp. 383, 398.

81. Patterson, *Politics of Illusion*, p. 206.

82. O Connor, *In Search of a State*, pp. 259–60.

83. My thanks to Marianne Elliott for this recollection.

84. Andy Pollak (ed.), *A Citizens' Inquiry: The Opsahl Report on Northern Ireland* (Dublin, 1993), pp. 400, 406ff, 409, 420–21; O Connor, *In Search of a State*, p. 260.

85. Seán Duignan, *One Spin on the Merry-go-round* (Dublin, 1995), pp. 96–7.

86. Dean Godson, *Himself Alone: David Trimble and the Ordeal of Unionism* (London, 2004), p. 115.

87. O Connor, *In Search of a State*, pp. 263, 246, 263.

88. John Coakley (ed.), *Changing Shades of Orange and Green: Redefining the Nation in Contemporary Ireland* (Dublin, 2002), p. 152.

89. At the National Press Club in New York, 16 Oct. 1963: reported in *Irish Independent*, 17 Oct. 1963.

90. Kevin Rafter, *Martin Mansergh: A Biography* (Dublin, 2002), p. 108.

91. Notably Noël Dorr, Dermot Nally, Dermot Gallagher, Tim Dalton, Paddy Teahon and Seán Ó hUiginn.

92. Rafter, *Martin Mansergh*, pp. 201, 204.

93. Eamonn Mallie and David McKittrick, *Endgame in Ireland* (London, 2002), p. 147.

94. The climax had been the St Patrick's Day 1977 statement by Tip O'Neill, Daniel Moynihan, Hugh Carey and Ted Kennedy, condemning support of the IRA by Irish-Americans. A 'Friends of Ireland' organization had evolved, from which derived the powerful Ireland Funds. Lillis in fact wrote the first draft of Jimmy Carter's speech on Ireland, 30 May 1977 (Murray, *John Hume*, p. 230).

95. Rafter, *Martin Mansergh*, p. 224; Reynolds airily told him not to expect the IRA to produce saints.

96. Ibid., p. 230.

97. As he stated on RTÉ, 19 Feb. 2005.

98. Speech at the Woodrow Wilson School of Politics and International Affairs, Princeton, New Jersey, 25 Sept. 2001.

99. Lynch, *Pity for the Wicked*, p. 2.

100. Rafter, *Martin Mansergh*, p. 248.

101. Mansergh himself noted this in a paper given at the conference 'Constitution-making and Conflict in Divided Societies' at Bellagio in 1999.

102. Rafter, *Martin Mansergh*, pp. 253–4.

103. Lynch, *Pity for the Wicked*, p. 16.

104. O'Doherty, *Trouble with Guns*, p. 173.

105. John Bruton's experience, as relayed to the Woodrow Wilson Institute, 25 Sept. 2001; see n. 98 above.

106. See, among others, Kenneth Bloomfield, *A Tragedy of Errors: The Government and Misgovernment of Northern Ireland* (Liverpool, 2007); Currie, *All Hell*, p. 10; English, *Armed Struggle*, pp. 145–7, 350–78; Hennessey, *Origins of the Troubles*, pp. 375–6 and conclusion.

107. For a thoughtful alternative view, see Chapters 11–13 in John McGarry and Brendan O'Leary, *The Northern Ireland Conflict: Consociational Engagements* (Oxford, 2004), pp. 323–403.

108. It is instructive to read the astute Michael McInerney in *Irish Times*, 30 Mar. 1970, praising Chichester-Clark for putting a wide range of reforms into place without delay (one man one vote, phasing out B-Specials, disarming the RUC, ending the Special Powers Act, setting up the Central Housing Authority, reorganizing local government, accepting the Cameron and Hunt reports); McInerney believed that the 'crisis was over'.

109. See Peter Shirland, 'Northern Ireland: A Reminder from the Present' in Colin Coulter and Steve Coleman (eds.), *The End of Irish History? Critical Reflections on the Celtic Tiger* (Manchester, 2003), pp. 192–207, and Peter Shirlow and Brendan Murtagh, *Belfast: Segregation, Violence and the City* (London 2006), dealing with patterns of increased sectarianism since the Good Friday Agreement reinforced ethnic chauvinism.

110. UTV interview of Jan. 1970, transcript in NAI 2001/6/513.

111. Garret FitzGerald, *Ireland in the World: Further Reflections* (Dublin, 2005), Chapter 10; Frank Miller, *David Trimble: The Price of Peace* (Dublin, 2004), p. 84.

112. 'A Guide to Political Neuroses', *Encounter* (June 1953), p. 26.

113. *American Way*, 11 Jan. 2002.

114. *VIP*, Issue 39, Sept. 2002.

115. Cormac Ó Gráda, *A Rocky Road: The Irish Economy from the 1920s* (Manchester, 1997), pp. 54–5, 134–5.

116. Jimmy Steel, cited in Peter Taylor, *Provos: The IRA and Sinn Féin* (London, 1997), pp. 45–6.

CHAPTER 5: HOW THE SHORT STORIES
BECAME NOVELS

1. Sam Smyth, *Thanks a Million, Big Fella* (Dublin, 1997), p. 97.

2. Noel Ignatiev, *How the Irish Became White* (London, 1996). On this phenomenon, see Sean Campbell, ' "What's the story?" Rock Biography, Musical "Routes" and the Second-Generation Irish in England', *Irish Studies Review*, Vol. 12, No. 1 (Apr. 2004), pp. 63–76.

3. *Hot Press*, Vol. 2, No. 1 (11–30 May 1979).

4. See Gerry Smyth, *Noisy Island: A Short History of Irish Popular Music* (Cork, 2005), pp. 2–3.

5. See Eamon Dunphy, *Unforgettable Fire: The Story of U2* (London, 1987), p. 213.

6. Dec. 1984. For Waters's account, see *Jiving at the Crossroads* (Belfast, 1991), pp. 130ff. While Haughey's malevolence towards his perceived enemies and liberal swearing shocked the pious, the general conclusion was that the interview made him more 'human'.

7. Moynagh Sullivan, 'Boyz to Menz(own)', *Irish Review*, No. 34 (2006), p. 61; for the showband connection, Smyth, *Noisy Island*, p. 112.

8. Smyth, *Noisy Island*, p. 133.

9. See Geraldine Moane, 'Colonialism and the Celtic Tiger: Legacies of History and the Quest for Vision' in Peadar Kirby, Luke Gibbons and Michael Cronin (eds.), *Reinventing Ireland: Culture, Society and the Global Economy* (London, 2002), pp. 109–23.

10. 'Branding India' in *Seminar* [Delhi] (Jan. 2004).

11. See John Waters's influential *Irish Times* columns and his book *An Intelligent Person's Guide to Modern Ireland* (London, 1997). For an ex-

cellent critique, Michael Boss, 'Mysticism and the Politics of Feeling: The Enduring Dream of an Authentic Ireland', *Times Change* (Spring–Summer 1999), pp. 11–16.

12. The Café Belge, though it had closed after Geldof's grandfather's day. The quotation comes from *Hot Press*, Vol. 1, No. 4 (21 July 1977); the autobiography is *Is That It?* (London, 1986).

13. *Irish Times*, 11 Oct. 2003.

14. Gerry Smyth, *Noisy Island*, pp. 10–11.

15. *Hot Press*, Vol. 2, No. 16 (25 Jan.–7 Feb. 1979).

16. Inès Praga Terente, 'U2 and Irishness' in Rosa González (ed.), *The Representation of Ireland/s: Images from Outside and from Within* (Barcelona, 2002), p. 80, and John Waters, *Race of Angels: Ireland and the Genesis of U2* (Belfast, 1994), p. 186.

17. See Fintan O'Toole, 'Unsuitables from a Distance: The Politics of Riverdance' in *The Ex-Isle of Erin: Images of a Global Ireland* (Dublin, 1997), pp. 143–56.

18. Boss, 'Mysticism and the Politics of Feeling', p. 1.

19. Victoria Mary Clarke, *A Drink with Shane MacGowan* (London, 2001), pp. 187, 274–80.

20. Report in the *Irish Times*, 23 Jan. 1998, quoted in Michael Cronin and Barbara O'Connor, 'From Gombeen to Gubeen: Tourism, Identity and Class in Ireland 1949–1999' in Ray Ryan (ed.), *Writing in the Irish Republic: Literature, Culture, Politics 1949–1999* (London, 2000), p. 177.

21. An exception is Eric Zuelow's first-rate doctoral thesis, 'The Tourism Nexus: Tourism and National Identity since the Irish Civil War' (University of Wisconsin–Madison, 2004), which uses a vast range of contemporary sources to bring a cultural and political interpretation to the subject.

22. Eamonn Slater, 'When the Local Goes Global' in Eamonn Slater and Michel Peillon (eds.), *Memories of the Present: A Sociological Chronicle of Ireland 1997–1998* (Dublin, 2000), pp. 247ff.

23. See Diane Negra, 'Consuming Ireland', *Cultural Studies*, Vol. 15, No. 1 (2001), pp. 76–97.

24. Spurgeon Thompson, 'The Post-colonial Tourist: Irish Tourism and Decolonization since 1850' (Ph.D., Notre Dame, 2000), quoted in Zuelow, 'The Tourism Nexus', p. 241.

25. See John Fanning, *The Importance of being Branded: An Irish Perspective* (Dublin, 2006), pp. 235ff.

26. Tourism Traffic Act (1983), quoted in Zuelow, 'The Tourism Nexus', p. 173.

27. Cronin and O'Connor, 'From Gombeen to Gubeen', pp. 170–71.

28. Fanning, *Importance of being Branded*, p. 253.

29. Zuelow, 'The Tourism Nexus', pp. 218ff, 233.

30. Michael Cronin and Darryl Adair, *The Wearing of the Green: A History of St Patrick's Day* (London, 2002), pp. 184–5.

31. Cronin and O'Connor, 'From Gombeen to Gubeen', p. 165.

32. Kevin Kearns, 'Dublin's Crumbling Fair City', *Geographical Magazine*, Vol. 55, No. 2 (Feb. 1983); Frank McDonald, *The Destruction of Dublin* (Dublin, 1985); Stephen A. Royle, 'The Historical Legacy in Modern Ireland' in R. W. C. Carter and A. J. Parker (eds.), *Ireland: Contemporary Perspectives on a Land and Its People* (London, 1989), pp. 113–43.

33. *Irish Times* Magazine, 19 May 2001.

34. See Frank McDonald and James Nix, *Chaos at the Crossroads* (Kinsale, 2005), pp. 184ff.

35. Ibid., p. 193.

36. By John Waters, scourge of Dublin 4; ibid., p. 150. For earlier quotes, see pp. 125–7.

37. Plan-A-Home Ireland, *Cottages and Holiday Homes: A Book of Architectural Designs* (Donegal [n.d.]).

38. See my *The Irish Story: Telling Tales and Making It Up in Ireland* (London, 2001), Chapters 2 and 12.

39. Dermot Bolger, *The Journey Home* (London, 1990), pp. 292–3.

40. 'Martyrs and Metaphors' in Dermot Bolger (ed.), *Letters from the New Island* (Dublin, 1991), p. 45. The essay was first written for the Kate O'Brien Weekend in 1985.

41. See particularly *Magill*, Vol. 8, No. 7 (Feb. 1985), for an immense article on the Supreme Court and its part in changing Irish life.

42. *The Heather Blazing* (London, 1992; 1993 ed.), p. 178.

43. Quoted in Ray Ryan, 'The Republic and Ireland: Pluralism, Politics and Narrative Form' in Ray Ryan (ed.), *Writing in the Irish Republic: Literature, Culture, Politics 1949–1999* (London, 2000), p. 84. Also see Ryan, *Ireland and Scotland: Literature and Culture, State and Nation 1966–2000* (Oxford, 2002), for a slightly fuller repetition of the same material. On the effect of Bolger's intervention see Ferdia Mac Anna, 'The Dublin Renaissance: An Essay on Modern Dublin and Dublin Writers', *Irish Review*, No. 10 (Spring 1991), pp. 14–30.

44. Declan Kiberd, *Inventing Ireland* (London, 1995), p. 610.

45. Anthony Giddens, *Modernity and Self-Identity: Self and Society in the Late Modern Age* (Cambridge, 1995), p. 54.

46. 'The Elephant of Irish Fiction', *Irish Review*, No. 30 (Spring–Summer 2003), p. 134.

47. My thanks to Julia Crampton and Rob Tobin.

48. O'Toole, *Ex-Isle of Erin*, p. 108.

49. Quoted in Edna Longley and Declan Kiberd, *Multi-Culturalism: The View from the Two Irelands* (Cork, 2001), p. 43.

50. Moane, 'Colonialism and the Celtic Tiger', p. 121.

51. Cormac Ó Gráda, 'Famine Trauma and Memory', a paper read at a meeting of An Cumann le Bealoideas Éireann, 6 Nov. 2000; Niall Ó Ciosáin, 'Famine Memory and the Popular Representation of Scarcity' in I. McBride (ed.), *History and Memory in Modern Ireland* (Cambridge, 2001).

52. For a suggestive overview, see Margaret Kelleher, 'The Field Day Anthology and Irish Women's Literary Studies' in *Irish Review*, No. 30, pp. 82–94.

53. See Joe Cleary, 'Modernization and Aesthetic Ideology in Contemporary Irish Culture' in Ryan, *Writing in the Irish Republic*, pp. 105–29.

54. *The Irish Language in a Changing Society: Shaping the Future*, quoted in Tony Crowley, *Wars of Words: The Politics of Language in Ireland 1537–2004* (Oxford, 2005), p. 186.

55. Nuala Ní Dhomhnaill, 'The Yeast in the Bread: The Rise in Culture: The Role of Irish in Contemporary Ireland' in Robert J. Savage (ed.), *Ireland in the New Century: Politics, Culture and Society* (Dublin, 2003), pp. 202–3.

56. Manchán Magan, 'Cá bhfuil na Gaeilgeoirí?', *Guardian*, 5 Jan. 2006.

57. Colum Kenny, 'Súil Eile' in *Moments That Changed Us* (Dublin, 2005), pp. 244–8.

58. Edna Longley, 'Irish Poetry and Internationalism: Variations on a Critical Theme' in *Irish Review*, No. 30 (Spring–Summer 2003), p. 59.

59. 'House of "The Dead" Rises Again', *Irish Times*, 3 Jan. 2004.

60. Kiberd, *Inventing Ireland*, p. 7.

61. Tom Dunne, *Rebellions: Memoir, Memory and 1798* (Dublin, 2004).

62. See my 'Something to Hate: Intimate Enmities in Irish History', *Irish Review*, No. 30 (Spring–Summer 2003), pp. 1–12.

63. Patrick O'Mahony and Gerard Delanty, *Rethinking Irish History: Nationalism, Identity and Ideology* (Basingstoke, 2001), p. 177.

64. 'The Fading of Traditional Nationalism in the Republic of Ireland' in J. Coakley (ed.), *Changing Shades of Orange and Green* (Dublin, 2002), p. 129. Also see J. Coakley's conclusion in the same volume and Catherine Frost, 'Is Post-Nationalism or Liberal-Culturalism behind the Transformation of Irish Nationalism?' in *Irish Political Studies*, Vol. 21, No. 3 (Sept. 2006), pp. 277–95.

65. Mainly publicized in the *Sunday Business Post* at the time, this organization is mentioned in Ryan, *Writing in the Irish Republic*, p. 237.

66. Tom Hayden, *Irish on the Inside: In Search of the Soul of Irish America* (New York and London, 2002).

67. *Memory Ireland: Insights into the Contemporary Irish Condition* (Harmondsworth, 1985), p. ix.

68. Ibid., pp. 174–5.

69. *Irish Times*, 27 May 1997.

70. *Irish Times*, 23 Dec. 2000.

71. 'Rebel Tours' were advertised in 2002 (targeting visiting American students, among others) on http://www.yoursay.i.e. univstudy.htm.

72. Ann Marie Hourihane, *She Moves through the Boom* (Dublin, 2000), p. 18.

73. A. J. Saris and others, 'Horses and the Culture of Protest in West Dublin' in Slater and Peillon, *Memories of the Present*, pp. 126–7.

74. Negra, 'Consuming Ireland', p. 85.

75. Ian S. Wood, *Crimes of Loyalty: A History of the UDA* (Edinburgh, 2006), pp. 286–7. Also *The Times*, 3 Dec. 2002. Duddy announced that he intended to revive his act as a fundraiser for paramilitary prisoners. 'I'll probably be wearing a flowing dress, as gaudily coloured as possible. I'll have my black handbag over my shoulder of course and the fishnet stockings will be back on. They always used to go for that, screaming "Higher, Samantha, higher!" A loyalist colleague remarked, "He wasn't so bad in the Seventies, but I dread to think what he'll be like now. His cheeks have gone a bit ruddy, but we'll see what he looks like when he gets the wig on."

76. 'Frontiers of Writing' in *The Redress of Poetry: Oxford Lectures* (London, 1995), pp. 186–203.

77. From *General Admission* (Oldcastle, 2006), p. 94.

CONCLUSION: THE STRANGE DEATH OF ROMANTIC IRELAND

1. *The Complete Plays of Bernard Shaw* (one-volume edition, London, 1931), pp. 917–18.

2. Paddy Logue (ed.), *Being Irish* (Dublin, 2000), p. xvii.

3. See Daniel P. Moynihan, 'The Irish' in Daniel P. Moynihan and Michael Glazier (eds.), *Beyond the Melting Pot* (Cambridge, Mass., 1963), p. 256.

4. Joe Joyce and Peter Murtagh, *The Boss: Charles J. Haughey in Government* (Dublin, 1983), p. 83.

5. From 'Patriotic Suite' in John Montague, *Collected Poems* (Oldcastle, 1995), p. 67.

6. Quoted in *Sunday Tribune*, 11 Nov. 2001, from an RTÉ interview of 15 Oct. 1997.

Index